Guide to Campus-Business Linkage Programs

Guide to Campus-Business Linkage Programs

Education and Business Prospering Together

Second Edition

Authors

DOROTHY C. FENWICK
Executive Secretary, Accrediting Commission
National Association of Trade and Technical Schools

JAMES R. MYERS
Dean of Instruction
Florida Junior College,
Jacksonville, Florida

P. ANTHONY GIORGIO
Executive Vice President
Griffin Institute
Windsor, Connecticut

ROBERT J. KOPECKY
Management Development
Division
Henry Ford Community College
Dearborn, Michigan

LAWRENCE G. LLOYD
Associate Dean of Instruction
Moorpark College
Moorpark, California

American Council on Education • Macmillan Publishing Company
NEW YORK

Collier Macmillan Publishers
LONDON

Copyright © 1986 by Macmillan Publishing Company and American Council on Education
The American Council on Education/Macmillan Series in Higher Education

All rights reserved. No part of this book may be reproduced or transmitted in any form or by any means, electronic or mechanical, including photocopying, recording, or by any information storage and retrieval system, without permission in writing from the Publisher.

Macmillan Publishing Company
A Division of Macmillan, Inc.
866 Third Avenue, New York, N.Y. 10022

Collier Macmillan Canada, Inc.

Library of Congress Catalog Card Number:

Printed in the United States of America

printing number
1 2 3 4 5 6 7 8 9 10

Library of Congress Cataloging-in-Publication Data
Main entry under title:

Guide to campus-business linkage programs.

    Rev. ed. of: Directory of campus-business linkages / Dorothy C. Fenwick. 1st ed. 1983.
    Includes index.
    1. Employer-supported education—United States.
2. Employer-supported education—United States—Directories.   I. Fenwick, Dorothy C.   II. American Council on Education.   III. Fenwick, Dorothy C. Directory of campus-business linkages.
HF5549.5.T7G84   1986   378'.103   85-23925
ISBN 0-02-910600-1

Preface

The concept of campus-business linkages is one that has undergone rapid growth since its conception. Campus-business linkages are multipurpose and multidimensional. However, one purpose and dimension, common to all linkage programs, is the need to build a reciprocal relationship between the institution of higher education and the business with well-defined mutual expectations and realistic goals within the framework of the needs and demands of the business and the educational services of the institution.

This book has two parts. Part I presents the three phases of campus-business linkages, namely the (1) predevelopment phase; (2) development phase; and (3) postdevelopment phase. Chapter 1 deals with the predevelopment phase which consists of developing a rationale, obtaining the support of the institution of higher education, and assessing the needs of the marketplace. Chapters 2–5 deal with the development phase which consists of activities and decision-making processes that ultimately result in a linkage program. Those processes, of course, are program construction, curriculum development, program implementation, and program evaluation. Chapter 6 deals with the postdevelopment phase of campus-business linkages which consists of planning follow-up activities for ongoing linkage programs, acquiring institutional commitment to the concept of campus-business linkages, and promoting campus-business linkages in the marketplace. Part I of this book, Chapters 1–6, is more or less a "how to" develop, implement, and maintain campus-business linkages.

Special appreciation and thanks are due Dr. Shirley P. Myers, Florida Junior College at Jacksonville, for the graphical depiction of the *three phases of campus-business linkages* and the *four components of a linkage program*, as well as for her painstaking effort at editing Part I of this book.

Part II of this book, presents the *Directory of Campus-Business Linkages*.

Contents

Part I

1 PREDEVELOPMENT PHASE OF CAMPUS-BUSINESS LINKAGES	3
Introduction	3
Rationale for CBL	3
Who Initiates CBL?	4
Why Initiate CBL?	5
CBL and the Organizational Structure of the Institution	6
Is the CBL office's perception of its place in the institution in harmony with the institution's perception of it?	6
Internal Advisory Committee for CBL	8
IMIS	8
Procedure Manual for CBL	9
Assessment of the External Environment of the Institution	10
Market Potential	10
Competition	12
Cost Effectiveness of CBL	13
2 LINKAGE PROGRAM CONSTRUCTION	15
Defining the Program	15
Audience	16
Program Goals	18
Selection and Involvement of People	18
Specify Program Peculiarities and Features: Program Design	19
Resources, Costs, and Deadlines	20
The Construction Meeting	20
Agenda for the Construction Meeting	21

Preparing the Formal Proposal 22
    Purpose of the Proposal 22
    Cost Profile 23
    Sign-offs, Comments, and Signatures 23

Presenting the Formal Proposal 23
    Cover Letter 23

Patience, Persistence, and Professionalism 24

3 CURRICULUM DEVELOPMENT 25

Issues Involved in Curriculum Development 25
    Quality 26
    Delivery 27
    Evaluation 28

Selecting and Organizing Content and Learning Experiences 29
    Developing a New Program 29
    Modifying an Existing Program 30

4 IMPLEMENTATION OF A LINKAGE PROGRAM 31

Putting into Effect the Linkage Program 31
    Writing a Contract 31
    Signing the Contract 34

Twelve Steps to Successful Program Implementation 35

1. Notify Individuals or Groups Involved or Affected by the Acceptance of the Linkage Program Proposal 35
2. Issue Faculty Contracts 35
3. Visit the Facilities Where Instruction Will Take Place 35
4. Acquire Appropriate Equipment 36
5. Obtain Necessary Instructional Materials 36
6. Assign Special Staff as Required 36
7. Maintain Lines of Communication 37
8. Prepare Public Relations Materials 37
9. Plan for Registration 37
10. Start the First Class Enthusiastically 38
11. Involve Faculty in Monitoring Procedures 38
12. Implement Program Evaluation 39

Monitoring the Linkage Program	39
Who? What? When? Where? Why? and How?	39
Methods of Monitoring	40

5 PROGRAM EVALUATION 41

Gathering Evaluative Data	42
Formal Methods for Data Collection	42
Informal Methods for Data Collection	42
Making a Judgment Based on an Analysis of the Data	42
Standards for Evaluation	43
Determining if the Judgment is Valid	44
Sharing the Results of the Evaluation	45
Follow-up Evaluations	45

6 POSTDEVELOPMENT PHASE OF CAMPUS-BUSINESS LINKAGES 46

The Three Phases of CBL	46
Postdevelopment Phase	48
Follow-up Activities for Ongoing Programs	48
Planning Additional Linkage Programs	49
Institutional Support and Commitment	49
CBL as a Permanent Concept	49
Promoting CBL in the Marketplace	50

INDEX 267

Part II

LIST OF FIGURES

Fig. 1.1.	A Typical Organizational Structure for a CBL office.	7
Fig. 2.1.	The Four Components of a Linkage Program.	16
Fig. 3.1.	Issues Involved in the Curriculum Development Process of CBL.	26
Fig. 6.1.	The Three Phases of CBL.	47

PART I

CHAPTER ONE

Predevelopment Phase of Campus-Business Linkages

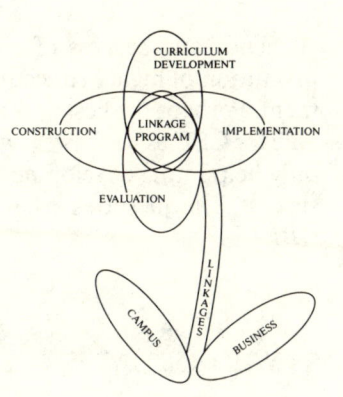

INTRODUCTION

Many relationships exist between institutions of higher education and private businesses. Depending upon the time, the place, and the people involved, the relationship may be harmonious or antagonistic, it may be uninterrupted or fragmentary, or it may be a reciprocal relationship with well-defined mutual expectations and realistic goals. The 1980s may or may not produce new relationships between institutions and businesses, but it will produce a synergy, a combined and correlated effort, to address a major challenge of the decade: the development of human resources.

Institutions of higher education and private businesses, no matter how large or how small, are becoming increasingly more interdependent. This chapter deals with the predevelopment phase of *Campus-Business Linkages* (CBL). That is, it lays the foundation for the rationale of CBL, provides some insight into the realities involved in determining where CBL fits into the organizational structure of the institution, and discusses the major aspects of the necessary assessment of the external environment, the marketplace for CBL.

Moreover, this chapter stresses that without the support and commitment of the institution to the concept of CBL, there is little hope for the success of linkage programs.

RATIONALE FOR CBL

Before discussing the process involved in developing CBL, there are several issues that need to be examined. These issues are critical to the subsequent efficiency and success of any linkage program regardless of the size of the institution of higher education or the market potential of its external environment. Perhaps the best approach to these issues, which are related to the rationale for CBL, is to answer two questions, keeping in mind that the answers not only help in the development of the rationale but serve as early indicators for success. The questions to be answered are, *Who initiates CBL?* and *Why initiate CBL?*

WHO INITIATES CBL?

A linkage program may be initiated by the President of the institution, by the Vice President for Academic Affairs, by the Faculty Senate, by the Board of Trustees, or by a particular Dean of Instruction. The real concern is not *who* initiates CBL, but *how much power* (financial, political, or personal) the initiator has. Organizational clout is necessary to guarantee support, continuity, and success of CBL. Without a major commitment from a powerful individual or group, linkage programs are doomed. Every effort must be made to identify the sources of support and to ascertain the degree of power these sources have within the institution.

Determining where power lies within an institution will vary among the institutions of higher education. The easiest and most efficient way of determining the power of an individual or group is to study the decision-making process of the institution.

If an open-management decision-making situation exists where decisions are the result of interactions among interested parties with affected parties contributing to the discussions, then it is usually easy to determine the power of the participants and to measure the extent of their commitment and support for CBL.

If a closed-management decision-making situation exists where only a few people are actually involved in the decision-making process and decisions are made at the top of the power structure with limited participation by interested or affected parties, then it is much more difficult to determine the commitment and support for CBL even though the power of the individual or group is known.

The importance of the support and commitment of the institution of higher education to CBL cannot be overemphasized. It is our contention that institutional commitment and support must exist before the *first* attempt to develop a linkage program is made. Campus-business linkages should become an integral part of the institution's mission, and information pertaining to CBL must circulate among administrators, faculty, and staff of the institution to ensure a broad support base. Linkage programs are vulnerable if they are not built upon a solid foundation of institutional support and commitment.

WHY INITIATE CBL?

The second question that relates to the development of the rationale for CBL addresses the *why* of CBL. The answer to this question depends on both the internal and the external reasons for the development of linkage programs. Knowing *why* CBL are initiated is as important as knowing *who* initiated them. The reasons, whether internal or external or both, may differ among the institutions, but knowing *why* is important because it brings into focus the direction, tone, and extent of participation in CBL.

Internal Reasons. Among the numerous reasons underlying the support and commitment of an institution to initiate CBL are internal reasons such as:

1. An expected or real decline in the enrollment of traditional students
2. A desire for new income sources both in tuition and development dollars
3. An interest in the expansion of educational opportunities for nontraditional students
4. Innovative curriculum development by faculty
5. A desire to expand the communication network between the academic and business communities
6. A desire to change the image of the institution in the community it serves
7. Faculty and staff development through exposure to new environments and challenges

External Reasons. There are also external reasons that influence the decision to initiate CBL, but these are more difficult to identify and are often known only to the initiator or to top administrators. Some of the possible external reasons are:

1. Real or anticipated changes in the economic development of the community
2. Specific human resource needs or training demands from private businesses or labor organizations
3. Encouragement by the Board of Trustees, advisory committees, or governmental agencies
4. Cooperative initiatives among other institutions of higher education in the community
5. Decline in student enrollment due to increased competition from other academic and nonacademic institutions

6. The need to change the image of the institution in the community due to preconceived or misconceived notions

The importance of understanding the relationship between the support and commitment of the institution and the linkage program has been stressed. Central to the understanding of this commitment is the identification of *who* initiated CBL and the reasons *why* CBL was initiated. These two concerns should be carefully examined by the individual or group having the responsibility for linkage programs.

CBL AND THE ORGANIZATIONAL STRUCTURE OF THE INSTITUTION

Determining where to place CBL organizationally begins with an examination of the organizational structure of the institution of higher education. The position of CBL within the institution is significant because it will affect the credibility, efficiency, productivity, and visibility of the concept of CBL. The position of CBL may vary among institutions due to differences in their organizational structures. That is, an institution does not need to have a particular organizational structure for CBL to function successfully. It is critical, however, to know *where* CBL actually fits in the organizational structure because this awareness helps to define the operational parameters and thereby helps to avoid internal territorial conflicts that affect the effectiveness of linkage programs.

IS THE CBL OFFICE'S PERCEPTION OF ITS PLACE IN THE INSTITUTION IN HARMONY WITH THE INSTITUTION'S PERCEPTION OF IT?

Clearly, this is a question that must be answered. A dual focus should be considered by the leadership of the institution as it ponders the establishment of a CBL office. This duality involves critical realities that require attention, comprehension, and management.

Organizational Realities. Organizational realities are couched in and shaped by the organizational structure of the institution, its mission, its leadership, and its faculty. Questions that must be answered by every institution comtemplating CBL include: (1) What are the responsibilities of the CBL office?; (2) Where is the CBL office in the institution's organizational structure? The answers may vary somewhat from one institution to another. There may be arguments within institutions as to whether the responsibilities of the CBL office include research and development, marketing, and administration of linkage programs and as to whether the CBL office should be line or support, central or peripheral. There may be persistent differences, but it is important that they be openly discussed so that a common understanding can be reached.

Budgetary Realities. The obvious and the most pervasive of the critical realities is *money. What are the budgetary realities?* Once again the answers will vary. For some institutions the CBL office may become part of the overhead, while others may consider it a profit-center or as a pass-through. There are other issues germane to the functional aspects of the CBL office which are related to resource allocation and control such as staffing, space, budget size, and income control. The issue of budgetary control will most likely be hotly debated, but it is the responsibility of the individuals involved to make sure decisions are made to enhance the success of CBL.

An Organizational Structure for a CBL Office. Figure 1.1 shows a typical organizational structure for a CBL office. The principal function of a CBL office is to serve as an overall coordinating agency for linkage programs. The quality of linkage programs will be a direct outgrowth of the efficiency of the CBL office and will depend on the degree of clarity surrounding the scope and magnitude of the responsibilities of the CBL office. Therefore, it is important that the CBL office's perception of its place in the organization is in harmony with the institution's perception of its place within the organizational structure.

As suggested by the organizational structure for a CBL office, the CBL *coordinator* is responsible to the institution for the operation of the CBL office. The CBL *curriculum specialist* reports to the CBL *coordinator* on all matters involving curriculum development, implementation, evaluation, and modification. The CBL *public relations specialist* reports to the CBL *coordinator* on matters such as market potential, competition, company profiles, media releases, and CBL presentation packages. The CBL *public relations specialist* also attends meetings of local groups and is directly involved in making contact with businesses. An *Internal Management Information System* (IMIS) *specialist* reports to the CBL *coordinator* on all matters involving the collection and management of CBL information.

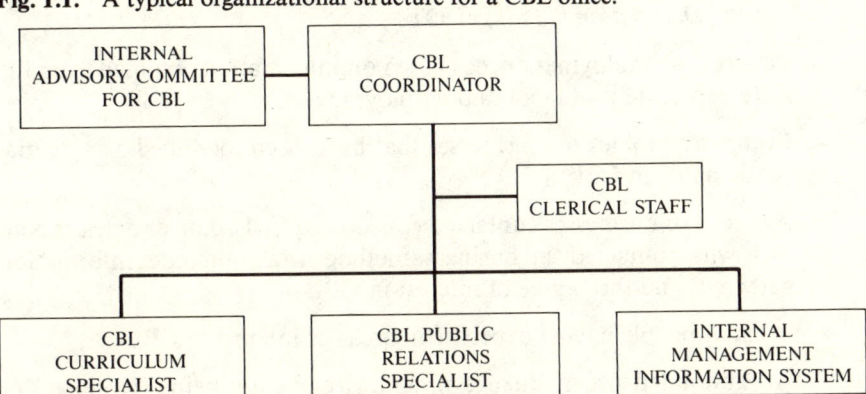

Fig. 1.1. A typical organizational structure for a CBL office.

INTERNAL ADVISORY COMMITTEE FOR CBL

The establishment of an *internal advisory committee* which includes individuals or groups interested in the development of CBL who have expertise in budgeting, marketing, administrative policies, curriculum, instruction, or information management is recommended. This committee would identify the pupose and responsibilities of the CBL office and make appropriate budgetary recommendations. It would also serve to:

1. Assist in the selection of faculty and staff for involvement in linkage program development
2. Establish compensation and pricing guidelines consistent with the policies of the institution
3. Outline evaluation and staffing procedures and policies
4. Assist in the development of marketing strategies
5. Assist in the dissemination of information concerning CBL

IMIS

Another function of a CBL office is to develop and maintain an IMIS. Record keeping, whether manual or computerized, is an area of concern because of the need for rapid retrieval of marketplace information. An IMIS should provide immediate access to the following information about the external environment of the institution of higher education:

1. A list of businesses with 25 or more employees classified according to *Standard Industrial Classifications* (SIC)
2. A list of typical job titles, based on SIC codes matched with the *Dictionary of Occupational Titles* (DOT)
3. Patterns of employment needs based on information obtained from the state department of labor and employment
4. Company profiles on businesses that have been identified as potential participants in CBL
5. A record of businesses contacted concerning CBL, date or dates of contact, who contacted the business, method used, outcome, information gathered, and the degree of interest in CBL
6. A list of people having expertise in areas of interest to CBL
7. An annotated list of linkage programs currently being developed or

implemented, and previously developed and implemented by the competition in the marketplace

8. Date when information was last updated on each file

The IMIS should also provide institutional information with respect to CBL. Information such as:

1. A list of administrators, faculty, and staff having expertise in areas of interest to CBL

2. An annotated list of linkage programs developed and implemented by the institution, or currently being developed and implemented

3. Fiscal records and cost effectiveness of linkage programs once they are implemented and evaluated

Many of the initial tasks of the CBL office staff involve collecting information for the IMIS specialist to organize and store for future reference.

PROCEDURE MANUAL FOR CBL

A *Procedure Manual* for the CBL office should be developed to provide guidance for individuals or groups interested in initiating CBL, as well as to provide guidance for the CBL staff. It should be written in clear, precise language and use the step-by-step approach with numerous samples of finished products. Among the items that should be included in the manual are:

1. The rationale for CBL

2. An organizational chart of the institution

3. An organizational chart of the CBL office

4. Descriptions of staff positions and the responsibilities of the position

5. Samples of letters of introduction, follow-up contact letters, and letters acknowledging meetings

6. A sample proposal for a linkage program that satisfies legal, fiscal, and geographical requirements imposed by the state on the institution and consistent with the mission of the institution

7. Samples of budgets using state-generated funds and at least one budget which is not solely dependent on state funds

8. Samples of contracts for linkage programs approved by the institution

9. Typical instructional costs information or college credit and noncollege credit classes

10. Guidelines for pricing linkage programs
11. Company profile forms with procedures for gathering the information
12. Samples of designs for program evaluations
13. Procedures for updating IMIS
14. Guidelines for follow-up of initial contacts with businesses
15. An information list that must be fed to the IMIS for storing

Naturally, it will take time to develop a *Procedure Manual* for the CBL office and it is possible that linkage programs will be developed and implemented long before the manual is completed. A loose-leaf binder should be used to store the various parts of the manual until it has been completed, evaluated, and revised. With the binder, the manual can be easily revised and additions or deletions can be readily made. The CBL coordinator is responsible for the development of the *Procedure Manual*.

ASSESSMENT OF THE EXTERNAL ENVIRONMENT OF THE INSTITUTION

When contemplating the development of CBL, the institution must acquire an accurate picture of the external environment. This is necessary because the external environment represents the marketplace for linkage programs. Without an assessment of the needs of private businesses in the external environment, the prospect for the development of a successful linkage program is very slim. It is imperative that marketplace research precede any *formal* announcement of a linkage effort because it will influence the magnitude, focus, and timing of such an effort. It is quite possible that after the assessment of the needs of businesses is conducted, the institution would be ill advised to proceed with CBL.

Three aspects are included in the assessment of the external environment: market potential, competition, and the cost effectiveness of CBL. However, the basis for the *go* or *no go* decision will vary among institutions since the decision must be based upon the institution's unique expectations and its mission.

MARKET POTENTIAL

One dimension of CBL development is the need to build a reciprocal relationship with well-defined mutual expectations and realistic goals within the framework of the needs and demands of business and the available resources of the institution. This requires the ability to balance market demand with resource supply. To do this, it is necessary to understand the nature and extent of market demand and to have knowledge of the institution's available resources.

Determining the nature and extent of market demand can be done formally or informally. Some institutions gather information about the marketplace informally through advisory groups consisting of administrators, faculty, staff, and representatives from private business. Other institutions gather information using a more formal approach through surveys, interviews, and phone calls asking private businesses to provide information about their human resources, products, or services. Both approaches require an awareness of what business activity and economic development is underway or contemplated, so it is always wise to review local newspapers and other available sources of information.

Sources of Information. Active solicitation of information by the institution of higher education is a must to obtain an accurate assessment of its external environment. The *Chamber of Commerce* is probably the most common vehicle for obtaining valuable marketplace information, as is the local chapter of the *American Society for Training and Development* (ASTD). Other sources of information include *professional associations, trade organizations,* and some *civic organizations.*

Formal participation is encouraged, that is, the institution should:

1. Ascertain membership information and meeting schedules of the Chamber of Commerce, ASTD, professional associations, trade organizations, and other appropriate civic organizations

2. Select with great care the best qualified individual to attend meetings as the representative of the institution

3. Instruct its representative to gather information about potential marketplace needs, attitudes toward the institution, and potential linkages

4. Be aware that arrogance is the fastest way to destroy market potential

With this approach some good business contacts will be developed and some useful marketplace information gathered.

Company Profiles. Specific questions about the businesses in the marketplace need to be answered before the nature and extent of market demands can be determined. Among those questions, the ones most useful in the development of company profiles are as follows:

1. How many white-collar, blue-collar, and pink-collar employees are in the company?

2. What products or services are provided by the company?

3. How does the company organize its human resources?

4. How much company support is given to human resource development?

5. How extensive is the human resource development?

6. Are there human resource specialists or other company officials interested in the cooperative development of human resources?

7. What are the training priorities within the company for white-collar, blue-collar, and pink-collar employees?

8. Are there existing physical facilities available for a cooperative training effort?

9. Have there been other cooperative efforts with academic or nonacademic institutions? If so, by whom and were they successful?

10. Are there employees who are graduates of the institution or are presently enrolled?

There are two main purposes for developing company profiles, namely (1) to aid in the development of an overall picture of the marketplace showing the specific needs of its human resources and; (2) to provide the necessary background information on a company so that individuals who contact the company can talk intelligently about possible human resource problems.

Although the information obtained by way of company profiles is sent to the IMIS specialist for storage, there should be a backup source for the information. It is suggested, especially if record keeping is computerized, that files be established for the targeted businesses and that they contain copies of the company profile and written communications to or from the company. Campus-business linkages coordinators may want a *small* business file which consists of information on businesses employing less than 200 employees and a large business file because there are differences in the kind of educational services required and the types of people involved.

There is a final step in determining the nature and extent of market potential. Representatives from the institution and from business must meet and exchange information concerning the needs of businesses and the available resources of the institution. Often businesses and trade organizations have developed their own training programs, but will welcome any assistance the institution can provide. The importance of a cooperative approach is emphasized as is the importance of productive personal interactions that can prove valuable for both sides involved in CBL.

COMPETITION

Information about market potential is essential as is information about potential *market share*. Competition exists in the external environment of the institution of higher education. A major challenge facing the institution in the development of CBL is to identify the available market share. Perhaps the most effective approach to gathering market share information is to know:

1. The available resources and the resource potential of the competition
2. The comparative quality of existing CBL or similar programs
3. The competitive activities of other institutions, professional associations, trade organizations, and internal training programs within businesses

That is, the institution must find out which linkage programs the other institutions of higher education as well as the nonacademic institutions and organizations are providing or could provide businesses. This is best done by being on the mailing lists of the competition, reviewing their advertisements, calling them directly to ask specific questions, and participating in area conferences and meetings.

The extent and nature of competition will vary by marketplace. However, it should not be a major deterrent to CBL if the potential linkage programs have resource bases that are solid and consistent. Often the best approach is to identify potential CBL that are modifications of specific on-campus programs that are significantly better than the competition. By emphasizing the quality and success of the on-campus program, credibility is lent to the potential linkage program. Once a linkage is made, other CBL can be systematically developed.

Generally speaking, most institutions will find they are in an *open-market* situation or possibly the only game in town. How the institution will meet its competition is a major issue that should be reconciled before the development of CBL.

COST EFFECTIVENESS OF CBL

One of the most difficult tasks during the predevelopment phase of CBL is the establishment of a budgetary structure within which the cost effectiveness of CBL can be measured. The profit motive of each linkage program must be identified. CBL profit motives may vary from that of a public service venture to that of generating *real profit* to off-set an anticipated shortfall in either tuition or governmental subsidy.

Linkage programs will have costs similar to those of on-campus programs. While the cost amounts may vary among CBL the cost categories will generally remain constant. Therefore, by using a standardized cost/revenue form that categorizes costs with respect to faculty and staff salaries, instructional materials, travel, advertising, space rental, administrative overhead, institutional overhead, and other costs, each linkage program can be evaluated for cost effectiveness by the same budgetary criteria used for on-campus programs.

Accurate records and uniform budgetary procedures are essential. The quality of the linkage program, the number of businesses served, and the enhancement of the institution's image are important, but the ability to generate *real profit* somehow helps to convince even the severest critics of linkage programs that CBL are a worthwhile endeavor. This does not mean that the profit motive is the only basis for the institution's commitment and support of the concept of CBL, but experience has suggested that profit often tips the scales in favor of continued support and commitment.

Regardless of the bottom-line focus, a budgetary structure should be established that allows the CBL office to measure and demonstrate the cost effectiveness of CBL.

CHAPTER TWO

Linkage Program Construction

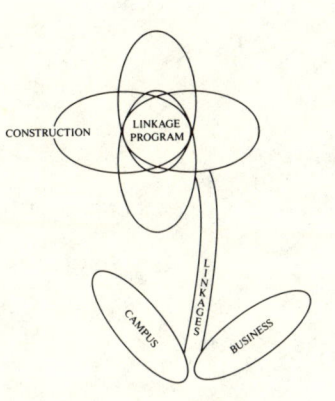

A linkage program consists of four essential components: (1) program construction; (2) curriculum development; (3) program implementation; and (4) program evaluation. Program construction consists of the decision-making process that determines the nature and design of the program; curriculum development consists of selecting and organizing content and learning experiences consonant with the nature and design of the program; program implementation is the process of putting into effect the program produced by the construction and curriculum development processes; and program evaluation consists of the assessment of the linkage program. Although these four components are discussed sequentially and discretely, they are neither discrete nor sequential, but occur concurrently and in combination with each other. The relationships among the four components of a linkage program are graphically demonstrated in Figure 2.1. The linkage program is shown as the intersection of its four components which in turn are shown as the overlapping processes involved in CBL.

This chapter deals with the major decision-making areas that constitute the construction component of a linkage program. Development, implementation, and evaluation are dealt with in Chapters 3, 4, and 5, respectively.

DEFINING THE PROGRAM

Before the first draft of a proposal for a potential linkage program can be written, the institution must:

1. Identify the audience
2. Establish program goals

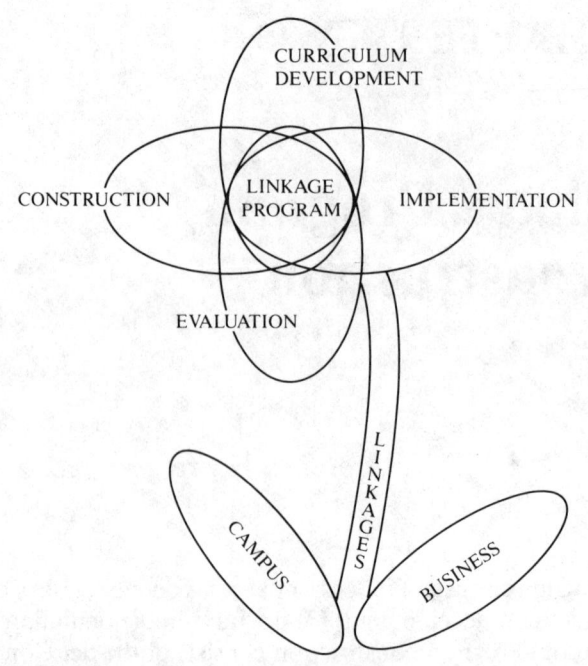

Fig. 2.1. The four components of a linkage program

3. Obtain a consensus on selection and involvement of people
4. Specify program peculiarities, if any exist, and features
5. Determine the necessary resources, costs, and deadlines

That is, the institution must define the program.

AUDIENCE

The *audience,* a term used to define the extent of the linkage effort, may be a single business or a group of businesses. Although decisions regarding the participation of the audience are usually settled externally, by officials of the targeted businesses, the individual or group initiating a linkage program must have a specific audience in mind. Most likely, the audience will be one that has been identified by the assessment of the external environment, or through contacts with the Chamber of Commerce, ASTD, professional associations, and civic organizations.

After an annotated list of the potential audience has been made, the next step is to contact the businesses listed. This is an important step, but one that shouldn't be too difficult. From the list, select those about which the most information is available or those that are most likely to participate in CBL and decide which method to use for initial contacts: telephone calls, letters, or cold calls.

Initial Contacts by Telephone. Telephone calls are very effective if conducted properly. Their purpose is twofold, namely (1) to make an appointment to meet with and discuss educational services of the institution that may be useful to the business; and (2) to gather information. When making initial contacts by telephone, there are several *caller do's* and *caller don'ts:*

1. *Do* review the company profile before making the telephone call.
2. *Do* prepare an outline of the information you want to convey or gather.
3. *Do* identify yourself and the name of the institution you represent.
4. *Do* make notes during the conversation.
5. *Don't* try to give details about possible CBL over the telephone.
6. *Don't* ask to have your call returned if the person you wanted to speak to is not in or busy; ask for a "best time" to call back.
7. *Do* use the call back option; it keeps you in control.

Initial Contacts by Letter. Letters are often the best but not the fastest way of making initial contacts with businesses. Letters are successful if they reach and if they are read by the appropriate official of the business. Therefore, letters should be addressed to specific persons or specific job titles within the targeted businesses and they should be concise! The primary purpose of the letter is to arrange a meeting to discuss the educational services of the institution which involve human resource development in areas that may be of interest to the business.

Initial Contact by Cold Calls. Cold Calls are unannounced visits to places of business. Whether the business official is *in* and has the *time to talk* is unpredictable. Cold calls are not recommended as a method of making initial contacts with large, formally structured businesses or corporations, but cold calls can be effective when making initial contacts with small businesses that are not formally structured and are less likely to respond to letters. Some of the negative aspects of cold calls are:

1. Time is wasted if no one is available to talk or if everyone is too busy to talk.
2. Company officials may think the cold caller is insensitive to their busy schedules.
3. Dropping in unannounced may be viewed as inconsiderate.
4. If company officials agree to talk it is quite possible that their attention is not undivided.

Whichever method is chosen for making an initial contact with a targeted business, *follow-up* is important. Follow up a telephone call with a letter verifying the agreed upon time, place, and date of the meeting. Follow up an unanswered letter with a telephone call or another letter. Follow up cold calls with letters thanking business officials for their time and verifying any arrangements that may have been made for another meeting.

PROGRAM GOALS

Are the *perceived* needs the *real* needs of the business? Answering this question requires the ability to recognize existing or potential problems within the business which can be solved through human resource development. It may take both the business and the institution of higher education, working together in an open and trusting environment, to identify the real needs and to derive program goals from these needs.

SELECTION AND INVOLVEMENT OF PEOPLE

It should be obvious that the selection and involvement of people depends on both the audience and the goals of the linkage program. Similarly, it should be obvious that it would be unrealistic for an institution to attempt to *actively involve* everyone interested or affected by the linkage program — administrators, faculty, staff, and human resource specialists or others from the targeted business — because there would be so many people involved that nothing would get done. A group consisting of specialized personnel, selected faculty, selected administrators, and representatives or contact people from the audience is needed.

The institution's CBL coordinator assisted by the Internal Advisory Committee for CBL would be the most likely person to select people from the institution to be involved. Human resource specialists or other interested officials from the audience may choose to be actively involved or designate certain employees of the company to be involved in the development of the linkage program. Whoever is brought into the construction, curriculum development, implementation, and evaluation processes must have the necessary expertise and the necessary authority to work on the linkage program. It is extremely important to select and involve people who have the power to make *go* or *no go* decisions. Many linkage programs remain on the drawing table because the people involved did not have the power to authorize its implementation, thereby wasting time, talent, and money.

SPECIFY PROGRAM PECULIARITIES AND FEATURES: PROGRAM DESIGN

Distinguishing features and program peculiarities, if they exist, must be identified and tentatively agreed upon so that both the targeted business or business and the institution have a working idea of the type of linkage program to be developed. Among the features that affect program design are:

1. Contract versus open-market classes
2. College credit versus noncollege credit status
3. On-site versus on-campus instruction
4. Training versus education

In many instances, the potential audience will make the choice after both the advantages and disadvantages are discussed, and the overall effect of each on the design of the program.

Contract Classes Versus Open-Market Classes. Contract classes are classes in which the enrollment is limited to persons employed by the company with which the contract was made. In comparison, anyone can enroll in *open-market* classes; being employed by the company with which the contract was made is not a condition for enrollment.

College Credit Versus Noncollege Credit. College credit status versus noncollege credit status may be a moot point. For some businesses college credit is a must while for others there is no particular preference. Cost usually enters into any credit versus noncredit discussion. College credit classes tend to be more expensive than noncollege credit classes since the institution has less flexibility when it comes to scheduling, staffing, course content, and cost; but at the same time they tend to generate more revenue for the institution.

On-site Instruction Versus On-campus Instruction. The location of classes is negotiable. As a matter of convenience for its employees, the company may stipulate that on-site instruction take place. Usually costs are reduced if the company provides the facilities. However, some companies prefer on-campus instruction because they want their employees to be exposed to an academic environment or they want to encourage their employees to interact with a cross-section of people.

On-site instruction may not be an option when the audience consists of several businesses. Unless, of course, it can be arranged for the linkage program to be conducted in facilities provided by one of the businesses and have the employees from the other businesses attend. If such an arrangement cannot be made there are two options, namely (1) use on-campus instruction; or (2) rent a site convenient to all concerned.

RESOURCES, COSTS, AND DEADLINES

Other topics that need to be addressed before the first draft of a proposal for a linkage program can be written are resources, costs, and deadlines. Resources necessary for the development and implementation of the linkage program must be identified and a tentative agreement reached as to which resources the institution will provide and which resources the business will provide. Once the resources are determined, an estimate of direct and indirect costs can be made. The profit motive of the linkage program must be known and considered when making cost estimates. The break-even point should be known or at least estimated at this point if the linkage program is to generate a profit.

Finally, a timetable should be established showing not only the sequence of events, but the deadlines for the completion of the development and the implementation of the linkage program.

THE CONSTRUCTION MEETING

The purpose of the construction meeting is to gather information needed to make the necessary decisions that will determine the nature and design of the linkage program and ultimately define the program. Attendance at this meeting should be held to a minimum. At this point, the only people who need to be involved are the CBL coordinator from the institution and the human resource specialist or training director from the business, but more often than not, these individuals will bring others to the meeting as resource people. Whoever said, "Too many cooks spoil the soup" must have been a CBL coordinator before becoming a chef.

Prior to the meeting the CBL coordinator, as well as anyone else from the institution who plans to attend, should:

1. Review the company profile

2. Understand as much as possible about the product or services provided by the company

3. Acquire knowledge about the available resources of the institution and its willingness to use these resources in a linkage program

4. Prepare a list of questions designed to gather the information needed to make decisions regarding the nature and design of the program

Most company officials have had a very limited experience with institutions of higher education. They seldom equate flexible, tailor-made programs and contracted services with educational institutions, but rather see them as rigid structures featuring sequential courses for degree-seeking students. It is very important that this impression of rigidity be dispelled and the educational services of the institution portrayed as flexible and capable of being customized to meet their specific needs.

AGENDA FOR THE CONSTRUCTION MEETING

The topics for discussion that should be included on the agenda of the construction meeting are (1) audience; (2) needs; (3) program goals; (4) selection and involvement of people; (5) program features; and (6) resources, costs, and deadlines. Each of these topics was discussed earlier in this chapter and in the discussions several questions were raised. The following are examples of questions that should be raised at the construction meeting and, if possible, answered.

1. What is the likelihood of the company participating in a linkage program?
2. What human resource problems are encountered by the company?
3. What can the institution of higher education do to help solve these problems?
4. What are the training needs of the company?
5. What can the institution do to assist the company in their training programs?
6. What should be the goals of the linkage program?
7. Approximately how many employees will participate in a linkage program?
8. What company official will be actively involved in the development and implementation of the program?
9. What resources will be provided by the company? By the institution?
10. Will the employees be selected to participate or will it be up to them to enroll in the program?
11. What are the educational backgrounds of the participating employees?
12. Who pays tuition costs, the company or the employees?
13. Who makes the final decision that authorizes the employees to participate in the program?
14. What features should be included in the program: contract or open-market classes, credit or noncredit classes, on-site or on-campus instruction?

15. What deadlines, if any, exist for program development, for program implementation?
16. What criteria will be used to evaluate the program?

Be discrete, but find out as much as possible about the needs of the business and determine whether or not the institution has the necessary resources to satisfy the needs.

PREPARING THE FORMAL PROPOSAL

The proposal for a linkage program is the first written document to be presented to the company for consideration. To a large degree, the proposal will determine whether the linkage program is accepted or rejected. Considerable effort should be made to prepare a "first class" document because the quality of the proposal will, in effect, be the basis for the company's opinion of the quality of the linkage program.

Readability is essential. The proposal should be written in universally understood terms avoiding the temptation to use educational jargon. It should be specific enough to answer the company's question: What can this institution of higher education do for me? Yet, it should be general enough to protect the linkage program from competitive pilfering or from adoption by the company without the resources of the institution.

PURPOSE OF THE PROPOSAL

The purpose of the proposal is to convey a clear picture of (1) the nature and design of the linkage program; (2) the requirements and procedures by which the program will be developed, implemented, and evaluated; (3) the role and responsibilities of both the institution and the company with respect to the program; (4) the costs involved in the development and implementation of the program; and (5) the timetable for the program.

To convey a clear picture of the nature and design of the program, the proposal must identify the audience, state program goals, provide a criterion for the selection and involvement of people, and specify the features of the program. Procedures for the development, implementation, and evaluation should be stated briefly along with any requirements about quality control, delivery, staffing, and deadlines. Similarly, the role and responsibilities of the institution during the curriculum development, program implementation, and program evaluation processes, as well as the role and responsibilities of the company must be stated as explicitly as possible. Conflicts can be avoided by making certain that there are no areas in which the responsibilities of the institution and company overlap or are not covered in the proposal.

COST PROFILE

A cost profile should be developed along sound lines while allowing for some flexibility during negotiations. Many businesses are only interested in the aggregate figure, the bottom line, while others want specifics. Either way, a cost profile is an appropriate way to help eliminate budgetary oversights. This is one part of the proposal that should be as accurate as possible. There will be negotiations that change cost figures, but the bottom line of the cost profile should be something with which the institution can live. It is extremely important to list all items for which specific costs could not be determined in time for the proposal and to state that they are not included in the aggregate cost as presented.

SIGN-OFFS, COMMENTS, AND SIGNATURES

The proposal should provide adequate space for comments, sign-offs, and signatures. Spaces for comments by company officials should be provided in each major area of the proposal, as well as at the conclusion of the document.

PRESENTING THE FORMAL PROPOSAL

During the preparation of the proposal, lines of communication were opened and probably used to verify or clarify certain aspects of the linkage program. By the time the proposal is completed, it should be known, for certain, who has the authority within the company to accept the proposal. Ideally, this person was actively involved in the program construction process and is aware that a linkage program proposal is forthcoming.

COVER LETTER

The proposal with an accompanying cover letter is sent to the human resource specialist or to the company official with whom the CBL coordinator has been dealing. Usually the tone of the letter sets the tone for the proposal. The letter should state that it accompanies a *working copy* of the proposal and it should welcome any suggestions, comments, or questions concerning the proposal. Since business officials are accustomed to meeting and setting deadlines, it is quite proper to ask that the proposal be returned by a certain date. Be sure to use the phrase *working copy* because it implies that the institution is willing to negotiate. Therefore, it is less likely that the proposal will be rejected on the first reading.

PATIENCE, PERSISTENCE, AND PROFESSIONALISM

Patience, persistence, and professionalism play as important a role in the development of CBL as they do in any other worthwhile venture. *Patience* is required now, because the proposal may cover areas with which the human resource specialist is unaccustomed, and decisions in these areas may have to be made by officials in the company who have not been actively involved in the program construction process. *Persistence* was required to get this far along in the development of a potential linkage program and will be required to complete the remaining tasks if the proposal is accepted. *Professionalism* was expected by those persons encountered during the program construction process because of the confidence and respect with which institutions of higher education are viewed. The methods and manner of CBL coordinators when dealing with business officials must be above-board and inspire the same confidence and respect that already is accorded the institution they represent.

CHAPTER THREE

Curriculum Development

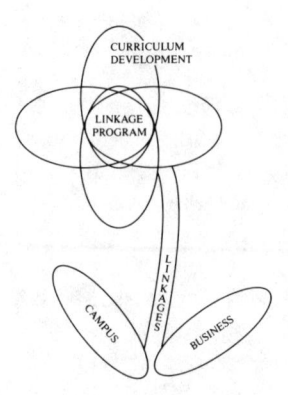

The second component of a linkage program is curriculum development which consists of selecting and organizing content and learning experiences. Like program construction, curriculum development refers to a process. Curriculum development is related to program construction, but it is distinguishable from it by the nature of the decisions. Although program construction and curriculum development are discussed sequentially and discretely, the processes usually overlap in that (1) development and construction decisions are being made at the same time; and (2) development decisions may effect the design of the program and construction decisions may effect the selecting and organizing of content and learning experiences. In many instances, curriculum development precedes curriculum construction.

ISSUES INVOLVED IN CURRICULUM DEVELOPMENT

It has been said that issues should not be seen as threats, but as opportunities for gaining new insights. If this is true, then among the curriculum developers for the linkage program there should be at least one opportunist. The issues involved in the curriculum development process of CBL have been classified into three categories: (1) quality; (2) delivery; and (3) evaluation. As shown in Figure 3.1, the issue of quality deals with the content, learning experiences, and instructional materials developed for or used in the linkage program; issues involving delivery include location, methods of instruction, and faculty; and evaluation issues that must be dealt with are goals versus roles, and types of evaluation for CBL.

```
                    ┌─────────────────────────┐
                    │   MAJOR ISSUES INVOLVED │
                    │            IN           │
                    │  CURRICULUM DEVELOPMENT │
                    └─────────────────────────┘
                                 │
         ┌───────────────────────┼───────────────────────┐
         │                       │                       │
    ┌─────────┐            ┌──────────┐           ┌────────────┐
    │ QUALITY │            │ DELIVERY │           │ EVALUATION │
    └─────────┘            └──────────┘           └────────────┘
         │                       │                       │
  ┌────────────┐           ┌──────────┐            ┌─────────┐
  │  CONTENT   │           │          │            │  GOALS  │
  │     &      │           │ LOCATION │            │    &    │
  │  LEARNING  │           │          │            │  ROLES  │
  │EXPERIENCES │           └──────────┘            └─────────┘
  └────────────┘                │                       │
         │                      │                       │
  ┌────────────┐           ┌──────────┐            ┌─────────┐
  │ MATERIALS  │           │ METHODS  │            │         │
  │    FOR     │           │    OF    │            │  TYPES  │
  │INSTRUCTION │           │INSTRUCTION│           │         │
  └────────────┘           └──────────┘            └─────────┘
                                │
                           ┌──────────┐
                           │ FACULTY  │
                           └──────────┘
```

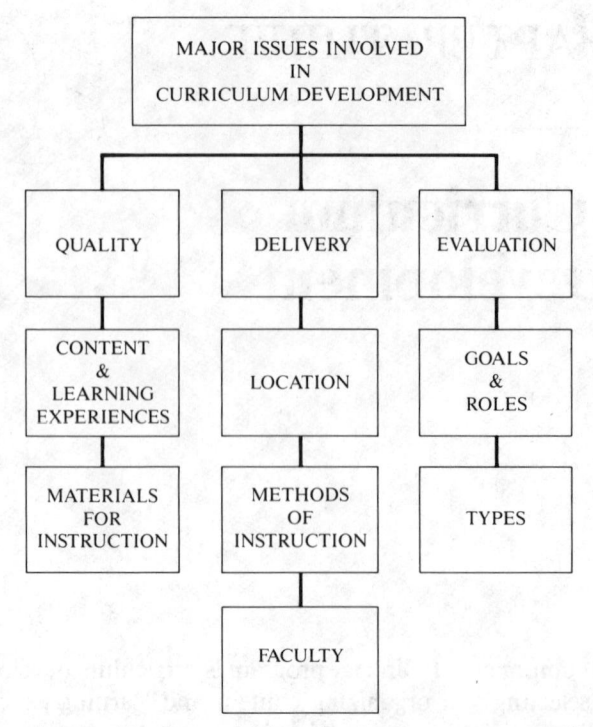

Fig. 3.1. Issues involved in the curriculum development process of CBL.

QUALITY

While quality is expected throughout the development and implementation of the linkage program, there are two areas in the curriculum development process that deserve special mention.

Content and Learning Experiences. To begin with, the difficulty of maintaining a good correspondence between the goals of the program and the specific objectives formulated to attain the goals must be recognized and accepted as a challenge. There is no clear-cut relationship between program goals and content, nor is there one between program goals and learning experiences or content and learning experiences. Goals, content, and learning experiences are interrelated, so decisions about any one of them will have a bearing on decisions about the others. Thus, the quality of the selected content and learning experiences should be measured in terms of their ability to achieve the goals of the linkage program. Moreover, there should be no conspicuous inconsistencies between goals and content, goals and learning experiences, and content and learning experiences!

Instructional Materials. The quality of a linkage program also depends on the quality of the instructional materials used. When on-site instruction takes place, it is wise to have the CBL coordinator and the selected faculty members visit the site to determine if appropriate instructional materials are available, and, if not, the source for supplying them. To insure quality in linkage programs that rely on technical devices, instructional assistants should be available to assist faculty with acquisition, preparation, and maintenance chores. Dated instructional materials should be avoided!

DELIVERY

Curriculum development requires resolving issues involving the delivery system and the overall design of the linkage program. The organization of content and learning experiences indirectly depends on the system through which it will be delivered, but the delivery system directly depends on the design of the linkage program.

Location. Do the advantages of on-campus instruction outnumber the advantages of on-site instruction? Does on-site instruction contribute to or get in the way of achieving program goals? Questions like these require answers prior to making on-site versus on-campus decisions. Sometimes location decisions will be made based on convenience and other times they will be based on necessity. In both cases, the training-education dichotomy enters into the decision-making process and affects the selection and organization of learning experiences.

Methods of Instruction. Methods of instruction will vary among linkage programs and have little effect on selecting and organizing learning experiences. However, college credit versus noncollege credit status greatly affects the content of the program and to a lesser degree affects the method of instruction. Most likely, the curriculum developer will have little say about how the developed curriculum should be taught. The choice of methods tends to be in the domain of the instructor as it, quite possibly, should be. Consequently, the developed curriculum must be flexible enough for use in a number of different educational settings and consonant with the design of the program. There are exceptions. When curriculum is developed to meet training needs unique to a particular business, the curriculum developer should consider the uniqueness of the needs and develop the curriculum accordingly.

Faculty. The faculty's primary role in the curriculum development process is that of teaching the developed curriculum. This does not, of course, dismiss the possibility or the probability of release time for faculty to participate in the development process. It does, however, emphasize that faculty influence is the greatest in the classroom where applicability and feasibility of the developed curriculum are tested.

Selection of faculty should be based on:

1. Their ability to adapt to new teaching situations
2. Their compatibility with the audience which may or may not consist of traditional students

3. Their attitude toward the concept of CBL

4. Their willingness to revise their teaching techniques and instructional materials

5. Their interest in keeping pace with technological and professional advances

A great deal of tact and diplomacy is required when selecting faculty for the linkage program. There is always the possibility of the " 'fish-out-of-water' " problem when the linkage program involves on-site instruction. That is, the "best" on-campus instructor might be "less than satisfactory," to put it politely, as an on-site instructor. The success or failure of the linkage program may well be in the hands of its faculty. Remember, there is no such thing as faculty-proof curriculum!

EVALUATION

Since no single method of evaluation can be proposed and no specific criterion can be established for the evaluation of all curricula, curriculum developers are faced with the goals versus roles of evaluation issue.

Goals and Roles. The principal goal of evaluation is to evaluate the finished curriculum. This goal can be achieved by measuring the performance of the curriculum against established criteria or by comparing the performance of the curriculum with a similar curriculum. Once again, the training-education dichotomy enters into the decision-making process. Criteria, usually in the form of standardized achievement tests exist and can be adopted as a means of evaluating curriculum developed for the purpose of education. However, curriculum developed for the purpose of training is usually evaluated by measuring its performance against a similar curriculum. That is, if the linkage program is for the purpose of training, with prescribed skills as outcomes, then institutions must be able to convince businesses that they can *do it better*. So, the performance of the curriculum will be measured against the company's previous training program or its potential training program. It should be noted that *doing it better* sometimes means *doing it cheaper,* so cost enters into this form of evaluation.

Numerous roles are played by evaluation. Evaluation plays a motivational role for some students and a coercive role for others. For faculty, the role of evaluation is more like a control device. From the institution's point of view, the role of evaluation is that of classifying students. Whereas curriculum developers view the role of evaluation as a means of ongoing improvement of the curriculum which is consistent with the principal goal of evaluation.

Types of Evaluation. Two types of evaluation exist: (1) formative and (2) summative. Formative evaluation takes place throughout the curriculum development process; in contrast, summative evaluation takes place at the end of the process. Success or failure of linkage programs depends on the results of summative evaluations which make formative evaluations a priority of curriculum developers. The *first* attempt at CBL must be a relatively successful one! Information should be obtained, by means of formative evaluation, that can be used to *form* a better curriculum and that information should be used to form a success-oriented curriculum.

SELECTING AND ORGANIZING CONTENT AND LEARNING EXPERIENCES

Do the specific objectives, formulated from the goals, of the linkage program require the development of a new curriculum? Is there an existing on-campus, or off-campus, program that can be modified to meet the specific objectives of the linkage program? Often the curriculum development process for linkage programs is one of modifying an existing program rather than developing a new program.

DEVELOPING A NEW PROGRAM

The specific objectives of the linkage program indicate the attitudes to be developed, the concepts to be learned, and the skills to be mastered. The analysis of the needs of the audience determines where the emphasis will lie. Together they provide the impetus for selecting and organizing content and learning experiences, as well as an overall picture of the finished curriculum.

There are criteria other than objectives and needs that should be considered when selecting and organizing content and learning experiences. Significance, validity, continuity, design, sequence, and strategies are a few. For example, continuity of learning must be considered when organizing content and learning experiences, if optimum learning is to occur.

In addition to problems that normally occur in the selection and organization decision-making process, there are problems resulting from the involvement of noneducators—business officials or training directors—in the development of curriculum. These problems are inevitable particularly when the purpose of the linkage program is training, since the involvement of training directors or others from the business is crucial to the success of the program. After all, they are the ones who ultimately evaluate the program and not necessarily in terms of the achievement of objectives, but, more often than not, in terms of productivity, on-the-job injuries, personnel turnover, absenteeism, attitude, and so on. Do not attempt to develop training programs without the *active* involvement of training directors, possibly shop foreman and others, in the four essential components of the linkage program in general, and the selection and organization of content and learning experiences in particular. The reverent attitude regarding the institution of higher education which most likely prevails among noneducators in the marketplace does not preclude their belief that educators, for the most part, know little, if anything, about the *real world* training needs of businesses. Remember the " 'ivory tower' " syndrome!

MODIFYING AN EXISTING PROGRAM

The task of selecting and organizing content and learning experiences, when modifying an existing program, is less complex than it would be for developing a new program even though the criteria involved are the same. The most obvious difference is that of creativity or having to start from "scratch." The framework formulated by either the state or the audience within which the selection and organization of content and learning experiences takes place is the same in both instances. The task becomes one of picking and choosing rather than determining the actual structure of the content, and sequencing the learning experiences consistent with the structure. It would be in the best interest of the institution making a *first* attempt at CBL to select an audience for which an existing program can be modified. Primarily because the time spent on the curriculum development component of the linkage program could be put to better use in the program implementation component. Finally, active involvement of the company is almost as important when modifying a program as it is when developing a new program.

CHAPTER FOUR

Implementation of a Linkage Program

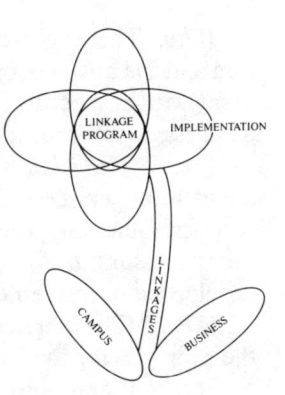

Implementation, the third component, is the process of putting into effect the linkage program. As indicated by the schema for linkage programs, the implementation component is not sequential, but overlaps each of the other three components of a linkage program. One of the main tasks of program implementation is to provide feedback to the construction and curriculum development processes which, when evaluated, can be used to revise and improve the curriculum.

PUTTING INTO EFFECT THE LINKAGE PROGRAM

Before a linkage program can be implemented, a contract must be written and signed. A *contract* is an agreement between two or more parties for the performance of services at a fixed cost. Two acts are involved in a contract: (1) making an offer; and (2) accepting the offer. For CBL, the proposal for the linkage program represents the act of *making an offer* and signing the contract represents the act of *accepting the offer*.

WRITING A CONTRACT

There are several important questions which must be answered when writing a contract. Who? What? When? Where? Why? and How? provide the heart of a news story. Similarly, the answers to Who? What? When? Where? Why? and How? provide the heart of a contract.

Who? The *who* in contract writing refers to the institution of higher education and the business participating in the linkage program. It involves an agreement with respect to the roles and responsibilities of the institution and the business as set forth in the proposal for the linkage program.

What? The *what* in contract writing requires an explicit statement of the educational services to be performed by the institution and a fixed cost for those services. Generally, the *what* refers to the sections in the proposal that describe the nature and design of the linkage program; the requirements for program development, implementation, and evaluation; and the cost of the program.

When? The *when* in contract writing deals with the timetable included in the proposal for the linkage program. *When* the services will begin, *when* the services will end, and *when* the services will be paid for, are usually critical factors in accepting the proposal and signing the contract. Any flexibility in the starting and ending dates must be agreed upon and appear as part of the contract. The timetable should be a realistic one within which the described educational services can be performed by the institution and the stipulated compensation can be paid by the business.

Where? The *where* in contract writing is usually a statement designating the location at which the services will be performed: on-campus, on-site, or in an agreed upon rented facility as set forth in the proposal.

Why? The *why in* contract writing is related to the goals of the linkage program which, most likely, appear in the proposal as the statement of purpose for the program. The *why of* contract writing is important and should be mentioned because of the peacekeeping role played by the contract. Since an underlying purpose of a contract is to settle disputes before they occur, stipulations for any, and probably all, possible areas of conflict should be included in the contract.

How? The *how* in contract writing is answered by the proposals stated procedures for development, implementation, and evaluation. The procedures and regulations set forth in the proposal may be considered, by some, the "nuts and bolts" of the program because they hold together the program's components.

Contract Negotiations. Formal proposals for linkage programs are seldom, if ever, accepted *as is.* Changes with respect to requirements, responsibilities, procedures, and costs should be expected. As previously indicated, the proposal for the linkage program represents the act of making an offer and that is the first step in writing the contract.

The second step is for the parties involved to negotiate the terms of the contract. That is, the answers to the questions Who? What? When? Where? Why? and How? must be mutually agreed upon by representatives from the institution and the business. Negotiations may occur in a single meeting or a series of meetings.

In the first session for contract negotiations, the *working copy* of the proposal is critically reviewed. Negotiators for the institution of higher education must:

1. Be aware of the items in the proposal that are nonnegotiable.
2. Be well versed in both the language and the intent of the proposal.
3. Have the authority to make minor changes on negotiable items.
4. Be prepared for a financial review and have the authority to resolve minor fiscal disputes.
5. Tactfully reject any suggested additions or changes that might lessen the program's chance for success or may not be educationally sound.
6. Determine if there is a likelihood of an increase or decrease in the number of employees participating in the program.

The negotiation of a contract can be a bittersweet experience that depends on the personalities of the people involved. The number of sessions needed for contract negotiations varies directly with the number of items that must be *checked out* before the negotiator can commit the institution to the requested changes. If an agreement can be reached during the first session, then negotiations are over and preparations are made for writing the contract.

Language of a Contract. Since a contract is an agreement involving a fixed cost for specific services, the language used must be precise. When planning the language of a contract, there are several points that must be considered and included in the contract by way of the language.

Increases or Decreases in the Number of Employees Participating in the Linkage Program. If during negotiations it is determined that an increase in the number of employees participating in the linkage program is likely to occur, then a provision is needed to address the costs involved. One way of addressing the costs is to include a formula for computing potential cost overruns due to increased participation as a provision of the contract if it is not already provided for in the budget section of the proposal. Another way is to prevent such costs from occurring by limiting participation. That is, a provision that states that the institution will provide instruction for up to x *number* of students. Similarly, if the anticipated enrollment does not occur, the language of the contract must indicate some type of shared responsibility or hold the business totally responsible for recruiting and enrolling up to x *number* of students.

On-site Instruction and Instructional Materials. When on-site instruction is to occur, the language of the contract should address the adequacy of the facilities provided and the instructional materials. For example, a provision of the contract may be "the business will provide an instructional facility capable of providing a comfortable teaching environment." A second provision should state that the business will provide all classroom facilities, instructional aids, and technical assistance for the preparation of required instructional media at no cost to the institution, except as noted in the budget section of the proposal.

Major Changes in the Contract. A statement, acceptable to both the business and the institution, should be in the contract to address the possibility of major changes being proposed by either party. Usually, a simple statement, asserting that major changes will necessitate the suspension of services and the renegotiation of the contract, is sufficient.

Monitoring and Evaluation of Program Implementation. The language of the contract should also address monitoring and evaluation processes. Sometimes, particularly if the purpose of the linkage program is training, periodic visitation by the company's training director or human resource specialist is stipulated to ensure the effectiveness of the linkage program. But usually, only the cooperation of the company with the institution's monitoring and evaluation efforts is required.

Cancellation of the Contract. When a contract is made for an indefinite period of time, it remains in effect until cancelled. The language of the contract must include a provision that states how the involved parties can cancel the contract. One such statement is: "This contract can be cancelled by either party with ten days written notice." However, an additional provision should be included in the contract which asserts that in the event of cancellation, the conditions of the contract will remain in effect until the end of the term in which the written notification was received. A statement such as that would protect both the institution and the business.

SIGNING THE CONTRACT

Patience, persistence, and professionalism have paid off again. Both parties involved in the negotiations have indicated their mutual acceptance of the proposal, which now becomes part of the contract. The third and last step of contract writing is signing the contract. Forms for contracts will vary with respect to the type of services to be provided and the business receiving the services. The contract is basically an agreement to accept the proposal along with any additions, changes, or modifications. Any actual changes written on the proposal itself should be initialed by both parties; sign offs on the proposal should be signed by the negotiators, and it should be determined whether a complete rewrite of the proposal is necessary or if an amendment to the proposal is sufficient.

A rewrite of the proposal may require another session for contract negotiations because it, in effect, represents the act of making a second offer which opens the door for more negotiations. So, unless numerous changes have been made, it is better to amend the original proposal.

The contract, attached to the proposal, must be presented to appropriate chief executive officers of the institution for their signatures and to similar officials in the business for their signatures. Seldom do CBL coordinators, human resource specialists, or training directors have the authority to legally commit their institutions or businesses to a linkage program.

TWELVE STEPS TO SUCCESSFUL PROGRAM IMPLEMENTATION

Program implementation should be the most rewarding component of the linkage program. The proposal has been accepted, a contract signed, and all the time and effort put into the construction and curriculum development processes is finally paying off. The challenge now is to deliver the educational services designed to satisfy the needs or to solve human resource problems of the business and to provide feedback that can be used to revise and improve the curriculum.

The gap between theory and practice can become painfully obvious during program implementation. Particularly if the faculty and staff responsible for implementing the program have not been involved in the construction and curriculum development processes. The following 12 steps are suggested not only to help keep the gap between theory and practice from widening, but to help implement the linkage program successfully.

1. Notify Individuals or Groups Involved or Affected by the Acceptance of the Linkage Program Proposal.

Once the proposal has been accepted and a contract signed, everyone involved in or affected by the linkage program should be notified. Administrators, faculty, and staff who invested their time and talents need to know that the proposed program is underway and the proposed timetable is in effect. The institution informs its people and the business informs theirs. Together, they decide whether or not they want to publicly acknowledge their joint education or training program.

2. Issue Faculty Contracts.

Faculty contracts should be issued and decisions that were made during the selection of faculty for involvement in the linkage program, especially in curriculum development, need to be implemented. Be sure all faculty contracts are signed by full-time and part-time faculty and instructors from the company. It is a good idea to hire the teaching staff early, so they can participate in the curriculum development process. By having the faculty contribute in decision-making processes, some of the responsibility for the success or failure of the program rests with them, which, most likely, will be reflected in their teaching.

3. Visit the Facilities Where Instruction Will Take Place.

Visit the facilities where instruction will take place whether it is on-campus, on-site, or in a rented facility. During the visit the following questions should be answered: Is the space allotted for implementation of the linkage program suitable for both the method of instruction and the anticipated enrollment? Does the facility adequately provide for *creature comforts* such as lighting, heating and cooling, restrooms, food service, and parking? Are the existing furniture and equipment adequate for the program? Are instructional materials readily available?

Campus-business linkages coordinators, selected faculty, and human resource specialists or training directors should walk through the facilities to jointly determine what, if any, modifications are necessary for program implementation. A diagram showing table or desk arrangement, equipment, and the physical features of the facility should be drawn.

4. Acquire Appropriate Equipment.

Any special equipment needed to support classroom instruction or training should be available prior to the first day of classes. Faculty should be encouraged to familiarize themselves with the equipment and develop contingency plans for use when equipment malfunctions. Backup equipment may be needed for overhead projectors, tape recorders, and other audio-visual equipment. The faculty should provide a list of support equipment needed along with the date and time needed.

5. Obtain Necessary Instructional Materials.

The preparation of instructional materials is a lengthy process, as is the reproduction of instructional materials and the acquisition of textbooks and shop supplies. Everything should be obtained before the first day of classes so that they can be organized, inspected, and delivered to the faculty. *All* instructional materials should be of good quality, current, and appropriate for the level of instruction of the program. A class outline that is complete, accurate, and free of typographical errors is a must. The quality of the materials used in the classroom creates a first impression for the quality of instruction.

6. Assign Special Staff as Required.

As a general rule, when beginning a new linkage program, it is better to be overstaffed than understaffed. Be certain to have on-site staff to assist the faculty when problems occur. Don't operate on the assumption that what appears flawless on paper will, in fact, be just as flawless in practice. Usually, just the opposite is true. A major problem that exists in CBL is *taking for granted* that everything will work out.

7. Maintain Lines of Communication.

Lines of communication must be open between the institution and the company. Encourage the company to be actively involved if that was agreed upon in the contract. Communicate openly and freely. Be receptive to requests for written progress reports and inform the company of any modifications being made as the result of evaluative data gathered during the monitoring process. Include faculty in meetings scheduled for the purpose of reporting progress, preventing misinformation and dissension, or changing the curriculum.

8. Prepare Public Relations Materials.

When an innovative, exciting linkage program has been developed and is being implemented successfully, people should know about it. This is where the public relations specialist is valuable. Public relations involves the dissemination of promotional materials to three groups: (1) internal operations; (2) the external environment; and (3) businesses targeted for potential CBL.

Internal Operations. Internal operations refers to the institution of higher education. It is amazing how many institutions have outstanding linkage programs, yet, very few people within the institution are aware of them. Effective use of internal publications, such as faculty and staff newsletters, is recommended as a way of developing awareness of CBL and the linkage program being implemented.

The External Environment. Newspapers, radio and television, professional magazines, and speaking engagements at civic or social functions are among the many ways of informing the public about successful implementation of CBL. Be sure that *all* press releases are approved by company officials prior to dissemination. Tact and diplomacy are needed when dealing with companies that do not like publicity written by others. Try to avoid *telling all* unless both the institution and the business are willing to share the information with the public!

Businesses Targeted for Potential CBL. Businesses identified as prospective clients for CBL are the third group that should be informed about successful implementation of a linkage program. This group is most likely to be involved in future linkage programs and the most effective way to get their attention is by sharing the success of the linkage program being implemented. Usually the success is shared with the group by means of word-of-mouth during formal meetings of the Chamber of Commerce, ASTD, professional associations, trade organizations, and other civic organizations.

9. Plan for Registration.

Plans for registration must be consistent with registration policies at the institution. For linkage programs involving noncollege credit classes, the registration should be done during the first meeting of the class. For linkage programs involving college credit classes, registration can be done during the first meeting with the aid of someone from the registrars office or it can be done through normal registration procedures. Registration is affected by the conditions set forth in the proposal. Conditions such as: how tuition fees are to be paid—by the company or by the employees, whether the classes are contract or open market, and limitations on enrollment, if they exist.

Early registration is encouraged, since it provides enrollment figures, time to iron out problems that occur during registration, and there is usually a less hectic atmosphere. Remember, a well-informed registration team can handle concerns and questions, solve problems, and promote goodwill.

10. Start the First Class Enthusiastically.

First impressions are as important in linkage programs as they are anywhere else. In addition to planning for an easy-going registration, plan for flawless meetings on the first day of classes. It is imperative that:

1. All faculty be present and prepared to teach
2. The instructional materials be available and of good quality
3. The classroom be comfortable and suitable for the type of instruction that is to take place
4. No last minute room changes occur
5. The first day of class meetings reinforce the institution's commitment to the linkage program
6. Nontraditional students be treated as mature, experienced adults and not as traditional students
7. Instruction begins as soon as introductions and registration tasks are completed

11. Involve Faculty in Monitoring Procedures.

Monitoring the linkage program is important to ensure that the program is on the right track. Faculty should be involved in the monitoring procedure because they are in the best position to determine the applicability and feasibility of the curriculum and to implement any changes in the curriculum. Potential major problems can be averted by making minor changes while implementation is in progress.

12. Implement Program Evaluation.

Evaluation is necessary to see if the linkage program has fulfilled the conditions of the contract. All aspects of the linkage program must be evaluated, the results tabulated, and changes made in the curriculum to improve the program. The evaluation process begins with the collection of evaluative data and ends with program modification based on the analysis of the data. This will be discussed in detail in Chapter 5.

MONITORING THE LINKAGE PROGRAM

Monitoring refers to the ongoing review of the educational services to guarantee that the provisions of the contract are being met. The actual procedures for monitoring should be determined immediately after signing the contract. Some businesses prefer to be actively involved in monitoring, which requires an arrangement of shared responsibilities; others prefer to leave the monitoring up to the institution which requires the development of a procedure for reporting any irregularities and remedies. The concept of monitoring should be included in the contract, but actual procedures can be an addendum, noting the times, places, and methods.

Monitoring is a protective procedure. It provides an early warning system that alerts the business or institution of program implementation problems and allows for corrective actions to be taken to solve the problems. Monitoring is necessary to keep the implementation of the linkage program on track and going smoothly. For monitoring to be successful, the Who? What? When? Where? Why? and How? questions must be answered.

WHO? WHAT? WHEN? WHERE? WHY? AND HOW?

There should be a mutual agreement on *who* is going to carry out the monitoring procedure: the institution, the business, or an outside consultant. It should be clear as to *what* needs to be monitored to satisfy the requirements of the contract. A schedule should be developed showing *when* and *where* the monitoring will take place. The *why* of monitoring results in a checklist of things to look for during the monitoring procedure. These things are:

1. Being on track with respect to the timetable agreed upon in the proposal

2. The attainment of objectives, that is, curriculum effectiveness

3. The degree to which the objectives are being achieved

4. Discrepancies between conditions stated in the contract and actual conditions during implementation

5. Information that is useful for program evaluation

The procedures agreed upon are the *how* of linkage program monitoring.

Although monitoring procedures will vary among linkage programs with respect to form and method of data collection, information obtained through monitoring should be organized and presented in a format that is relatively easy to understand and interpret. Modifications should be made during the implementation process if the need to modify is indicated by the results of monitoring.

METHODS OF MONITORING

Monitoring may be as simple as asking faculty, staff, and students how things are going or as complicated as administering standardized tests with student achievement compared to national norms. Faculty must be receptive to the monitoring procedures and not view it as an evaluation of their teaching, but rather as a means of providing feedback to curriculum developers so that the program can be revised and improved. Regular meeting with administrators, faculty, and staff of the linkage program should be scheduled to discuss the results of monitoring and ways to improve the program.

CHAPTER FIVE

Program Evaluation

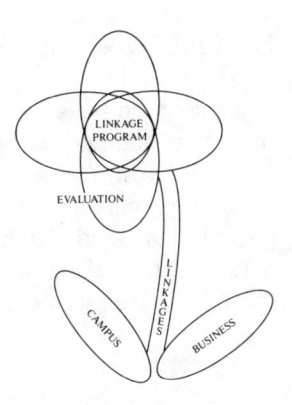

The fourth component, program evaluation, consists of an assessment of the linkage program. It is a summative, rather than a formative, evaluation in that it takes place after the program has been implemented and provides a final judgment on the success or failure of the program. Program evaluation, like program construction, curriculum development, and program implementation is a process; a process that includes (1) gathering evaluative data; (2) making a judgment based on an analysis of the data; and (3) determining if the judgment is valid. For the purposes of CBL, the focus of evaluation is on student achievement which is usually referred to as *product evaluation* as opposed to *comprehensive evaluation* which involves intangibles such as thought processes, esthetic development, and moral values.

Usually, the institution of higher education is held responsible for evaluating the linkage program, but special conditions may be imposed, by the business, on the evaluation process. It is very important that the contract for the linkage program address evaluation in terms of assigning responsibility for the process and stating the expected outcomes which provide a bench mark for the program.

Program evaluation should be based on more than just an assessment of student achievement. It should include evaluations of objectives, teaching methods, and instructional materials. Administrators, faculty, students, and employers are involved in the evaluation process, some actively, others passively. Administrators, most likely, are concerned about the overall success or failure of the program to achieve its goals. Faculty are concerned about the success or failure of the students to achieve the objectives of the program. Students tend to be concerned about how much they have learned. Employers are concerned with practical applications resulting from the linkage program such as changes in work habits, increased productivity, decreased down-time of equipment, or performance on national or state license examinations.

GATHERING EVALUATIVE DATA

Evaluation constitutes a value judgment based on data obtained formally through pencil-and-paper tests, or informally through skills checklists, attitude scales, interest inventories, observations, rating scales, and so on. Decisions about the procedures used to collect data for evaluation should be made with respect to the kind of linkage program implemented. That is, whether to collect data using formal methods, informal methods, or a combination of both formal and informal directly depends on the nature and design of the linkage program.

FORMAL METHODS FOR DATA COLLECTION

Pencil-and-paper tests are the most efficient and effective way of gathering student achievement data; standardized tests are preferred over nonstandardized or teacher-made tests. Standardized tests are the most dependable means for obtaining achievement data because (1) they are easy to administer; (2) their validity has been established; (3) they provide national norms; and (4) they can be used to measure progress. Unfortunately, they are seldom used to gather CBL data due to the uniqueness of the objectives of linkage programs. So, despite the possible shortcomings, teacher-made tests are among the most frequently used methods of data collection for linkage programs.

INFORMAL METHODS FOR DATA COLLECTION

Many linkage programs require a combination of formal and informal methods for gathering evaluative data. For the most part, data are collected objectively by using teacher-made tests and subjectively by using skills checklists or rating scales. Every effort must be made to develop teacher-made tests that are objective and reliable. Similarly, every effort must be made to achieve greater objectivity and dependability in skills checklists, rating scales, or any other informal instrument developed for data collection.

The gathering of evaluative data should not be limited to sources of data for product evaluation, but should also include data gathered from the linkage program. Questions concerning the relevance of different aspects of the program should be answered during the evaluation process.

MAKING A JUDGMENT BASED ON AN ANALYSIS OF THE DATA

Evaluation data must be gathered with the goal of evaluation in mind. To measure the performance of the program against criteria that were established during program construction, it is necessary to gather data that can be interpreted and analyzed with respect to the criteria. Both the nature of the data and the purpose for which it is to be used should be considered when interpreting evaluative data. To avoid problems that are inherent in data interpretation, cooperation is needed between faculty who collect the data and staff who share the responsibility for interpreting it.

STANDARDS FOR EVALUATION

Judgments regarding the degree to which the goals of the linkage program have been achieved are usually based on standards for evaluation. For some linkage programs, a *minimum level standard* is set and all employees participating in the program are expected to master the objectives at that level. When the evaluation criterion is a minimum level standard, data collections and data interpretation are relatively simple tasks. Data are collected by way of a skills checklist which does not involve grading or by way of pencil-and-paper tests using a pass-fail system. The linkage program is successful if *all* employees achieve *all* the prescribed skills at the minimum level. Minimum level standards are recommended for linkage programs that are for the purpose of training.

There are linkage programs for which a *maximum level standard* should be set as the evaluation criterion. Theoretically, all employees participating in the program can achieve at the established level, but in reality only a few actually do. The judgment in this case is, for the most part, a determination of the employee's productive, technical, or intellectual ability, rather than a judgment of success or failure of the linkage program. That is, employees who fail to achieve at the maximum level are graded accordingly and those who achieve at the maximum level are viewed as highly capable. The maximum level standard is also appropriate for linkage programs that are for training purposes where grading or sorting of employees is required. Primarily, data are collected by means of pencil-and-paper tests and when the results are interpreted they can be used to revise and improve the linkage program. It should be noted that a maximum level standard tends to penalize anyone with low grades even though it may later be determined that the maximum level was set too high. The most obvious difference between minimum level standards and maximum level standards is that minimum level standards judge the program's success or failure whereas maximum level standards judge the employee's ability.

For many linkage programs a *relative standard* is accepted as the evaluation criterion. This standard judges each employee with respect to the overall performance of the group. While a relative standard tends to promote a highly competitive atmosphere that may be undesirable, interpretation of the evaluative data provides some insight into the strengths and weaknesses of the linkage program. For example, if the employees participating in the program consistently do poorly on pencil-and-paper tests, then the objectives, content, method of instruction, and validity of the tests need to be reexamined and, most likely, revised. Meanwhile, no one is penalized with low grades because the grades are adjusted upward or "curved" with respect to the overall performance of the group.

The *multiple standard,* which consists of measuring the growth that takes place during the employee's participation in the linkage program, is not recommended. It is only mentioned here for informational purposes. The multiple standard is an individualized measurement, probably the "fairest" standard to use, but there is little opportunity to use it as an evaluation criterion because of data collection and interpretation problems. Although the multiple standard appears to apply to some linkage programs, it would be better to use a minimum level standard.

In most cases, a combination of standards for evaluation is used when developing the criteria for program evaluation; but regardless of which choice is made, the performance of the linkage program must be measured against the criteria and data must be collected and interpreted with respect to the criteria.

One final note on making judgments based on an analysis of the data: The importance of analyzing evaluative data in light of the total picture cannot be overemphasized. Often, it is necessary to develop a profile of group attainment of the objectives to "see" the strengths and weaknesses of the linkage program. Remember, the purpose of evaluation is twofold: A judgment is required to determine if the conditions of the contract were met, and if the linkage program needs to be revised or improved.

DETERMINING IF THE JUDGMENT IS VALID

To determine if the judgment is valid, it must be determined if the data on which the judgment is based were valid; to determine if the data were valid it must be determined if the instruments used to collect the data were valid. That is, if the data collected by the instruments actually described what it said it was describing, then a judgment based on that data is valid. Among the many factors that jeopardize the validity of evaluations are:

1. Program objectives are vague and can not be translated into recognizable behaviors.

2. Tests used to gather evaluative data do not measure what they are suppose to measure.

3. Informal instruments used to gather evaluative data do not serve a clear purpose.

4. Failure to develop a group profile so patterns of strengths and weaknesses of group achievement can be interpreted as strengths and weaknesses of the program.

5. Evaluation lack comprehensiveness.

6. There is a lack of consistency between evaluation and program objectives.

Clearly, validity of evaluations of linkage programs is an important issue that needs to be addressed, but usually it is an issue that is frequently overlooked because every aspect of the evaluation process must be scrutinized.

SHARING THE RESULTS OF THE EVALUATION

Evaluation is necessary to determine if the specific objectives of the linkage program actually resulted in the attainment of program goals. In addition, an evaluation indicates whether the institution's perception of what the linkage program should accomplish is consistent with the company's perception of what the linkage program did accomplish.

Once the linkage program has been evaluated, the results should be shared with CBL administrators and staff, participating faculty, and appropriate or interested officials from the business. Sometimes, even when the results of an evaluation are positive, there are minor disappointments that surface during the evaluation presentation. These disappointments should be given immediate attention, because at this point, it is important that everyone concerned be pleased with the results of the linkage program, thereby, establishing the credibility of the educational services of the institution with respect to CBL.

FOLLOW-UP EVALUATIONS

Both the institution and the business can obtain valuable information from a follow-up evaluation of the linkage program. Businesses may want to justify the participation of their employees in the program in terms of cost versus benefits. In essence, the question for which the business is seeking an answer is: Do the benefits derived from the participation of employees in the program outweigh the cost of the program? The institution may want to document the success of the linkage program by collecting evidence such as greater productivity, improved communication skills, increased profits, upward mobility, job skill improvement, enlightened attitude, or whatever else is pertinent to the program.

Follow-up evaluations can also influence decisions regarding program modifications.

CHAPTER SIX

Postdevelopment Phase of Campus-Business Linkages

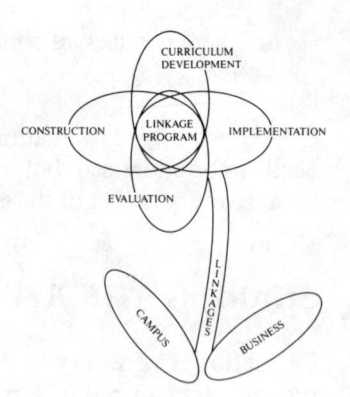

In Chapters 1–5, the concept of CBL has gone from theory to practice and the decision-making processes involved have been presented as occurring during the predevelopment phase or the development phase of CBL. There is still another phase of CBL that needs to be discussed, namely the postdevelopment phase which includes decisions and activities that occur after a linkage program has been successfully implemented.

THE THREE PHASES OF CBL

Figure 6.1 graphically depicts the three phases of CBL. The predevelopment phase, which consists of developing a rationale for CBL consonant with the mission of the institution, obtaining institutional support and commitment for the concept of CBL, and assessing the marketplace to determine if there were existing human resource problems that indicate a need for CBL, were discussed in Chapter 1. In Chapters 2–5 the activities and decision-making processes of the development phase of CBL were discussed. That is, the development phase of CBL consists of program construction, curriculum development, program implementation, and evaluation of the linkage program. This chapter deals with the postdevelopment phase of CBL which consists of activities that occur *after* the first successful attempt at CBL. Activities involved in follow-up for ongoing linkage programs, institutional support and commitment, and promotion of CBL in the marketplace are discussed.

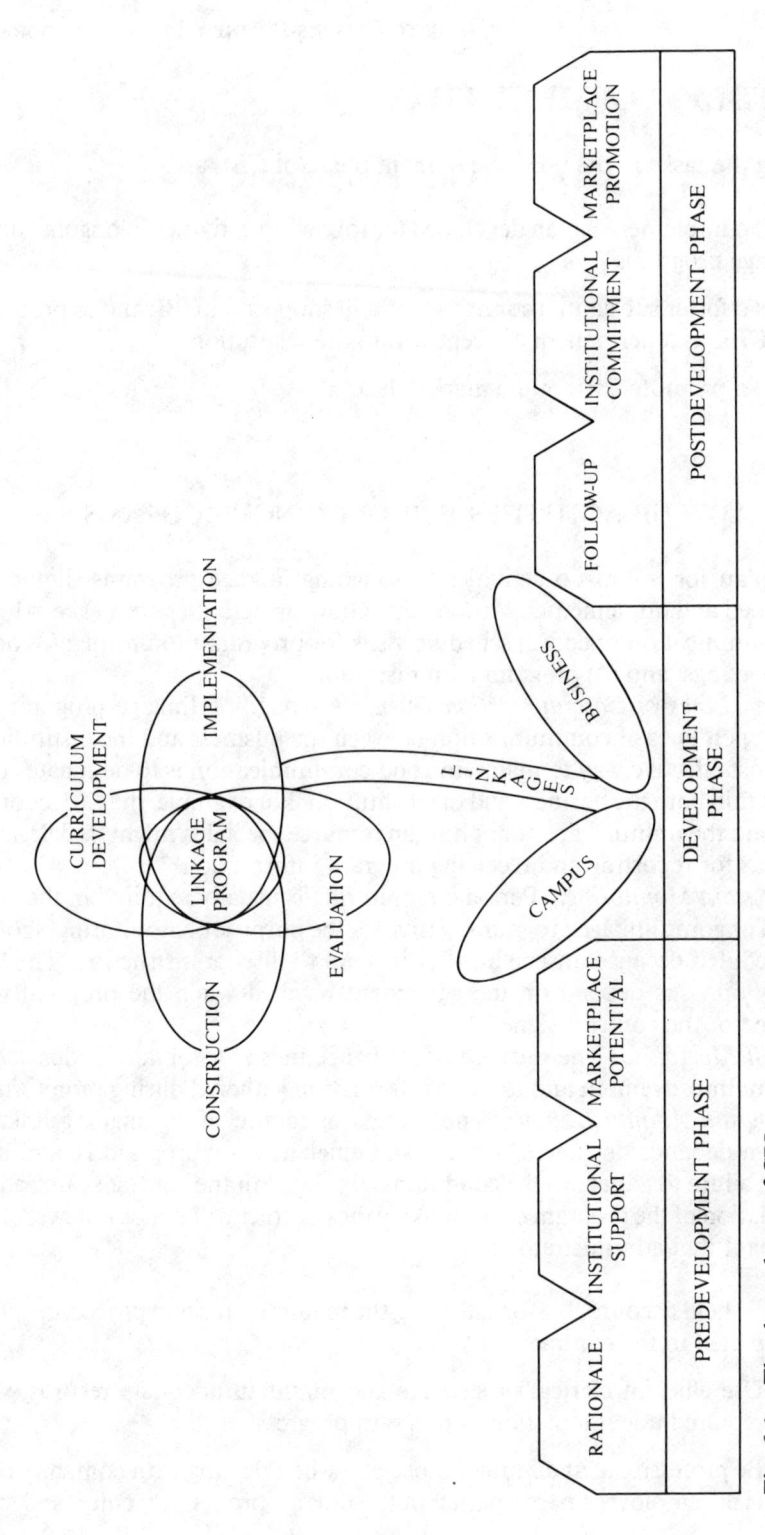

Fig. 6.1. The three phases of CBL.

POSTDEVELOPMENT PHASE

Among the tasks in the postdevelopment phase of CBL are:

1. To implement a plan developed for follow-up activities in ongoing linkage programs

2. To foster substantial commitment and support for CBL and to promote CBL as a permanent concept within the institution

3. To promote CBL in the marketplace

FOLLOW-UP ACTIVITIES FOR ONGOING PROGRAMS

A plan for follow-up activities for ongoing linkage programs should be developed and implemented. Among the follow-up activities are: (1) keep lines of communication open; (2) schedule visits for program monitoring; (3) hold staff meetings; and (4) program administration.

Keep Lines of Communication Open. An ongoing linkage program requires open lines of communication between the business and the institution. The most effective way to maintain good communication is to designate contacts within both the business and the institution. For example, the CBL coordinator and the training director or human resource specialist might be delegated the tasks for reporting and receiving program information.

Program Monitoring. Periodic monitoring is usually required in the contract of ongoing linkage programs. Visits, for the purpose of monitoring, should be scheduled because unscheduled visits tend to disrupt instruction. The frequency of visits depend on the agreement reached when the proposal was accepted or the contract signed.

Staff Meetings. The purpose of staff meetings is to obtain feedback for program improvement and to share information gathered during monitoring.

Program Administration. The success or failure of an ongoing linkage program depends on how effectively and efficiently the program is administered. Failure to adhere to the conditions stipulated in the contract can lead to cancellation of the program or most likely the contract will not be renewed. It is important that administrators:

1. Be held accountable for satisfying the requirements and procedures stipulated in the contract

2. Use efficient clerical procedures and maintain adequate records with required documentation of program progress

3. Be professional at all times, especially when dealing with company officials, employees participating in the linkage program, faculty, and staff

PLANNING ADDITIONAL LINKAGE PROGRAMS

CBL do not occur one-at-a-time. Although it is convenient to discuss linkage programs as though they are developed one-at-a-time, in practice they occur concurrently. Consequently, it should be remembered that CBL coordinators, specialists, and staff are usually involved with more than one linkage program and each program will probably be in different phases of development. Businesses identified as potential participants in CBL are approached using the methods described in the predevelopment phase of CBL and it is not necessary to complete one linkage program before starting another.

INSTITUTIONAL SUPPORT AND COMMITMENT

It was our contention in Chapter 1 that institutional support and commitment exist prior to the first attempt at CBL and that CBL should become an integral part of the institution's mission. During the postdevelopment phase, one of the challenges is to substantially increase the support and commitment to CBL within the institution.

Economic Development and CBL. Cooperation between business and institutions of higher education is not a new concept, but it is a concept that has gained favorable attention during the last few years. The attention, for the most part, has been due to the economic turbulence experienced recently in the United States, and by the gradual reduction in government funding for education which resulted in economical hardships for some programs offered by the institution. Campus-business linkages, in many instances, have become a necessary and effective tool for the economic survival of various educational services. Today, even as the economic climate improves, businesses and institutions are considering the possibility of developing long-term reciprocal relationships that will, from an economic standpoint, benefit both.

CBL AS A PERMANENT CONCEPT

Are CBL an answer to declining enrollment? For many institutions currently involved in CBL, the answer is *yes*. For other institutions just beginning to initiate CBL, the answer is, "*I hope so!*" Institutions of higher education are confronted with the problem of declining enrollment. In contrast, businesses are confronted with the problem of increasing costs for in-house training or retraining of employees. Campus-business linkages appear to be a solution for both problems and as the number of institutions that are willing to modify programs to meet the training needs of business increases, the concept of CBL will become unquestionably more permanent.

Measuring the Extent of Commitment and Support. The extent of commitment and support for the concept of CBL can be measured by the amount of exposure linkage programs receive before becoming official programs of the institution. The answers to the following questions will provide a bench mark for determining the extent of institutional commitment and support:

1. Was the Board of Trustees informed of this outward focus?

2. Did the Academic Deans and faculty participate in the development of linkage programs?

3. Are support units informed of the potential impact of linkage programs?

4. Are decisions to implement linkage programs announced publicly through media releases?

If the answers to most of these questions are *yes,* then the concept of CBL has a solid foundation of institutional support and commitment that greatly enhances the chances for success of linkage programs.

PROMOTING CBL IN THE MARKETPLACE

When the first attempt at CBL results in a successful linkage program and the credibility of the educational services of the institution with respect to CBL is established, it is time to begin to skillfully promote the concept of CBL in the marketplace.

Developing a CBL Presentation Package. A presentation package should be developed to promote CBL. It should contain handout materials that can be given to training directors, human resource specialists, or other people within the targeted business. The distributed materials must be attractive and interesting, and encourage thought-provoking questions or comments. The information presented should be self-explanatory and portray the educational services of the institution in the most favorable light.

The CBL presentation package should be printed professionally with color utilized to enhance the overall appearance, as well as to focus attention on key points of information. The institution must be willing to spend some money on the presentation package and to spend some time updating it through the addition of new materials as they are developed. Among the ideas suggested as possible starting points for a CBL presentation package are:

1. A brochure that answers the Who? What? When? Where? Why? and How? of CBL

2. A portfolio of CBL with overviews of linkage programs successfully implemented and outlines of potential linkage programs

3. An annotated list of linkage programs that could be developed and tailored to meet specific needs

4. Brochures containing general information on other educational services offered by the institution of higher education

5. A CBL press packet containing press releases, pictures of linkage programs being implemented, newspaper articles about CBL, and magazine features referring to CBL

The materials developed for the promotion of CBL in the marketplace should be similar in design and quality to materials developed to promote other educational services of the institution. Special attention should be given to the role of CBL within the institution and the educational services offered by the institution to businesses in the marketplace. It should be emphasized that through CBL, cost-effective, efficient, and specialized training programs can be provided to meet almost any human resource needs of businesses.

Building a Credible Reputation for CBL. One of the outcomes of successfully implementing linkage programs is credibility in the marketplace. As indicated before, institutions of higher education are often viewed as lacking when it comes to understanding the *real world* needs of business. So a very important promotional activity is to build a credible reputation for the institution with respect to CBL using successful linkage programs as the foundation. Other factors that influence the institution's credibility are professionalism, open and effective communications, and knowledge of the marketplace. Sometimes asking the right question is more important than knowing all the answers! Such is the case for CBL. Institutions, attempting CBL for the first time, will want to spend more time trying to ask the right questions then trying to find all the answers.

PART II

A-1 STONE AND MASONRY
with
CALIFORNIA BAPTIST COLLEGE

BS DEGREE FOR BUSINESS EXECUTIVES

COMPANY CONTACT:
Bob Pentz
President
A-1 Stone and Masonry
9660 Arlington Avenue
Riverside, CA 92504

INSTITUTIONAL CONTACT:
Bob Jabs
Business Administration
California Baptist College
8432 Magnolia
Riverside, CA 92504
(714) 689-5771

PROGRAM DESCRIPTION/OBJECTIVES:
Opportunity for company employees to pursue coursework towards an undergraduate degree in business.

PROGRAM INITIATED:
1982

LENGTH OF STUDY FOR PARTICIPANT:
18 months

LENGTH OF CONTRACT:
18 months

LOCATION:
On campus

PARTICIPANTS:
25 employees

PROGRAM COSTS PROVIDED BY:
Institution: $2500 per person
Company: $2500 per person

PRINTED MATERIALS AVAILABLE FROM:
Institution

ABBOTT DIAGNOSTICS DIVISION
with
COLLEGE OF LAKE COUNTY

SUPERVISORY TRAINING FOR SCIENTIFIC PERSONNEL

COMPANY CONTACT:
Joanne Roberts
Training Specialist
Diagnostics Division
Abbott Laboratories
Abbott Park, IL
(312) 937-3578

INSTITUTIONAL CONTACT:
Keri Thiessen
Training & Development Consultant
Center for Economic Development
College of Lake County
19351 W. Washington
Grayslake, IL 60030
(312) 223-3615

PROGRAM DESCRIPTION/OBJECTIVES:
To introduce the concepts and practical applications of supervisory skills specifically desired for technical and scientific personnel.

PROGRAM INITIATED:
1982

LENGTH OF STUDY FOR PARTICIPANT:
16 weeks

LENGTH OF CONTRACT:
16 weeks

LOCATION
Abbott Park, Illinois

PARTICIPANTS:
Number: 16
Type: Scientific Managers

PROGRAM COSTS PROVIDED BY:
Company

PRINTED MATERIALS AVAILABLE FROM:
Institution

ADAMS-RUSSELL, HEWLETT PACKARD AND MICROWAVE ASSOCIATES
with
TUFTS UNIVERSITY

MICROWAVE ENGINEERS

COMPANY CONTACT:
John Gillespie, Jr.
Bay State Skills Corporation
   representing
Adams-Russell, Hewlett Packard and Microwave Associates
McCormack Office Building
One Ashburton Place
Room 2110
Boston, MA 02108
(617) 727-5431

INSTITUTIONAL CONTACT:
Arthur Uhlir
Department of Electrical Engineering
Tufts University
Medford, MA 02155
(617) 628-5000

PROGRAM DESCRIPTION/OBJECTIVES:
A graduate level program in microwave engineering specialist training.

PROGRAM INITIATED:
1982

LENGTH OF STUDY FOR PARTICIPANT:
1 academic year

LENGTH OF CONTRACT:
14 months

LOCATION:
Tufts University

PARTICIPANTS:
16 engineers

PROGRAM COSTS PROVIDED BY:
Institution: $38,686
Company: $48,850
Other Source: $48,121 (Bay State Skills Corporation)

PRINTED MATERIALS AVAILABLE FROM:
Company

UNIVERSITY CITY SCIENCE CENTER
with
200 COMPANIES AND 30 EDUCATIONAL INSTITUTIONS

ADVANCED TECHNOLOGY CENTER OF SOUTHEASTERN PENNSYLVANIA (ATC/SEP)

PROGRAM DESCRIPTION OBJECTIVES:
Economic development in advanced technology enterprises through joint university industry research and development, employment and training, and business assistance for entrepreneurs.

LENGTH OF CONTRACT:
September–August, 1984–85

LOCATION:
Southeastern Pennsylvania

PROGRAM COSTS PROVIDED BY:
Institutions: $3.9 million
Company: $9.9 million
Participants: $5.0 million
Other sources: $1.27 million

PRINTED MATERIALS AVAILABLE FROM:
ATC/SEP

ADVANCED TECHNOLOGY LABS
with
SEATTLE COMMUNITY COLLEGE DISTRICT

ELECTRONICS TRAINING PROGRAM

COMPANY CONTACT:
David Kinne
Advanced Technology Labs
13208 Northrup Way
Bellevue, WA 98905
(206) 641-5410

INSTITUTIONAL CONTACT:
Thomas F. Ris
Director
Contract Education Service
Seattle Community College

District
Seattle, WA 98119
(206) 587-4199

PROGRAM DESCRIPTION/OBJECTIVES:
To use resources at a time when state funding was cut to train entry level, CETA-eligible employees and upgrade women by using district's expertise and resources in the field of high technology.

PROGRAM INTIATED:
1981

LENGTH OF STUDY FOR PARTICIPANT:
1 academic year

LENGTH OF CONTRACT:
2 years

LOCATION:
North Seattle Community College

PARTICIPANTS:
70 pre- and on-job trainees in high technology areas

PROGRAM COSTS PROVIDED BY:
Company: $23,500

PRINTED MATERIALS AVAILABLE FROM:
Not available

AKRON CITY HOSPITAL
with
KENT STATE UNIVERSITY

MANAGEMENT DEVELOPMENT PROGRAM

COMPANY CONTACT:
Ralph DeCristoforo
Akron City Hospital
525 East Market
Akron, OH 44309
(216) 375-3121

INSTITUTIONAL CONTACT:
Karen Rylander
Director, Continuing Education
Kent State University
327 Rockwell Hall
Kent, OH 44242
(216) 672-3100

PROGRAM DESCRIPTION/OBJECTIVES:
Pragmatic approach to the following management concepts: planning and control, motivation, leadership and conflict resolution, organizational communications, decision making.

PROGRAM INITIATED:
1982

LENGTH OF STUDY FOR PARTICIPANT:
20 hours

LENGTH OF CONTRACT:
20 hours

LOCATION:
Local hotel

PARTICIPANTS:
90 department managers

PROGRAM COSTS PROVIDED BY:
Company: 100%

PRINTED MATERIALS AVAILABLE FROM:
Institution

AKRON CITY HOSPITAL
with
KENT STATE UNIVERSITY

SUPERVISORY DEVELOPMENT PROGRAM

COMPANY CONTACT:
Ralph DeCristoforo
Akron City Hospital
525 East market
Akron, OH 44309
(216) 375-3121

INSTITUTIONAL CONTACT:
Karen Rylander
Director, Continuing Education
Kent State University
327 Rockwell Hall
Kent, OH 44242
(216) 672-3100

PROGRAM DESCRIPTION/ OBJECTIVES:
Pragmatic approach to the following management concepts: planning and control, motivation, leadership and conflict resolution, organizational communications, decision making.

PROGRAM INITIATED:
1982

LENGTH OF STUDY FOR PARTICIPANT:
20 hours

LENGTH OF CONTRACT:
20 hours

LOCATION:
Local hotel

PARTICIPANTS:
140 department supervisors

PROGRAM COSTS PROVIDED BY:
Company: 100%

PRINTED MATERIALS AVAILABLE FROM:
Institution

ALABAMA DEPARTMENT OF MENTAL HEALTH
with
ALABAMA DEPARTMENT OF EDUCATION

ALABAMA MENTAL HEALTH TECHNOLOGY LINKAGE PROGRAM

COMPANY CONTACT:
Helen Paulette Brignet
Human Resource Development Specialist
Office of Planning and Staff Development
Alabama Department of Mental Health
Montgomery, AL 36130
(205) 834-4350

INSTITUTIONAL CONTACT:
Howard Gundy
Chancellor
Postsecondary Education
Alabama Department of Education
817 South Court Street
Montgomery, AL 36104
(205) 832-3340

PROGRAM DESCRIPTION/ OBJECTIVES:
To upgrade work skills of incumbent human services workers in the Alabama Department of Mental Health.

PROGRAM INITIATED:
1978

LENGTH OF STUDY FOR PARTICIPANT:
2 academic years

LENGTH OF CONTRACT:
1 year with renewal option

LOCATION:
5 community colleges and 9 Department of Mental Health facilities

PARTICIPANTS:
Approximately 100 employees of the Alabama Department of Mental Health

PROGRAM COSTS PROVIDED BY:
Institution: Employee release time
Company: Record keeping, facility supervision
Participant: Books

PRINTED MATERIALS AVAILABLE FROM:
Company

BRONX COMMUNITY COLLEGE
with
ALEXANDER DEPARTMENT STORES, INC.

SELF IMPROVEMENT PROGRAM

COMPANY CONTACT:
Robert Ronph
Corporation Training Manager
E. 58th Street & Lexington Ave.
New York, NY 10022
(212) 572-8328

INSTITUTIONAL CONTACT:
Rafael Infante
Director, Contracts and Training
Continuing Education
Bronx Community College
University Avenue and 181 Street
Bronx, NY 10453
(212) 220-6424

PROGRAM DESCRIPTION/ OBJECTIVES:
To upgrade the management skills of middle-level managers employed by Alexander's

LENGTH OF STUDY FOR PARTICIPANT:
1 semester

LENGTH OF CONTRACT:
12 months with renewal option

LOCATION:
Alexander's store at 3rd Avenue and 58th Street

PARTICIPANTS:
Number: 50 annually
Type: mid-management

PRINTED MATERIALS AVAILABLE FROM:
Institution
Dean Symour Reisin
Dean of Continuing Education & Grants

**ALLIED BENDIX AEROSPACE
with
FLORIDA JUNIOR COLLEGE AT JACKSONVILLE**

BLUEPRINT READING AND SOLDERING

COMPANY CONTACT:
Carl Knapp
Personnel
Allied Bendix Aerospace
P.O. Box 17880
Jacksonville, FL 32245-7880
(904) 739-4197

INSTITUTIONAL CONTACT:
Dr. James R. Myers
Instructional Dean
Occupational Education
Florida Junior College at Jacksonville
101 West State Street
Jacksonville, FL 32202
(904) 633-8284

PROGRAM DESCRIPTION/ OBJECTIVES:
To familiarize employees with schematics and techniques used in assembly processes.

PROGRAM INITIATED:
1981

LENGTH OF STUDY FOR PARTICIPANT:
40 hours

LENGTH OF CONTRACT:
Open-ended

LOCATION:
Florida Junior College—Downtown Campus

PARTICIPANTS:
Number: 30–35 per class 3–4 times a year
Type: Employees

PROGRAM COSTS PROVIDED BY:
Participant: 100%

PRINTED MATERIALS AVAILABLE FROM:
Institution and Company

**ALUMINUM COMPANY OF AMERICA
with
MARYVILLE COLLEGE**

AFFILIATE ARTISTS

COMPANY CONTACT:
Elton R. Jones
Manager, Tennessee Public Relations
Aluminum Company of America
P.O. Box 9128

Alcoa, TN 37701
(615) 977-3490

INSTITUTIONAL CONTACT:
Robert A. Ellis, Jr.
Vice President for Development
Maryville College
Maryville, TN 37801
(615) 982-6412

PROGRAM DESCRIPTION/ OBJECTIVES:
To expand audiences for the performing arts, to support the career development of young professional performers, and to offer American business the opportunity to invest in the cultural life of the communities.

PROGRAM INITIATED:
1979

LENGTH OF STUDY FOR PARTICIPANT:
42 days

LENGTH OF CONTRACT:
7 months

LOCATION:
Maryville College

PARTICIPANTS:
1 invited artist

PROGRAM COSTS PROVIDED BY:
Institution: $5,739.00

PRINTED MATERIALS AVAILABLE FROM:
Institution

ALUMINUM COMPANY OF AMERICA ROCKDALE WORKS
with
TEXAS STATE TECHNICAL INSTITUTE

APPRENTICE TRAINING PROGRAM

COMPANY CONTACT:
Bill Eckert
Manager, Maintenance
ALCOA-Aluminum Company of America
P.O. Box 472
Rockdale, TX 76567
(512) 466-5811

INSTITUTIONAL CONTACT:
J. Don Pierson
Coordinator of Curriculum
Instructional Administration
  Department
Texas State Technical Institute
Waco, TX 76705
(817) 799-3611, X293

PROGRAM DESCRIPTION/ OBJECTIVES:
To provide ALCOA Rockdale Works with an effective apprentice training program that is Rockdale Works job-oriented and emphasizes job performance.

PROGRAM INITIATED:
1981

LENGTH OF STUDY FOR PARTICIPANT:
6,000 hours

LENGTH OF CONTRACT:
Quarterly with renewal options

LOCATION:
Rockdale, TX

PARTICIPANTS:
50–100 craft apprentices in 10 craft areas

PROGRAM COSTS PROVIDED BY:
Company: 100%

PRINTED MATERIALS AVAILABLE FROM:
Institution and Company

AMANA REFRIGERATION COMPANY
with
IOWA STATE UNIVERSITY

ADULT HOME ECONOMICS EDUCATION PROGRAM

COMPANY CONTACT:
Dixie Trout
Director
Home Economics
Amana Refrigeration Company
Amana, IA 52203
(319) 622-5511

INSTITUTIONAL CONTACT:
Penny A. Ralston, Ph.D.
Associate Professor
Home Economics Education
Iowa State University
222C MacKay
Ames, IA 50011
(515) 294-6444

PROGRAM DESCRIPTION/OBJECTIVES:
Major purpose of the program is to provide students with a half-semester supervised practicum in the business setting. Students who work with a professional home economists have experiences in program planning.

PROGRAM INITIATED:
1976

LENGTH OF STUDY FOR PARTICIPANT:
8–9 weeks

LENGTH OF CONTRACT:
On-going

LOCATION:
Amana, Iowa 52203

PARTICIPANTS:
Number: 1–2 annually
Type: Undergraduate students

PROGRAM COSTS PROVIDED BY:
Institution: In-kind
Company: In-kind
Participant: Through student fees and tuition
Other Source: N/A

PRINTED MATERIALS AVAILABLE FROM:
Institution

AMERICAN ASSOCIATION OF RAILROADS
with
POLICE TRAINING INSTITUTE UNIVERSITY OF ILLINOIS

SPECIALIZED TRAINING FOR RAILROAD POLICE OFFICERS

COMPANY CONTACT:
Jesse E. Williamson
Director of Training and Project Development
Operations and Maintenance Department
Association of American Railroads
1920 I Street, NW
Washington, DC 20036
(202) 835-9288

INSTITUTIONAL CONTACT:
Clifford W. Van Meter
Director
Police Training Institute
University of Illinois
725 South Wright Street
Room 341
Champaign, IL 61820
(217) 333-2337

PROGRAM DESCRIPTION/OBJECTIVES:
Provide specialized police training to meet various needs of railroad police officers.

PROGRAM INITIATED:
1981

LENGTH OF STUDY FOR PARTICIPANT:
Normally 1 week (40 hours)

LENGTH OF CONTRACT:
No ongoing contract exists

LOCATION:
Police Training Institute

PARTICIPANTS:
100 police officers

PROGRAM COSTS PROVIDED BY:
Company: 100%

PRINTED MATERIALS AVAILABLE FROM:
Institution

AMERICAN FLETCHER NATIONAL BANK
with
INDIANA VOCATIONAL TECHNICAL COLLEGE

CUSTOMER SERVICE/ASSISTANT CERTIFICATION PROGRAM, MANAGEMENT TRAINING

COMPANY CONTACT:
Deanne Lane
Manager of Training
AFNB Training Center
American Fletcher National Bank
5704 West 86th Street
Indianapolis, IN 46278
(317) 639-7692

INSTITUTIONAL CONTACT:
Sue Beard
Director, Extended Services
Indiana Vocational Technical College
1315 East Washington Street
Indianapolis, IN 46202
(317) 635-6100, X68

PROGRAM DESCRIPTION/ OBJECTIVES:
To provide communication, human relations, and management skills for banking center managers and customer service personnel.

PROGRAM INITIATED:
1981

LENGTH OF STUDY FOR PARTICIPANT:
Not reported

LENGTH OF CONTRACT:
12 months renewable

LOCATION:
American Fletcher National Bank

PARTICIPANTS:
550 managers and customer service personnel

PROGRAM COSTS PROVIDED BY:
Company: 100%

PRINTED MATERIALS AVAILABLE FROM:
Not available

AMERICAN HEART ASSOCIATION
with
CENTRAL MICHIGAN UNIVERSITY*

TOWARD STRONG MANAGEMENT IN THE VOLUNTARY SECTOR

COMPANY CONTACT:
Susan Calkin
Associate Project Director
Degree Program (Training)
American Heart Association
7320 Greenville Avenue
Dallas, TX 75231
(214) 750-5329

INSTITUTIONAL CONTACT:
Larry Murphy
Director, Institute for Personal and Career Development
and
John Schleede
Professor of Marketing
School of Business Administration
Central Michigan University
Mt. Pleasant, MI 44859
(517) 774-3865

PROGRAM DESCRIPTION/ OBJECTIVES:
To establish a behaviorally based master's degree program in voluntary agency management designed to meet the needs of the practitioner.

PROGRAM INITIATED:
1982

LENGTH OF STUDY FOR PARTICIPANT:
3 years

LENGTH OF CONTRACT:
3-year FIPSE grant

LOCATION:
Varies, all over the country

PARTICIPANTS:
30 students per year + managers and staff

PROGRAM COSTS PROVIDED BY:
Company: 50%
Participant: 50%

PRINTED MATERIALS AVAILABLE FROM:
Company

* Representative entry—complete list available from institution.

AMERICAN HEART ASSOCIATION
with
MARYMOUNT COLLEGE OF VIRGINIA

DETERMINING THE EFFECT OF NON-PHARMACOLOGICAL TREATMENTS ON THE BLOOD PRESSURE OF BORDERLINE HYPERTENSIVES

COMPANY CONTACT:
Rick C. Marshall
Director of Medical and Community Programs
Northern Virginia Chapter
American Heart Association
4231 Markham Street, Suite 225
Annandale, VA 22003

INSTITUTIONAL CONTACT:
Dr. Wayne Lesko
Coordinator, Stress Management Center
Marymount College of Virginia
Arlington, VA 22207

LENGTH OF STUDY FOR PARTICIPANT:
Exercise program as prescribed

LENGTH OF CONTRACT:
1 year, with program funding to be continued by institution

PROGRAM COSTS PROVIDED BY:
Institution: $24,000
Company: $20,000
Participant: 0

AMERICAN INSTITUTE OF BANKING
with
MARSHALL UNIVERSITY

AMERICAN INSTITUTE OF BANKING

COMPANY CONTACT:
Ben Meredith
President, AIB Chapter
First Bank Cerido
P.O. Box 607
Cerido, WV 25507
(304) 453-1301

INSTITUTIONAL CONTACT:
Paul D. Hines
Vice President/Dean
Community College
Marshall University
16th Street and Hal Greer Blvd.
Huntington, WV 25701
(304) 696-3646

PROGRAM DESCRIPTION/ OBJECTIVES:
To provide area bank employees with the skills needed to function more effectively in their positions.

PROGRAM INITIATED:
1976

LENGTH OF STUDY FOR PARTICIPANT:
1 semester at a time

LENGTH OF CONTRACT:
1 year, renewable

LOCATION:
Marshall University

PARTICIPANTS:
100 bank employees annually

PROGRAM COSTS PROVIDED BY:
Company: 100%

PRINTED MATERIALS AVAILABLE FROM:
Not available

AMERICAN INSTITUTE OF BANKING (WASHINGTON CHAPTER)
with
MONTGOMERY COLLEGE

BANKING AND FINANCIAL MANAGEMENT

COMPANY CONTACT:
Jean Bathurst
Executive Director
American Institute of Banking
5010 Wisconsin Avenue
Suite B-8
Washington, DC 20016
(202) 362-5510

INSTITUTIONAL CONTACT:
Fred Saint
Instructional Dean
Institute of Applied Sciences
Montgomery College
Takoma Park, MD 20912
(301) 587-4090

PROGRAM DESCRIPTION/OBJECTIVES:
To provide an opportunity for people in banking to receive college credit for evaluated AIB courses toward an Associate in Arts degree from Montgomery College.

PROGRAM INITIATED:
1982

LENGTH OF STUDY FOR PARTICIPANT:
Differs with each individual

LENGTH OF CONTRACT:
Ongoing

LOCATION:
Takoma Park and Germantown campuses

PARTICIPANTS:
Unknown

PROGRAM COSTS PROVIDED BY:
Company: Tuition may be reimbursed by company
Participant: Tuition based on student residence

PRINTED MATERIALS AVAILABLE FROM:
Institution

AMERICAN INTERNATIONAL GROUP, INC.
with
BOROUGH OF MANHATTAN COMMUNITY COLLEGE

SHORT TERM TRAINING FOR AMERICAN INTERNATIONAL GROUP, INC.

COMPANY CONTACT:
Jannette Porta-Avalos
Training Specialist
American International Group, Inc.
70 Pine Street
New York, NY 10270
(212) 770-5107

INSTITUTIONAL CONTACT:
Sylvia Seidmann
Director of Company Training
Borough of Manhattan Community College
1633 Broadway

New York, NY 10019
(212) 262-2675

PROGRAM DESCRIPTION/OBJECTIVES:
To upgrade the educational level of employees in basic studies and office skills.

PROGRAM INITIATED:
1981

LENGTH OF STUDY FOR PARTICIPANT:
1 semester

LENGTH OF CONTRACT:
12 months

LOCATION:
American International Group

PARTICIPANTS:
300 clerical and secretarial employees annually

PROGRAM COSTS PROVIDED BY:
Other Source: $53,000 (vocational education grant from Albany)

PRINTED MATERIALS AVAILABLE FROM:
Institution

AMERICAN INSTITUTE OF BANKING, SOUTHSIDE CHAPTER
with
JOHN TYLER COMMUNITY COLLEGE

AMERICAN INSTITUTE OF BANKING

COMPANY CONTACT:
Mrs. Evelyn M. Lichvar
Education Committee Chairman
American Institute of Banking,
  Southside Chapter
c/o United Virginia Bank
898 East Washington Street,
Petersburg, VA 23803
(804) 541-2906

INSTITUTIONAL CONTACT:
Dr. Samuel Lee Hancock
Director
Division of Continuing Education
John Tyler Community College
13101 Jefferson Davis Highway,
Chester, VA 23831
(804) 796-4111

PROGRAM DESCRIPTION/OBJECTIVES:
The courses are designed to be relevant to the needs of the banking industry and enhance the long-term career objectives of bank employees.

PROGRAM INITIATED:
Spring, 1984

LENGTH OF STUDY FOR PARTICIPANT:
On-going and as needed

LENGTH OF CONTRACT:
10 instructional hours per 1 college credit

LOCATION:
Selected sites within college service area and on-campus

PARTICIPANTS:
Number: 40–50
Type: Local bank employees

PROGRAM COSTS PROVIDED BY:
Institution: Administrative leadership, instructors' salaries
Company: Coordination leadership
Participant: Time
Other Source: Local banks: tuition, textbooks

PRINTED MATERIALS AVAILABLE FROM:
Institution and Company

AMERICAN PSYCHOLOGICAL ASSOCIATION
with
UNIVERSITY OF HARTFORD

A.P.A. CONTINUING EDUCATION PROGRAM

COMPANY CONTACT:
Barbara Hammond
Director, Continuing Education Program
1200 Seventeenth Street N.W.
Washington, D.C. 20036
(202) 833-7600

INSTITUTIONAL CONTACT:
A.L. Zander
Director
Office of University College
Continuing Prof. Development
University of Hartford
200 Bloomfield Avenue
West Hartford, CT. 06117
(203) 243-4371

PROGRAM DESCRIPTION/ OBJECTIVES:
Provides psychologists' access to resources that:
A. Improve his or her own competence in professionally relevant ways.
B. Make possible the acquisition of new skills and knowledge required to maintain competence.
C. Strengthen the habits of critical inquiry and balanced judgment that denote the professional and scientific person.

PROGRAM INITIATED:
1983

LENGTH OF STUDY FOR PARTICIPANT:
1–2 days
N.A.

LOCATION:
University of Hartford

PARTICIPANTS:
Psychologists continuing their education and professional development beyond the level of graduate training.

PROGRAM COSTS PROVIDED BY:
Company and Participant

PRINTED MATERIALS AVAILABLE FROM:
Institution

AREA AUTOMOTIVE DEALERSHIPS
with
JOHN TYLER COMMUNITY COLLEGE

AUTOMOTIVE MANAGEMENT CERTIFICATE PROGRAM

COMPANY CONTACT:
Mr. H. Carter Myers
President & Owner
Heritage Chevrolet
P.O. Box AS
Chester, VA 23831
(804) 748-6461

INSTITUTIONAL CONTACT:
Dr. Samuel Lee Hancock
Director
Division of Continuing Education
John Tyler Community College
13101 Jefferson Davis Highway
Chester, VA 23831
(804) 796-4111

PROGRAM DESCRIPTION/ OBJECTIVES:
Designed to promote an understanding of the role and functions of an automobile dealership manager's position. The current or potential manager will be guided through courses covering the many phases of the workplace.

PROGRAM INITIATED:
Summer, 1984

LENGTH OF STUDY FOR PARTICIPANT:
2½ years.

LENGTH OF CONTRACT:
30 instructional hours each 3 months.

LOCATION:
John Tyler Community College

PARTICIPANTS:
Number: 45
Type: Individuals who are/will be promoted to rank of manager.

PROGRAM COSTS PROVIDED BY:
Institution: Administrative leadership and instructors' salaries
Company: Tuition
Participant: Time
Other Source: Technical and sales materials/major auto manufacturers

PRINTED MATERIALS AVAILABLE FROM:
Institution

PROGRAM INITIATED:
1976

LENGTH OF STUDY FOR PARTICIPANT:
2 years for Associate in Applied Science

LENGTH OF CONTRACT:
1 year, renewable

LOCATION:
Marshall University

PARTICIPANTS:
360 bank employees

PROGRAM COSTS PROVIDED BY:
Company: 100%

PRINTED MATERIALS AVAILABLE FROM:
Institution and Company

AMERICAN INSTITUTE OF BANKING
with
MARSHALL UNIVERSITY COMMUNITY COLLEGE

ASSOCIATE DEGREE IN BANKING AND FINANCE

COMPANY CONTACT:
Judy Lucas, President AIB Chapter
Security Bank
Huntington, WV 25701
(304) 522-8281

INSTITUTIONAL CONTACT:
Dr. Betty Joan Jarrell
Director, Div. of Bus. Tech.
Marshall University Community College
Huntington, WV 25701
(304) 696-3646

PROGRAM DESCRIPTION/OBJECTIVES:
To provide bank employees with skills needed to function more effectively in their positions and to provide skills necessary for advancement.

ARLINGTON COUNTY DEPARTMENT OF PUBLIC WORKS
with
MARYMOUNT COLLEGE OF VIRGINIA

VIDEOS TAPES

COMPANY CONTACT:
Mr. Dennis R. Johnson
Chief, Operations Division, DPW
1400 N. Courthouse Road
Arlington, VA 22201

INSTITUTIONAL CONTACT:
Dr. John Fry
Director, Human Resources Development Program
Marymount College of Virginia
Arlington, VA 22207

LENGTH OF STUDY FOR PARTICIPANT:
1 hour or as needed for mastery of equipment

LENGTH OF CONTRACT:
Continuing until 12 video tapes are produced

PROGRAM COSTS PROVIDED BY:
Institution: $20,000
Company: $24,000
Participant: 0

AT&T
with
MIDDLESEX COUNTY COLLEGE

CORPORATE COLLEGE

COMPANY CONTACT:
Diane Dorer
Personnel Department
Corporate Education Center
AT&T
P.O. Box 2016
New Brunswick, NJ 08903
(201) 699-2078

INSTITUTIONAL CONTACT:
Barbara L. Greene
Director of Extension Operations
Division of Continuing Education
Middlesex County College
Edison, NJ 08818
(201) 549-9898

PROGRAM DESCRIPTION/ OBJECTIVES:
To provide college credit courses that address job skills for employees at work site. Program generally addresses management skills with supplementary accounting and liberal arts courses.

PROGRAM INITIATED:
1968

LENGTH OF STUDY FOR PARTICIPANT:
1 semester to duration of program

LENGTH OF CONTRACT:
Duration of employee interest

LOCATION:
Corporate premises

PARTICIPANTS:
50 management and accounting personnel per semester

PROGRAM COSTS PROVIDED BY:
Institution: Salaries and administrative overhead
Company: Usually 100%
Participant: Usually reimbursed

PRINTED MATERIALS AVAILABLE FROM:
Institution

AMERICAN WATCHMAKERS INSTITUTE
with
OKLAHOMA STATE TECH

AMERICAN WATCHMAKERS INSTITUTE SOLID STATE WATCH REPAIR SEMINAR AND WORKSHOP SERIES

COMPANY CONTACT:
Milton Stevens
Executive Secretary
American Watchmakers Institute
P.O. Box 11011
Cincinnati, OH 45211
(513) 661-3838

INSTITUTIONAL CONTACT:
Gray Lawrence
Supervisor, Watch Micro-Instrument and Jewelry
Small Business Trades Department
Oklahoma State Tech
4th and Mission
Okmulgee, OK 74447
(918) 756-6211, X271

PROGRAM DESCRIPTION/ OBJECTIVES:
To upgrade skills and knowledge of watchmakers and students in repair of current styles of watches and provide student opportunities for contact with potential employer.

PROGRAM INITIATED:
1972

LENGTH OF STUDY FOR PARTICIPANT:
Not reported

LENGTH OF CONTRACT:
Not reported

LOCATION:
Not reported

PARTICIPANTS:
64

PROGRAM COSTS PROVIDED BY:
Company, 100%

PRINTED MATERIALS AVAILABLE FROM:
Institution

AMOCO PIPELINE COMPANY
with
OKLAHOMA STATE TECH

DIGITAL LOGIC

COMPANY CONTACT:
James R. Polston
Manager
AMOCO Pipeline Company
401 Eisenhower Lane
Lombard, IL 60148
(312) 932-5530

INSTITUTIONAL CONTACT:
Bill J. Lyons
Department Head
Electrical-Electronic Technology
Oklahoma State Tech
4th and Mission
Okmulgee, OK 74447
(918) 756-6211, X252

PROGRAM DESCRIPTION/ OBJECTIVES:
Provide an educational background that enables AMOCO employees to be more receptive to specialized training courses by the company.

PROGRAM INITIATED:
1978

LENGTH OF STUDY FOR PARTICIPANT:
2 weeks

LENGTH OF CONTRACT:
Not reported

LOCATION:
Oklahoma State Tech

PARTICIPANTS:
180–200

PROGRAM COSTS PROVIDED BY:
Company: 100%

PRINTED MATERIALS AVAILABLE FROM:
Not available

AMPEX CORPORATION
with
COLLEGE OF SAN MATEO

ELECTRONIC UPGRADE

COMPANY CONTACT:
Margaret Meyer
Personnel Training
Ampex Corporation
401 Broadway
Redwood City, CA 04063
(415) 367-2750

INSTITUTIONAL CONTACT:
James Petromilli
Project Director
Electronics Department
College of San Mateo
1700 West Hillsdale Blvd.
Building 19, Room 111
San Mateo, CA 94402
(415) 574-6228

PROGRAM DESCRIPTION/ OBJECTIVES:
The upgrade program is provided for electronic worker on site. The Project attends to both the need for higher tech skill training as well as to providing job opportunities to California's unemployed.

PROGRAM INITIATED:
1980

LENGTH OF STUDY FOR PARTICIPANT:
Variable total approximately 540 hours

LENGTH OF CONTRACT:
12 months with renewal option

LOCATION:
Ampex Corporation

PARTICIPANTS:
20 employees needing upgrading

PROGRAM COSTS PROVIDED BY:
Other Source: State of California

PRINTED MATERIALS AVAILABLE FROM:
Institution

AMSCO
with
JAMESTOWN COMMUNITY COLLEGE

METAL BRAKE OPERATION TRAINING

COMPANY CONTACT:
Bob Beckstrom
Plant Manager
Amsco
P.O. Box 549 Girts Road
Jamestown, NY 14701
(716) 484-1156

INSTITUTIONAL CONTACT:
Rose M. Scott
Continuing Education Assistant
Jamestown Community College
525 Falconer Street
Jamestown, NY 15701
(716) 665-5220

PROGRAM DESCRIPTION/OBJECTIVES:
To provide those individuals participating in this course with the necessary shop math and blueprint reading skills as well as safety techniques and hands-on training to perform their jobs as brake operators safely and more efficiently.

PROGRAM INITIATED:
Not reported

LENGTH OF STUDY FOR PARTICIPANT:
12 weeks

LENGTH OF CONTRACT:
12 months with option to review

LOCATION:
Amsco

PARTICIPANTS:
11 brake operators

PROGRAM COSTS PROVIDED BY:
Institution: 40%
Company: 20%
Other Source: 20%

PRINTED MATERIALS AVAILABLE FROM:
Not available

THE ANSUL COMPANY
with
UNIVERSITY OF WISCONSIN-MARINETTE COUNTY

RETIREMENT PLANNING SEMINAR

COMPANY CONTACT:
Carol Rickaby
Benefits Officer
Personnel Department
The Ansul Company
1 Stanton Street
Marinette, WI 54143
(715) 735-7411

INSTITUTIONAL CONTACT:
Mary S. Blazer
Continuing Education Coordinator
University of Wisconsin Extension
U.W. Center-Marinette
Bay Shore, Marinette, WI 54143
(715) 735-7477

PROGRAM DESCRIPTION/OBJECTIVES:
Preparing employees for retirement; reviewing company plan, psychology of retirement, health and safety, financial planning and best use of leisure time/educational opportunities.

DIRECTORY OF CAMPUS-BUSINESS LINKAGES 71

PROGRAM INITIATED:
1981

LENGTH OF STUDY FOR PARTICIPANT:
8 hours

LENGTH OF CONTRACT:
4 months

LOCATION:
Ansul Company

PARTICIPANTS:
50 company employees (management and hourly employees)

PROGRAM COSTS PROVIDED BY:
Institution: $100 (administrative)
Company: $800

PRINTED MATERIALS AVAILABLE FROM:
Institution and Company

APPLE COMPUTER
with
EVERGREEN VALLEY COLLEGE

DRAFTING TO INTERNATIONAL STANDARDS

COMPANY CONTACT:
Rose Gardner
Manager
Engineering Services
Apple Computer
10240 Bubb
Cupertino, CA 95014

INSTITUTIONAL CONTACT:
Andrew McFarlin
Engineering Instructor and Coordinator
Evergreen Valley College
3095 Yerba Buena Road
San Jose, CA 95135
(408) 274-7900, X6570

PROGRAM DESCRIPTION/ OBJECTIVES:
Designed to upgrade the technical skills of personnel through a non-credit experience.

PROGRAM INITIATED:
1982

LENGTH OF STUDY FOR PARTICIPANT:
1 course, 24 hours in 6–8 week period

LENGTH OF CONTRACT:
1 course per contract

LOCATION:
On-site

PARTICIPANTS:
Estimated 30 drafters and designers

PROGRAM COSTS PROVIDED BY:
Institution: 100% (formative stage)

PRINTED MATERIALS AVAILABLE FROM:
Not yet available

ARMSTRONG INTERNATIONAL CORPORATION*
with
WESTERN MICHIGAN UNIVERSITY

WESTERN MICHIGAN UNIVERSITY OFFICE OF PUBLIC SERVICE

COMPANY CONTACT:
Douglas Bloss
Armstrong International Corporation
900 Maple Street
P.O. Box 381
Three Rivers, MI 49093

INSTITUTIONAL CONTACT:
Jack S. Wood
Director
WESTOPS
Western Michigan University
Kalamazoo, MI 49008
(616) 383-0077

PROGRAM DESCRIPTION/ OBJECTIVES:
Provide up-to-date technical information as requested by business and industry in southwest Michigan.

PROGRAM INITIATED:
1981

LENGTH OF STUDY FOR PARTICIPANT:
9 months to date

LENGTH OF CONTRACT:
On-going

LOCATION:
Western Michigan University

PARTICIPANTS:
Indeterminate

PROGRAM COSTS PROVIDED BY:
Institution: 100%

PRINTED MATERIALS AVAILABLE FROM:
Institution

*Representative entry—complete list available from institution.

ASHLAND OIL*
with
MARSHALL UNIVERSITY

INFORMATION SERVICE TO BUSINESS, INDUSTRY, AND GOVERNMENT AGENCIES

COMPANY CONTACT:
Sharon Payne
Reference Librarian
Ashland Oil
Russell, KY 41169
(606) 329-3333

INSTITUTIONAL CONTACT:
Kenneth T. Slack
Director of University Libraries
Marshall University
Huntington, WV 25705
(304) 696-3120

PROGRAM DESCRIPTION/ OBJECTIVES:
Access to reference materials is provided to local businesses and governmental agencies through requests.

PROGRAM INITIATED:
1972

LENGTH OF STUDY FOR PARTICIPANT:
Not available

LENGTH OF CONTRACT:
Informal verbal agreement

LOCATION:
Marshall University

PARTICIPANTS:
Approximately 20–25 industries, agencies, etc.

PROGRAM COSTS PROVIDED BY:
Institution: 100% (with business support through charitable gifts)

PRINTED MATERIALS AVAILABLE FROM:
Not reported

*Representative entry—complete list available from institution.

ASSOCIATION OF SCHOOL BUSINESS OFFICIALS OF THE U.S. AND CANADA
with
MICHIGAN TECHNOLOGICAL UNIVERSITY

FINANCIAL AND MANAGERIAL ACCOUNTING AND REPORTING FOR SCHOOL SYSTEMS

COMPANY CONTACT:
Charles Stolberg
Director of Research
Association of School Business Officials
720 Garden Street
Park Ridge, IL 60068
(312) 823-9320

INSTITUTIONAL CONTACT:
Sam B. Tidwell
Professor of Accounting
School of Business and Engineering Administration
Michigan Technological University

Houghton, MI 49931
(906) 487-2668

PROGRAM DESCRIPTION/OBJECTIVES:
Provide educational opportunity for school business officials to study generally accepted accounting and financial reporting standards as they apply specifically to elementary and secondary school systems.

PROGRAM INITIATED:
1959

LENGTH OF STUDY FOR PARTICIPANT:
1-4 weeks (6 hours daily)

LENGTH OF CONTRACT:
As programs develop

LOCATION:
Michigan Technological University

PARTICIPANTS:
School business officials

PROGRAM COSTS PROVIDED BY:
Participant: 100%

PRINTED MATERIALS AVAILABLE FROM:
Company

ATEC INDUSTRIAL TRAINING, INC.
with
MT. WACHUSETT COMMUNITY COLLEGE

ATEC-MT. WACHUSETT HYDRAULICS

COMPANY CONTACT:
Alex Tremblay
President
Atec Industrial Training, Inc.
P.O. Box 512
Westford, MA 01886
(617) 692-8344

INSTITUTIONAL CONTACT:
Richard F. Fox
Dean, Continuing Education
Mt. Wachusett Community College
444 Greem Street
Gardner, MA 01440
(617) 632-8261

PROGRAM DESCRIPTION/OBJECTIVES:
To train in locating and repairing problems in a hydraulic system.

PROGRAM INITIATED:
1982

LENGTH OF STUDY FOR PARTICIPANT:
7 weeks at 2½ hours per week

LENGTH OF CONTRACT:
3 months with renewal option

LOCATION:
Mt. Wachusett Community College

PARTICIPANTS:
17 various applicants

PROGRAM COSTS PROVIDED BY:
Participant: $150

PRINTED MATERIALS AVAILABLE FROM:
Institution

ATLANTIC RICHFIELD COMPANY
with
OKLAHOMA STATE TECH

ELECTRICAL PRINCIPLES

COMPANY CONTACT:
Marcus O. Durham
Senior Analytical Engineer
Atlantic Richfield Company
P.O. Box 521
Tulsa, OK 74102
(918) 588-8200

INSTITUTIONAL CONTACT:
Bill J. Lyons
Department Head
Electrical-Electronic Technology
Oklahoma State Tech
4th and Mission
Okmulgee, OK 74447
(918) 756-6211, X252

PROGRAM DESCRIPTION/ OBJECTIVES:
To provide maintenance technicians with basic technical knowledge and skills with emphasis on motors and controls. Also an introduction to cathodic protection of pipeline systems.

PROGRAM INITIATED:
1978

LENGTH OF STUDY FOR PARTICIPANT:
Not reported

LENGTH OF CONTRACT:
Not reported

LOCATION:
Not reported

PARTICIPANTS:
30–36

PROGRAM COSTS PROVIDED BY:
Company: 100%

PRINTED MATERIALS AVAILABLE FROM:
Not available

ATLAS ENERGY GROUP
with
KENT STATE UNIVERSITY

GEOLOGY SHORT COURSE

COMPANY CONTACT:
John McNally
Atlas Energy Group
5201 Mahoning Road, NW
Warren, OH 44483
(216) 847-7202

INSTITUTIONAL CONTACT:
Karen Rylander
Director, Continuing Education
Kent State University
327 Rockwell Hall
Kent, OH 44242
(216) 672-3100

PROGRAM DESCRIPTION/ OBJECTIVES:
Topics covered included: basic concepts of geology, geological history of northeastern Ohio, and petroleum.

PROGRAM INITIATED:
1981

LENGTH OF STUDY FOR PARTICIPANT:
9 hours

LENGTH OF CONTRACT:
9 hours

LOCATION:
Kent State University

PARTICIPANTS:
30 employees

PROGRAM COSTS PROVIDED BY:
Company: 100%

PRINTED MATERIALS AVAILABLE FROM:
Institution

AULTMAN HOSPITAL
with
KENT STATE UNIVERSITY

EFFECTIVE BUSINESS WRITING

COMPANY CONTACT:
Ronald Lamb
Aultman Hospital
2600 6th Street, SW
Canton, OH 44710
(216) 438-6352

INSTITUTIONAL CONTACT:
Karen Rylander
Director, Continuing Education
Kent State University
327 Rockwell Hall
Kent, OH 44242
(216) 672-3100

PROGRAM DESCRIPTION/ OBJECTIVES:
Provides a practical review of the fundamentals of written communication for

professions in business and industry. It emphasizes the application of successful strategies for writing persuasive and efficient prose in the various business forms.

PROGRAM INITIATED:
1982

LENGTH OF STUDY FOR PARTICIPANT:
10 hours + 1 hour individual follow-up

LENGTH OF CONTRACT:
10 hours + 1 hour individual follow-up

LOCATION:
Aultman Hospital

PARTICIPANTS:
12 upper managers

PROGRAM COSTS PROVIDED BY:
Company: 100%

PRINTED MATERIALS AVAILABLE FROM:
Institution

AULTMAN HOSPITAL
with
KENT STATE UNIVERSITY

LISTENING SKILLS

COMPANY CONTACT:
Ronald Lamb
Aultman Hospital
2600 6th Street, SW
Canton, OH 44710
(216) 438-6352

INSTITUTIONAL CONTACT:
Karen Rylander
Director, Continuing Education
Kent State University
327 Rockwell Hall
Kent, OH 44242
(216) 672-3100

PROGRAM DESCRIPTION/ OBJECTIVES:
An overview of communication and active listening skills from both one-to-one and small group perspectives.

PROGRAM INITIATED:
1981

LENGTH OF STUDY FOR PARTICIPANT:
2 hours

LENGTH OF CONTRACT:
2 hours

LOCATION:
Aultman Hospital

PARTICIPANTS:
180 first-line supervisors

PROGRAM COSTS PROVIDED BY:
Company: 100%

PRINTED MATERIALS AVAILABLE FROM:
Institution

NOT REPORTED*
with
AURORA UNIVERSITY

MANAGEMENT APPLICATION PROJECT CLASS

COMPANY CONTACT:
Specific company not identified

INSTITUTIONAL CONTACT:
Donald M. Cassiday, Jr.
Dean of Graduate Studies
Aurora University
347 South Gladstone
Aurora, IL 60506
(312) 892-6844

PROGRAM DESCRIPTION/ OBJECTIVES:
To provide practical on-the-job management experience to graduate students enabling them to apply academic theory to real life while accomplishing real life tasks for their employers.

PROGRAM INITIATED:
1980

LENGTH OF STUDY FOR PARTICIPANT:
2 years

LENGTH OF CONTRACT:
2 years

LOCATION:
Aurora College

PARTICIPANTS:
140 junior to middle level managers annually

PROGRAM COSTS PROVIDED BY:
Institution: $15,000
Company: highly varied
Participant: $505/term or $1170/year

PRINTED MATERIALS AVAILABLE FROM:
Institution

* Representative entry—complete list available from institution.

AUTODESK, INC. AND BASICOMP, INC.
with
IOWA STATE UNIVERSITY-COLLEGE OF DESIGN

EVALUATING CAD SOFTWARE FOR APPLICATION IN DESIGN FIELDS

COMPANY CONTACT:
Joe Woodman
Education Director and
MaryAnn Zadfar
Public Relations Director
Autodesk, Inc.
150 Shoreline Highway, Building B
Mill Valley, CA 94941
(415) 331-0356

COMPANY CONTACT:
Rose Erickson
Chief Executive Officer
Basicomp, Inc.
4040 East McDowell, Suite 305,
Phoenix, AZ 85008
(602) 231-0450

INSTITUTIONAL CONTACT:
Mary Kihl
Associate Dean
College of Design
Iowa State University
134 College of Design
Ames, Iowa 50011
(515) 294-7427

PROGRAM DESCRIPTION/OBJECTIVES:
Evaluation of CAD software to determine the appropriateness to design fields and professional design in Architecture, Landscape Architecture, Interior Design, Graphic Design; Autodesk Interior Design and Basicomp.

PROGRAM INITIATED:
1984

LENGTH OF CONTRACT:
1 year renewable

LOCATION:
College of Design, Ames, Iowa 50011

PARTICIPANTS:
Number: 250+
Type: Design students

PROGRAM COSTS PROVIDED BY:
Institution

PRINTED MATERIALS AVAILABLE FROM:
Institution

B & D MINISTORAGE
with
CALIFORNIA BAPTIST COLLEGE

BS DEGREE FOR BUSINESS EXECUTIVES

COMPANY CONTACT:
Bob Pentz
B & D Ministorage
9660 Arlington Avenue
Riverside, CA 92504

INSTITUTIONAL CONTACT:
Dr. Robert K. Jabs
Div. of Business Administration
California Baptist College
8432 Magnolia Avenue

Riverside, CA 92504
(714) 689-5771
PROGRAM DESCRIPTION/ OBJECTIVES:
Opportunity for company employees to pursue coursework towards an undergraduate degree in business.
PROGRAM INITIATED:
1982
LENGTH OF STUDY FOR PARTICIPANT:
18 months
LENGTH OF CONTRACT:
18 months
LOCATION:
On campus
PARTICIPANTS:
15 employees
PROGRAM COSTS PROVIDED BY:
Institution: $7,000 per cluster
Company: $7,000 per person
PRINTED MATERIALS AVAILABLE FROM:
Institution

BATHGATE EMPLOYMENT COORDINATING OFFICE
with
BRONX COMMUNITY COLLEGE

COMMERCIAL UPGRADE TRAINING
COMPANY CONTACT:
Oilda Martinez
Director
Bathgate Employment Coordinator Office
3960 Third Avenue
Bronx, NY 10457
(212) 731-3937
INSTITUTIONAL CONTACT:
Rafael Infante
Director, Contracts & Training
  Continuing Education

Bronx Community College
University Avenue & 181 Street
Bronx, NY 10453
(212) 220-6424
PROGRAM DESCRIPTION/ OBJECTIVES:
To upgrade the technical English, commercial math and secretarial skills of potential employees of the Bathgate Industrial Park
LENGTH OF STUDY FOR PARTICIPANT:
18 weeks
LENGTH OF CONTRACT:
4 months
LOCATION:
Bronx Community College
PARTICIPANTS:
Number: 50
PROGRAM COSTS PROVIDED BY:
Other sources: $50,317
PRINTED MATERIALS AVAILABLE FROM:
Institution

BERING STRAITS NATIVE CORPORATION
with
NORTHWEST COMMUNITY COLLEGE

FINANCIAL AND MANAGERIAL PLANNING FOR VILLAGE CORPORATION
COMPANY CONTACT:
John Tetpin
Director
Village Services
Bering Straits Native Corporation
Nome, AK 99762
(907) 443-5252
INSTITUTIONAL CONTACT:
Nancy Mendenhall
Director, Community Services
Northwest Community College

Pouch 400
Nome, AK 99762
(907) 443-2201
PROGRAM DESCRIPTION/ OBJECTIVES:
Training for Village Corporation managers and board members.
PROGRAM INITIATED:
1982
LENGTH OF STUDY FOR PARTICIPANT:
1 week
LENGTH OF CONTRACT:
30 months
LOCATION:
Brevig Mission, Shaktoolik, AK
PARTICIPANTS:
8–10 corporate officers and board members
PROGRAM COSTS PROVIDED BY:
Institution: $7,000
Company: $4,000
PRINTED MATERIALS AVAILABLE FROM:
Not available

BESSER COMPANY
with
ALPENA COMMUNITY COLLEGE

BLOCKMAKERS' WORKSHOP
COMPANY CONTACT:
Lucas Pfeiffenberger
Manager, Research and Training Center
Besser Company
Johnson Street
Alpena, MI 49707
(517) 354-4111

INSTITUTIONAL CONTACT:
Alan Reed
Dean, Occupational Education
Applied Arts and Science
Alpena Community College
666 Johnson Street
Alpena, MI 49707
(517) 356-9021
PROGRAM DESCRIPTION/ OBJECTIVES:
To provide training to various levels of personnel involved in the blockmaking process. Courses have included concrete masonry technology, block production vibrapac, product handling, equipment control, preventive maintenance and block production bescopac.
PROGRAM INITIATED:
1964
LENGTH OF STUDY FOR PARTICIPANT:
1 to 6 weeks
LENGTH OF CONTRACT:
Ongoing
LOCATION:
Alpena Community College
PARTICIPANTS:
225 mechanical and electrical machine operators
PROGRAM COSTS PROVIDED BY:
Company: $210/student
Participant: $196–260/session (amount based on residency)
PRINTED MATERIALS AVAILABLE FROM:
Institution

BETHLEHEM STEEL CORPORATION
with
DUNDALK COMMUNITY COLLEGE

INSPECTOR PLANNER
COMPANY CONTACT:
Nelson Daniel
Training Foreman
Maintenance Dept.
Bethlehem Steel Corp.
Sparrows Point Plant

Sparrows Point, MD 21219
(301) 388-5685
INSTITUTIONAL CONTACT:
Dr. James Bruns
Chairman
Social Science Dept.
Dundalk Community College
7200 Sollers Point Road
Dundalk, MD 21222
(301) 522-5782
PROGRAM DESCRIPTION/ OBJECTIVES:
To provide training for a new position in operational/preventive maintenance. (combination of credit and non-credit courses)
PROGRAM INITIATED:
September, 1982
LENGTH OF STUDY FOR PARTICIPANT:
2 semesters
LENGTH OF CONTRACT:
Yearly
LOCATION:
Dundalk Community College
PARTICIPANTS:
Number: 90
Type: Full-time
PROGRAM COSTS PROVIDED BY:
Company 100%
PRINTED MATERIALS AVAILABLE FROM:
Institution 100%

BETHLEHEM STEEL CORPORATION
with
DUNDALK COMMUNITY COLLEGE

RESCUE TRAINING FROM CONFINED SPACES
COMPANY CONTACT:
Martin Mossa
Division of Safety Engineering
Bethlehem Steel Corporation
Sparrows Point, MD 21219
(301) 388-4408
INSTITUTIONAL CONTACT:
Norma S. Tucker
Director of Continuing Education
Dundalk Community College
7200 Sollers Point Road
Baltimore, MD 21222
(301) 282-6700
PROGRAM DESCRIPTION/ OBJECTIVES:
This program was designed to offer rescue training techniques for employees in an industrial setting who face the potential hazard of being trapped in a confined space during the conduct of their work.
PROGRAM INITIATED:
1982
LENGTH OF STUDY FOR PARTICIPANT:
16 hours
LENGTH OF CONTRACT:
2,000 workers (10 per class)
LOCATION:
Bethlehem Steel Plant
PARTICIPANTS:
40 workers per month
PROGRAM COSTS PROVIDED BY:
Institution: $272 per 16 hours
Company: $1.50 per hour
Other Source: State aid
PRINTED MATERIALS AVAILABLE FROM:
Institution

BIRMINGHAM BUSINESS COMMUNITY*
with
BIRMINGHAM-SOUTHERN COLLEGE

DIVISION OF ADULT STUDIES AND SPECIAL PROGRAMS
COMPANY CONTACT:
Specific company not identified

INSTITUTIONAL CONTACT:
Jim Watson
Director of Adult Studies
Birmingham-Southern College
Birmingham, AL 35254
(205) 328-5250, X386

PROGRAM DESCRIPTION/ OBJECTIVES:
To provide an evening degree-granting program and special programs to strengthen Birmingham-Southern College's relationship with the Birmingham business community. Program offers majors in 7 disciplines, special programs for women and retirees, and courses at 2 local hospitals.

PROGRAM INITIATED:
1978

LENGTH OF STUDY FOR PARTICIPANT:
Miniterms

LENGTH OF CONTRACT:
Ongoing

LOCATION:
Birmingham-Southern College campus

PARTICIPANTS:
277

PROGRAM COSTS PROVIDED BY:
Participant: 100%

PRINTED MATERIALS AVAILABLE FROM:
Institution

* Representative entry—complete list available from institution.

BIRMINGHAM (et al.) BUSINESS COMMUNITY*
with
BIRMINGHAM-SOUTHERN COLLEGE

EXPERIENTIAL LEARNING
COMPANY CONTACT:
Specific company not identified.

INSTITUTIONAL CONTACT:
Carrie Anna Pearce
Coordinator, Experiential Learning
Contract Learning Center
Birmingham-Southern College
Birmingham, AL 35254
(205) 328-5250, ext. 403

PROGRAM DESCRIPTION/ OBJECTIVES:
To provide individualized/experiential learning opportunities for students.

PROGRAM INITIATED:
1977

LENGTH OF STUDY FOR PARTICIPANTS:
Semester (4-1-4)

LENGTH OF CONTRACT:
Ongoing

LOCATION:
Birmingham-Southern College campus and environs.

PARTICIPANTS:
Number: 450–500
Type: Undergraduate students

PROGRAM COSTS PROVIDED BY:
Participant: 100%

PRINTED MATERIALS AVAILABLE FROM:
Institution

* Representative entry . . . complete list available from institution.

BIRMINGHAM BUSINESS COMMUNITY
with
BIRMINGHAM-SOUTHERN COLLEGE

DIVISION OF ADULT STUDIES
COMPANY CONTRACT:
Specific company not identified.

INSTITUTIONAL CONTACT:
Jeff Norrell
Division Chairman

Division of Adult Studies
Birmingham Southern College
Birmingham, AL 35254
(205) 328-5250, Ext. 386

PROGRAM DESCRIPTION/ OBJECTIVES:
To provide an evening degree-granting program and to strengthen Birmingham-Southern College's relationship with the business community. Program offers majors in 7 disciplines and courses at 1 local hospital.

PROGRAM INITIATED:
1975

LENGTH OF STUDY FOR PARTICIPANTS:
4 9-week terms

LENGTH OF CONTRACT:
Ongoing

LOCATION:
Birmingham-Southern College campus

PARTICIPANTS:
Number: 350
Type: Adult learners in a credit program.

PROGRAM COSTS PROVIDED BY:
Participant: 100%

PRINTED MATERIALS AVAILABLE FROM:
Institution

BIRMINGHAM CITY GOVERNMENT
with
BIRMINGHAM-SOUTHERN COLLEGE

PROJECT WORK-LEARN/ EDUCATION WORK RETREATS

COMPANY CONTACT:
Birmingham City Government
800 8th Avenue West
Box A-10
Birmingham, AL 35254

INSTITUTIONAL CONTACT:
Ned Moomaw
Dean
Birmingham-Southern College
Birmingham, AL 35254
(205) 328-5250, X200

PROGRAM DESCRIPTION/ OBJECTIVES:
Education/Work Retreats are designed to bring together faculty from the College and executives from various firms, agencies or organizations to address topics of mutual interest and to plan future collaborative activities.

PROGRAM INITIATED:
1977

LENGTH OF STUDY FOR PARTICIPANT:
2-day retreat

LENGTH OF CONTRACT:
2 days

LOCATION:
Held in resort area to insure relaxed exchange of ideas

PARTICIPANTS:
44 Birmingham City Council members, Mayor of Birmingham and Birmingham-Southern Faculty members

PROGRAM COSTS PROVIDED BY:
Institution: 100%

PRINTED MATERIALS AVAILABLE FROM:
Institution

BIRMINGHAM EXECUTIVES*
with
BIRMINGHAM-SOUTHERN COLLEGE

PROJECT WORK-LEARN/ EXECUTIVES IN RESIDENCE

COMPANY CONTACT:
Specific company not identified

INSTITUTIONAL CONTACT:
Jeff Norrell
Director of Adult Studies
Birmingham-Southern College
Birmingham, AL 35254
(205) 328-5250

PROGRAM DESCRIPTION/ OBJECTIVES:
Birmingham executives attend regular academic classes, special seminars, and contribute their expertise to the College. Personal and professional growth is emphasized.

PROGRAM INITIATED:
1977

LENGTH OF STUDY FOR PARTICIPANT:
2 weeks

LENGTH OF CONTRACT:
2 weeks

LOCATION:
Birmingham-Southern College campus

PARTICIPANTS:
45 Birmingham area business executives

PROGRAM COSTS PROVIDED BY:
Institution: 100%

PRINTED MATERIALS AVAILABLE FROM:
Institution

* Representative entry—complete list available from institution.

EMPLOYEES FROM AREA BUSINESSES*
with
BIRMINGHAM-SOUTHERN COLLEGE

PROJECT WORK-LEARN/THE SOUTHERN EXPOSURE-LISTENER PROGRAM

COMPANY CONTACT:
Specific company not identified

INSTITUTIONAL CONTACT:
H. Irvin Penfield
Dean
Birmingham-Southern College
Birmingham, AL 35254
(205) 328-5250, X200

PROGRAM DESCRIPTION/ OBJECTIVES:
Program was designed to provide employees of Birmingham business an opportunity to attend Birmingham-Southern College as "listeners." For a nominal fee, these employers are permitted to attend as many class sessions as they desire.

PROGRAM INITIATED:
1977

LENGTH OF STUDY FOR PARTICIPANT:
Ongoing each semester

LENGTH OF CONTRACT:
Ongoing

LOCATION:
Birmingham-Southern College

PARTICIPANTS:
As of 1981 over 75 Birmingham area employees and community persons

PROGRAM COSTS PROVIDED BY:
Participant: $10.00

PRINTED MATERIALS AVAILABLE FROM:
Institution

* Representative entry—complete list available from institution.

FIFTY SOUTHEASTERN EMPLOYERS
with
BIRMINGHAM-SOUTHERN COLLEGE, SAMFORD UNIVERSITY, AND UNIVERSITY OF MONTEVALLO

"THREE-IN-ONE PLACEMENT CONFERENCE"

COMPANY CONTACT:
Various employers participate from year to year, representing a variety of career industries—accounting, banking, sales, insurance, hospitals, government, etc.

INSTITUTIONAL CONTACT:
Judith A. Harrington
Coordinator of Career Counseling & Placement
Counseling Center
Birmingham-Southern College
Box A-10, 800 8th Avenue West
Birmingham, AL 35254
(205) 328-5250 (ext. 395)

PROGRAM DESCRIPTION/OBJECTIVES:
To provide a cost effective and time effective method for various employers to conduct employment interviews with graduates of three small liberal arts universities. To increase the visibility of capable liberal arts graduates with a variety of employers while also increasing the opportunities for students to learn of and be considered for specific employment opportunities.

PROGRAM INITIATED:
First conference, February 1983

LENGTH OF STUDY FOR CONTACT:
Year round planning, annual event.

LENGTH OF CONTRACT:
Program is developed on an ongoing basis. Some recruiters have participated 3 years in a row, some for the first time each year.

LOCATION:
Birmingham-Southern is host in 1986. Location rotates to each college every third year.

PARTICIPANTS:
50 employers, 140 seniors or recent graduates. Prescheduled interviews number over 700 on day of conference.

PROGRAM COSTS PROVIDED BY:
Employers pay a fee of $10 per recruiter to cover luncheon costs. Institutions fund program administratively.

PRINTED MATERIALS AVAILABLE FROM:
Brochures from institution. Recruitment literature from company.

LOCAL BUSINESS INDUSTRIES AND GOVERNMENT*
with
BIRMINGHAM-SOUTHERN COLLEGE

PROJECT WORK-LEARN/ VISITING PROFESSORS

COMPANY CONTACT:
Varies
800 8th Avenue West
Birmingham, AL 35254

INSTITUTIONAL CONTACT:
Carrie Anna Pearce
Coordinator/Experiential Education
Birmingham-Southern College
Birmingham, AL 35254
(205) 328-5250, X200

PROGRAM DESCRIPTION/OBJECTIVES:
To provide opportunities for Birmingham-Southern College faculty members to spend time working in a local business, industry, labor, governmental or professional positions.

PROGRAM INITIATED:
1977

LENGTH OF STUDY FOR PARTICIPANT:
4–6 weeks

LENGTH OF CONTRACT:
4–6 weeks

LOCATION:
On-the-job sites, Birmingham, AL

PARTICIPANTS:
45 full-time faculty representing departments such as English, Marketing, etc.

PROGRAM COSTS PROVIDED BY:
Institution: 100%

PRINTED MATERIALS AVAILABLE FROM:
Institution

* Representative entry—complete list available from institution.

BOILER MAKERS UNION LOCAL LODGE #5
with
NEW YORK CITY TECHNICAL COLLEGE, DIVISION OF CONTINUING EDUCATION

APPRENTICE PROGRAM FOR WELDING AND ASSOCIATED SKILLS

COMPANY CONTACT:
Joseph R. Gregorio, Jr.
President
Boiler Makers Union Local Lodge #5
320 Northern Blvd.
Great Neck, NY 11021
(516) 487-3404

INSTITUTIONAL CONTACT:
Fannie Eisenstein
Dean
Continuing Education
New York City Technical College
300 Jay Street
Brooklyn, NY 11201
(718) 643-8150

PROGRAM DESCRIPTION/OBJECTIVES:
140 hours of training for welding and associated skills including electric arc welding, oxy-acetylene cutting, including air carbonarc, tube cutting, electric arc welding (tubes), tungsten inert gas welding (TIG) and automatic welding (MIG).

LENGTH OF STUDY FOR PARTICIPANT:
140 hours

LENGTH OF CONTRACT:
14 weeks

LOCATION:
Voorhees

PARTICIPANTS:
8 welders

PROGRAM COSTS PROVIDED BY:
Company: 100%

PRINTED MATERIALS AVAILABLE FROM:
Institution

BROOKWOOD MEDICAL CENTER*
with
BIRMINGHAM-SOUTHERN COLLEGE

PROJECT WORK-LEARN/CAREER CONSULTANT PROGRAM

COMPANY CONTACT:
Carol Gillespie Grizzle
Psychologist
Brookwood Medical Center
Birmingham, AL 35209
(205) 879-7953

INSTITUTIONAL CONTACT:
Judy Harrington
Coordinator Career
Counseling and Placement
Birmingham-Southern College
Birmingham, AL 35254
(205) 328-5250, X403

PROGRAM DESCRIPTION/ OBJECTIVES:
The Career Consultant Program is designed to put college students in direct contact with people in local business, industrial, labor, governmental, educational, religious, and professional organizations. The contact may be through an individualized career information interview or as a campus speaker.

PROGRAM INITIATED:
1977

LENGTH OF STUDY FOR PARTICIPANT:
Ongoing; contacts scheduled as needed

LENGTH OF CONTRACT:
Ongoing

LOCATION:
Work site or campus

PARTICIPANTS:
Approximately 400 consultants from all areas of the work world

PROGRAM COSTS PROVIDED BY:
Institution: 100%

* Representative entry—complete list available from institution.

Continuing Education
Bronx Community College
University Avenue & 181 Street
Bronx, NY 10453

PROGRAM DESCRIPTION/ OBJECTIVES:
To provide a certified Home Health Aide Program

LENGTH OF STUDY FOR PARTICIPANT:
3 months

LENGTH OF CONTRACT:
1 year with renewal option

LOCATION:
Bronx Community College

PARTICIPANTS:
Number: 210 annually
Type: Displaced homemakers

PROGRAM COSTS PROVIDED BY:
Company: $15,000
Participant: 0
Other Sources: $80,000

PRINTED MATERIALS AVAILABLE FROM:
Institution

BRONX COMMUNITY HOME CARE
with
BRONX COMMUNITY COLLEGE

HOME HEALTH TRAINING PROGRAM

COMPANY CONTACT:
Suzanne Pincus
President
Bronx Community Home Care
78 E. 208 Street
Bronx, NY 10467
(212) 920-6582

INSTITUTIONAL CONTACT:
Rafael Infante
Director, Contracts & Training

BROWARD COUNTY HOSPITALS
with
BROWARD COMMUNITY COLLEGE

NURSING SPONSORSHIP PROGRAM*

COMPANY CONTACT:
Several hospitals

INSTITUTIONAL CONTACT:
Wanda Thomas
Director, Division of Allied Health Technologies
Broward Community College
3501 S.W. Davie Road
Ft. Lauderdale, FL 33314
(305) 475-6767

PROGRAM DESCRIPTION/OBJECTIVES:
To provide hospital employees and other persons the financial means to become an R.N. To increase the number of available R.N.'s in the county and specifically sponsoring hospitals.

PROGRAM INITIATED:
1979

LENGTH OF STUDY FOR PARTICIPANT:
2 years

LENGTH OF CONTRACT:
Continuous agreement

LOCATION:
Broward Community College Sponsorship Hospitals

PARTICIPANTS:
7 hospitals and 450 students per year

PROGRAM COSTS PROVIDED BY:
Institution: 50%
Company: 50%

PRINTED MATERIALS AVAILABLE FROM:
Institution

* Representative entry—complete list available from institution.

BROWN AND ROOT CORPORATION
with
NORTHLAND PIONEER COLLEGE

POWER PLANT CONSTRUCTION TECHNOLOGY

COMPANY CONTACT:
Ben May
Project Director
Brown and Root Corporation
Springerville, AZ 85938
(602) 337-2977

INSTITUTIONAL CONTACT:
Ronald E. Glenn
Director of Vocational Education
Northland Pioneer College
1200 Nermose Drive
Holbrook, AZ 86025
(602) 536-7871

PROGRAM DESCRIPTION/OBJECTIVES:
To provide training for employees of Brown and Root as they move from one phase of construction to the next.

PROGRAM INITIATED:
1981

LENGTH OF STUDY FOR PARTICIPANT:
Continuing

LENGTH OF CONTRACT:
Until project is completed in 1985

LOCATION:
Springerville, AZ

PARTICIPANTS:
260 construction workers yearly

PROGRAM COSTS PROVIDED BY:
Institution: $60,000 per year
Company: $50,000 per year which includes supplies, supervision, facilities and equipment; Tucson Electric also provides facilities not included in $50,000

PRINTED MATERIALS AVAILABLE FROM:
Institution and Company

BROWN & WILLIAMS TOBACCO COMPANY
with
GEORGIA INSTITUTE OF TECHNOLOGY

INDUSTRIAL SAFETY-NEW ATTITUDES FOR SUPERVISORS

COMPANY CONTACT:
Bob McKinley
Safety Manager
Safety
Brown & Williams Tobacco Company
P.O. Box 1056

Macon, GA 31298
(912) 743-0561

INSTITUTIONAL CONTACT:
Dr. Roberson
Director
Industrial Education
Georgia Institute of Technology
225 North Avenue, NW
Atlanta, GA 30332
(404) 894-3950

PROGRAM DESCRIPTION/ OBJECTIVES:
A brief series of presentations, exercises, and in-plant studies which reaffirm the front-line supervisor's responsibility in an effective safety program.

LENGTH OF STUDY FOR PARTICIPANT:
16 hours

LENGTH OF CONTRACT:
16 hours

LOCATION:
In-plant

PARTICIPANTS:
Number: 20
Type: Front-line supervisors

PROGRAM COSTS PROVIDED BY:
Institution: $765.00
Company: $1275.00

PRINTED MATERIALS AVAILABLE FROM:
Institution

BULOVA WATCH COMPANY
with
OKLAHOMA STATE TECH

BULOVA WATCH COMPANY SERIES OF ADVANCED REPAIR WORKSHOPS

COMPANY CONTACT:
Leo Helmprecht, Manager
Field Training Services
Bulova Watch Company
75-20 Astoria Blvd.
Jackson Heights, NY 11370
(212) 335-6000

INSTITUTIONAL CONTACT:
Gray Lawrence
Supervisor, Watch Micro-Instrument
 and Jewelry
Small Business Trades Department
Oklahoma State Tech
4th and Mission
Okmulgee, OK 74447
(918) 756-6211, X271

PROGRAM DESCRIPTION/ OBJECTIVES:
To foster closer relations within the industry and upgrade skills and knowledge of current watchmakers in the field. To expose students to the latest types and styles of watches produced in the industry as well as provide them opportunities for contact with potential employers.

PROGRAM INITIATED:
1965

LENGTH OF STUDY FOR PARTICIPANT:
Not reported

LENGTH OF CONTRACT:
Not reported

LOCATION:
Not reported

PARTICIPANTS:
64

PROGRAM COSTS PROVIDED BY:
Institution: 35%
Company: 65%

PRINTED MATERIALS AVAILABLE FROM:
Not available

BURROUGHS CORPORATION
with
ASSOCIATION OF AMERICAN COLLEGES

BUILDING BRIDGES BETWEEN BUSINESS ON CAMPUS

COMPANY CONTACT:
Bill Faught
Former Area Recruiting Manager
Burroughs Corporation
701 Columbia Drive
Sacramento, CA 95825
(916) 971-3458

INSTITUTIONAL CONTACT:
Kathryn Mohrman
Director, Office of National Affairs
Association of American Colleges
1818 R Street, NW
Washington, DC 20009
(202) 387-3760

PROGRAM DESCRIPTION/OBJECTIVES:
Program designed to acquaint middle-management personnel with liberal arts faculty in an effort to increase awareness of job opportunities and educational experiences for the benefit of future graduates.

PROGRAM INITIATED:
1981

LENGTH OF STUDY FOR PARTICIPANT:
1-day conference; informal networking continuing afterwards

LENGTH OF CONTRACT:
1 year

LOCATION:
Retreat settings

PARTICIPANTS:
30 faculty members from liberal arts disciplines, human resource managers and corporation trainers per meeting

PROGRAM COSTS PROVIDED BY:
Other Source: 100% (small grants from local business)

PRINTED MATERIALS AVAILABLE FROM:
Institution

BUTLER COUNTY HISTORICAL SOCIETY
with
BUTLER COUNTY COMMUNITY COLLEGE

EXCURSION INTO HISTORY "CIVIL WARFARE"

COMPANY CONTACT:
Charles Heilmann
President
Butler County Historical Society
409 Houser Drive
El Dorado, KS 67042
(316) 321-4196

INSTITUTIONAL CONTACT:
Larry DeVane
Dean of Liberal Arts and Sciences
Walborn Administration Building
Butler County Community College
El Dorado, KS 67042
(316) 321-5083, X110

PROGRAM DESCRIPTION/OBJECTIVES:
Opportunity for college and community to provide an educational experience for local citizens.

PROGRAM INITIATED:
Not reported

LENGTH OF STUDY FOR PARTICIPANT:
1 day

LENGTH OF CONTRACT:
Informal

LOCATION:
Butler County Community College

PARTICIPANTS:
1,000 local citizens

PROGRAM COSTS PROVIDED BY:
Institution: $3,000
Company: $3,000

Other Source: $300 (El Dorado Art Association)
PRINTED MATERIALS AVAILABLE FROM:
Institution

CADILLAC GAGE, DIVISION OF EXCELLO CORPORATION
with
EDISON STATE COMMUNITY COLLEGE

COMPUTER NUMERICAL CONTROL MACHINE OPERATIONS
COMPANY CONTACT:
Robert Wilson
Director of Personnel
Personnel and Training
Cadillac Gage Company
Greenville, OH 45331
(513) 548-3166

INSTITUTIONAL CONTACT:
Gary W. Wilson
Assistant Dean
Continuing Education
Edison State Community College
Piqua, OH 45356
(513) 778-8600

PROGRAM DESCRIPTION/OBJECTIVES:
To provide training on newer CNC machines for operators who are now using manual machines, and to upgrade the technical skills of the support staff.

PROGRAM INITIATED:
February, 1985

LENGTH OF STUDY FOR PARTICIPANT:
10 months

LENGTH OF CONTRACT:
One year

LOCATION:
In-Plant, Greenville, OH

PARTICIPANTS:
Number: 30
Type: Union and managerial support

PROGRAM COSTS PROVIDED BY:
Institution: Developmental costs
Company: Direct costs

PRINTED MATERIALS AVAILABLE FROM:
Institution and Company

CALCOT, LTD.*
with
CALIFORNIA STATE COLLEGE-BAKERSFIELD

COOPERATIVE EDUCATION PROGRAM
COMPANY CONTACT:
Mary Jo Pasek
Administrative Manager
Personnel
Calcot, Ltd.
P.O. Box 259
Bakersfield, CA 93302
(805) 327-5961

INSTITUTIONAL CONTACT:
Carolyn Hart-Tidwell
Coordinator
Cooperative Education Program
California State College-Bakersfield
9001 Stockdale Highway
Bakersfield, CA 93311-1099
(805) 833-2204

PROGRAM DESCRIPTION/OBJECTIVES:
Provide opportunity for students to gain relevant, career-related experience. Co-op students gain academic credit, experience in the working world, a salary commensurate with the profession, and have an exceptional opportunity to personally participate in career and management-related positions.

PROGRAM INITIATED:
1980

LENGTH OF STUDY FOR PARTICIPANT:
Minimum: 1 quarter

LENGTH OF CONTRACT:
Open

LOCATION:
California State College-Bakersfield

PARTICIPANTS:
Number: Unlimited numbers
Type: Juniors, seniors and graduates

PROGRM COSTS PROVIDED BY:
Institution: California State College-Bakersfield
Other Source: Federal grant monies

PRINTED MATERIALS AVAILABLE FROM:
Institution

* Representative entry—complete list available from institution.

CAMPBELL AND DARBY METALS*
with
TRI-COUNTY TECHNICAL COLLEGE

SHEET METAL FABRICATION

COMPANY CONTACT:
Barney Darby
Vice President
Campbell and Darby Metals
P.O. Box 73
Anderson, SC 29622
(803) 225-6906

INSTITUTIONAL CONTACT:
Ronald N. Talley
Director, Comprehensive Manpower Training
Tri-County Technical College
P.O. Box 587
Pendleton, SC 29670
(803) 646-8361

PROGRAM DESCRIPTION/OBJECTIVES:
To train persons in the layout and fabrication of products manufactured from sheet metal.

PROGRAM INITIATED:
1982

LENGTH OF STUDY FOR PARTICIPANT:
9 months

LENGTH OF CONTRACT:
9 months

LOCATION:
Tri-County Technical College

PARTICIPANTS:
20 sheet metal workers

PROGRAM COSTS PROVIDED BY:
Institution: Indirect
Company: Indirect
Other Source: $42,800 (federal job-training funds)

PRINTED MATERIALS AVAILABLE FROM:
Institution

* Representative entry—complete list available from institution.

CANADORE COLLEGE AND ST. CLAIR COLLEGE
with
CENTRAL MICHIGAN UNIVERSITY

CANADIAN COMMUNITY COLLEGE PROGRAM

COMPANY CONTACT:
Neil Cornthwaite
Applied Arts and Technology
Canadore College
P.O. Box 5001
North Bay, Ontario
Canada P1B 8K9
and

Joyce McInerney
1001 Grand Avenue West
Thames Campus
St. Clair College
Chatham Ontario
Canada N7M 5E4

INSTITUTIONAL CONTACT:
Lawrence R. Murphy
Director
Institute for Personal and Career
  Development
Central Michigan University
Mt. Pleasant, MI 48859
(517) 774-3865

PROGRAM DESCRIPTION/ OBJECTIVES:
To provide graduate level education program to Subject Matter Specialists currently teaching in Canadian community colleges.

PROGRAM INITIATED:
Not reported

LENGTH OF STUDY FOR PARTICIPANT:
22 months average

LENGTH OF CONTRACT:
Ongoing

LOCATION:
North Bay and Sudbury, Ontario

PARTICIPANTS:
70 faculty of Canadian Community College and public school teachers

PROGRAM COSTS PROVIDED BY:
Participant: 100%

PRINTED MATERIALS AVAILABLE FROM:
Institution

CAPE COD BANK AND TRUST COMPANY
with
CAPE COD COMMUNITY COLLEGE*

MANAGEMENT DEVELOPMENT PROGRAM

COMPANY CONTACT:
Irene Charles
Director of Personnel
Cape Code Bank and Trust Company
Off Station Avenue
South Yarmouth, MA 02664
(617) 775-3500

INSTITUTIONAL CONTACT:
Patrick E. Costello
Director
Center for Business and Industry
Cape Cod Community College
West Barnstable, MA 20668
(617) 362-2131, X414

PROGRAM DESCRIPTION/ OBJECTIVES:
To provide seminars, workshops and programs to meet the continual management training needs of local organizations.

PROGRAM INITIATED:
1981

LENGTH OF STUDY FOR PARTICIPANT:
Varies: 4 hours; 8 hour workshops; and seminars 6 week (15 hour) programs

LENGTH OF CONTRACT:
12 months

LOCATION:
Cape Cod Community College Campus

PARTICIPANTS:
10-15 per program of first line and middle level supervisors and managers

PROGRAM COSTS PROVIDED BY:
Institution: 10%
Company: 90%

PRINTED MATERIALS AVAILABLE FROM:
Institution

* Representative entry—complete list available from institution.

CAREER HORIZONS BOARD OF CONSULTANTS
with
EASTERN MICHIGAN UNIVERSITY

CAREER HORIZONS BOARD OF CONSULTANTS
COMPANY CONTACT:
Eugene R. Karrer
Chairman, Career Horizons Board of Consultants
300 Knobby View Drive
Holly, MI 48442
(313) 887-8417

INSTITUTIONAL CONTACT:
Laurence N. Smith
Vice-President for Student Affairs
Eastern Michigan University
101 Pierce Hall
Ypsilanti, MI 48197
(313) 487-2390

PROGRAM DESCRIPTION/ OBJECTIVES:
A comprehensive program to keep faculty and students in the university attuned to the changing nature of the world of work through the use of business leaders as consultants in short courses and seminars.

PROGRAM INITIATED:
1978

LENGTH OF STUDY FOR PARTICIPANT:
Not available

LENGTH OF CONTRACT:
Ongoing

LOCATION:
On campus

PARTICIPANTS:
40–50 consultants annually

PROGRAM COSTS PROVIDED BY:
Institution: $2,000
Company: In-kind
Participant: In-kind

PRINTED MATERIALS AVAILABLE FROM:
Institution

CENTER FOR INDUSTRIAL RESEARCH AND SERVICES
with
IOWA STATE UNIVERSITY

SMALL BUSINESS DEVELOPMENT CENTER
COMPANY CONTACT:
Louise Brinkman
State Director, SBDC
Center For Industrial Research and Services
Iowa State University
205 Engineering Annex
Ames, IA 50011
(515) 294-3420

INSTITUTIONAL CONTACT:
Jan A. DeYoung
Assistant Director, SBDC
Department of Economics
Iowa State University
East Hall
Ames, IA 50011
(515) 294-8069

PROGRAM DESCRIPTION/ OBJECTIVES:
Major thrust of the program is to provide business counseling to all types of small businesses. Also there are workshops for those planning to go into business, along with management courses and conferences to interest those already operating small businesses. Each center houses a management information library and is involved in developing and disseminating publications aimed at solving specific

business problems. Assistance is provided on most any phase of management, production or marketing. Selected topics include: developing business strategies for individual firms and towns, trade area analysis, improving management and profit structures, and training and motivating employees.

PROGRAM INITIATED:
1981

LENGTH OF STUDY FOR PARTICIPANT:
Varies with topic and participant

LENGTH OF CONTRACT:
12 month renewable

LOCATION:
Community based

PARTICIPANTS:
Approximately 4,000 members of the local business community

PROGRAM COSTS PROVIDED BY:
Other Source: Small Business Administration with state institution match

PRINTED MATERIALS AVAILABLE FROM:
Institution

CENTRAL BANK AND TRUST*
with
BIRMINGHAM-SOUTHERN COLLEGE

PROJECT WORK-LEARN/THE WORK AND CULTURE SEMINARS

COMPANY CONTACT:
Philip C. Jackson, Jr.
Chief Executive Officer
Central Bank and Trust
Birmingham, AL 35203
(205) 933-3000

INSTITUTIONAL CONTACT:
Bob Wingard
Director of Church Relations
Birmingham-Southern College
Birmingham, AL 35254
(205) 328-5250, X206

PROGRAM DESCRIPTION/ OBJECTIVES:
The purpose of the Work and Culture Seminar is to bring together the college community with business-professional-governmental leaders, to discuss areas where culture makes an impact on the working world.

PROGRAM INITIATED:
1978

LENGTH OF STUDY FOR PARTICIPANT:
Series of luncheons, usually 5 in 1 year

LENGTH OF CONTRACT:
Ongoing

LOCATION:
Birmingham-Southern College

PARTICIPANTS:
Varies, an average of 170 business leaders, professionals, civic leaders and representatives of the college community

PROGRAM COSTS PROVIDED BY:
Institution: 100%

PRINTED MATERIALS AVAILABLE FROM:
Institution

* Representative entry—complete list available from institution.

CENTRAL ILLINOIS LIGHT COMPANY*
with
BRADLEY-BUSINESS TASK FORCE

BRADLEY BUSINESS TASK FORCE

COMPANY CONTACT:
William Vogelsang
President
Central Illinois Light Company
300 Liberty Street
Peoria, IL 61602
(309) 676-5271

INSTITUTIONAL CONTACT:
Arthur Schwartz
Acting Director
Office of Research and Sponsored
   Programs
Bradley University
Peoria, IL 61625
(309) 676-7611, Ext, 341

PROGRAM DESCRIPTION/ OBJECTIVES:
Create a liaison between the Peoria business community and Bradley community so that business sector is aware of institutional resources and services.

PROGRAM INITIATED:
1982

LENGTH OF STUDY FOR PARTICIPANT:
Negotiable

LENGTH OF CONTRACT:
Open

LOCATION:
Peoria and Central Illinois

PARTICIPANTS:
Number: 70–90
Type: Business executives, university administrators.

PROGRAM COSTS PROVIDED BY:
Not reported

PRINTED MATERIALS AVAILABLE FROM:
Institution

* Representative entry—complete list available from institution.

CENTRAL STATES CONFERENCE OF BANKERS ASSOCIATIONS
with
UNIVERSITY OF WISCONSIN-MADISON

GRADUATE SCHOOL OF BANKING AT THE UNIVERSITY OF WISCONSIN-MADISON

COMPANY CONTACT:
Richard I. Doolittle
Executive Vice President
Prochnow Graduate School of Banking
122 West Washington Avenue
Madison, WI 53703
(608) 256-7021

INSTITUTIONAL CONTACT:
E. James Blakely
Acting Dean
School of Business and Graduate
   School of Business
University of Wisconsin-Madison
1155 Observatory Drive
Madison, WI 53706
(608) 262-1553

PROGRAM DESCRIPTION/ OBJECTIVES:
To provide bankers with a broad and fundamental understanding of significant banking, economic and monetary problems.

PROGRAM INITIATED:
1945

LENGTH OF STUDY FOR PARTICIPANT:
3 years

LENGTH OF CONTRACT:
3 years

LOCATION:
University of Wisconsin-Madison

PARTICIPANTS:
1,500 bank officers and officers of bank regulatory agencies

PROGRAM COSTS PROVIDED BY:
Institution: 5%
Company: 95%

PRINTED MATERIALS AVAILABLE FROM:
Company

COLLEGE FOR FINANCIAL PLANNING
with
UNIVERSITY OF HARTFORD

CERTIFIED FINANCIAL PLANNING PROGRAM

COMPANY CONTACT:
College for Financial Planning
9725 E. Hampden Avenue
Denver, CO 80231
(303) 755-7101

INSTITUTIONAL CONTACT:
A.L. Zander
Director
Office of University College/Cont. Prof. Development
University of Hartford
200 Bloomfield Avenue
West Hartford, CT 06117
(203) 243-4371

PROGRAM DESCRIPTION/OBJECTIVES:
Advance the knowledge, professionalism, public recognition and responsibility of persons who are or will be offering financial counseling, investment and risk management advice, counseling relating to retirement, tax or estate planning, or general personal financial planning and implementation.

PROGRAM INITIATED:
1983

LENGTH OF CONTRACT:
This will be an annual offering.

PARTICIPANTS:
A minimum of 10 candidates per class

PROGRAM COSTS PROVIDED BY:
Company and Participant

PRINTED MATERIALS AVAILABLE FROM:
Institution

CHAMPION INTERNATIONAL
with
FAIRFIELD UNIVERSITY

LUNCHTIME LECTURE SERIES

COMPANY CONTACT:
James Donohue
Associate Director
Champion International
1 Champion Plaza
Stamford, CT 06921
(203) 358-7000

INSTITUTIONAL CONTACT:
Alan Katz
Associate Professor
Politics Department
Fairfield University
North Benson Road
Fairfield, CT 06430
(203) 255-5411

PROGRAM DESCRIPTION/OBJECTIVES:
To make available intellectually stimulating ideas to a bright, interested adult audience. Presentations are arranged in series, i.e., four lectures on "America in the '80's" or eight lectures on the Renaissance.

PROGRAM INITIATED:
1981

LENGTH OF STUDY FOR PARTICIPANT:
Ranges from 25 lectures over a year to 1 or 2

LENGTH OF CONTRACT:
2 13-15 week semesters

LOCATION:
Corporate headquarters in Stamford, CT

PARTICIPANTS:
Approximately 50 ranging from clerical staff through corporate executives

PROGRAM COSTS PROVIDED BY:
Company: $4500.00

PRINTED MATERIALS AVAILABLE FROM:
Not reported

CHEN SCHOOL
with
RUTGERS, THE STATE UNIVERSITY OF NEW JERSEY

PRIMARY AFFILIATION

COMPANY CONTACT:
Regina Harris
Executive Director
Chen School
51 Rector Street
Newark, NJ 07102
(201) 624-1681

INSTITUTIONAL CONTACT:
Lucille Joel
Associate Dean for Clinical Affairs
College of Nursing
Rutgers, The State University of New Jersey
University Avenue
Newark, NJ 07102
(201) 648-5298

PROGRAM DESCRIPTION/OBJECTIVES:
Manpower sharing; student placement.

PROGRAM INITIATED:
1981

LENGTH OF STUDY FOR PARTICIPANT:
Academic year

LENGTH OF CONTRACT:
10 months

LOCATION:
Chen School and Rutgers

PARTICIPANTS:
1

PROGRAM COSTS PROVIDED BY:
Shared equally by exchange of time between company and institution

PRINTED MATERIALS AVAILABLE FROM:
Institution

CHESTERFIELD COUNTY, VIRGINIA
with
JOHN TYLER COMMUNITY COLLEGE

EFFECTIVE LOCAL GOVERNMENT SUPERVISION

COMPANY CONTACT:
Mr. Robert B. Galusha
Personnel Director
Personnel
Chesterfield County
P.O. Box 40
Chesterfield, VA 23832
(804) 748-1551

INSTITUTIONAL CONTACT:
Dr. Samuel Lee Hancock
Director
Division of Continuing Education
John Tyler Community College
13101 Jefferson Davis Highway
Chester, VA 23831
(804) 796-4111

PROGRAM DESCRIPTION/OBJECTIVES:
Program is designed to promote an understanding of the role and functions of a local government department first line supervisor.

PROGRAM INITIATED:
Winter, 1985

LENGTH OF STUDY FOR PARTICIPANT:
2½ years.

LENGTH OF CONTRACT:
30 instructional hours per 3 month period.

LOCATION:
On-site in Chesterfield County facilities.

PARTICIPANTS:
Number: 16
Type: Current or potential first line supervisors.

PROGRAM COSTS PROVIDED BY:
Institution: Administrative Leadership, Instructors' Salaries

Company: Tuition, Textbooks
Participant: Time
PRINTED MATERIALS AVAILABLE FROM:
Institution

CHESTERFIELD COUNTY, VIRGINIA
with
JOHN TYLER COMMUNITY COLLEGE

LOCAL GOVERNMENT MID-MANAGEMENT DEVELOPMENT
COMPANY CONTACT:
Mr. Robert B. Galusha
Personnel Director
Personnel
Chesterfield County
P.O. Box 40
Chesterfield, VA 23832
(804) 748-1551

INSTITUTIONAL CONTACT:
Dr. Samuel Lee Hancock
Director
Division of Continuing Education
John Tyler Community College
13101 Jefferson Davis Highway
Chester, VA 23831
(804) 796-4111

PROGRAM DESCRIPTION/ OBJECTIVES:
The managers will gain the necessary knowledge, skills, and abilities to be assertive and postive leaders of their respective departments. Candidates will translate prior experiences and skills into appropriate management behavior, strengthen management orientations, and identify leadership traits.

PROGRAM INITIATED:
Winter, 1985
LENGTH OF STUDY FOR PARTICIPANT:
2½ years.

LENGTH OF CONTRACT:
30 instructional hours per 3 month period.
LOCATION:
On-site at Chesterfield County facilities.
PARTICIPANTS:
Number: 20
Type: Mid-Level Managers
PROGRAM COSTS PROVIDED BY:
Institution: Administrative Leadership, Instructors' Salaries
Company: Tuition, Textbooks
Participant: Time
Other Source: N/A
PRINTED MATERIALS AVAILABLE FROM:
Institution

CHEVROLET MOTOR DIVISION
with
STATE UNIVERSITY COLLEGE AT BUFFALO

L-4 TRAINING PROJECT
(Training for the Future)
COMPANY CONTACT:
Richard Kujawa
Production Superintendent
Chevrolet Motor Division
General Motors
River Road
Tonawanda, NY 14150
(716) 879-5305

INSTITUTIONAL CONTACT:
William T. Ganley
Director, Center for Applied Research
State University College at Buffalo
1300 Elmwood Avenue, G.C. 409
Buffalo, NY 14222
(716) 878-4110

PROGRAM DESCRIPTION/ OBJECTIVES:
Quality of work life training, technical skills, instructional materials development, training skills.

PROGRAM INITIATED:
1981

LENGTH OF STUDY FOR PARTICIPANT:
40 hours instruction each

LENGTH OF CONTRACT:
9 months

LOCATION:
Chevy-Tonawanda plant, in-house

PARTICIPANTS:
3,000 hourly and salary employees

PROGRAM COSTS PROVIDED BY:
Institution: $74,500
Company: $1,000,000
Other Source: Private Industry Council, New York Education Departments

PRINTED MATERIALS AVAILABLE FROM:
Not reported

PROGRAM INITIATED:
1980

LENGTH OF STUDY FOR PARTICIPANT:
180 hours in half day increments

LENGTH OF CONTRACT:
12 month renewed annually

LOCATION:
Chevron, USA, Inc.

PARTICIPANTS:
16 plant maintenance personnel annually

PROGRAM COSTS PROVIDED BY:
Company: $15,200

PRINTED MATERIALS AVAILABLE FROM:
Institution

CHEVRON, USA, INC.
with
EL PASO COMMUNITY COLLEGE

MACHINING PROCESSES TRAINING PROGRAM

COMPANY CONTACT:
L.A. Wilson
Chief Engineer
Chevron, USA, Inc.
P.O. Box 20002
El Paso, TX 79998
(915) 722-1411

INSTITUTIONAL CONTACT:
Gregory F. Linden
Associate Dean
Community Services/Continuing Education
El Paso Community College
P.O. Box 20500
El Paso, TX 79998
(915) 594-2597

PROGRAM DESCRIPTION/ OBJECTIVES:
To provide machining processes skills development training.

CHRYSLER LEARNING INC.
with
CENTRAL MICHIGAN UNIVERSITY

COMPANY CONTACT:
Walter Hempel
Academic Affairs
Chrysler Learning, Inc.
1200 E. McNichols
Highland Park, MI 48203
(313) 956-1578

INSTITUTIONAL CONTACT:
Dr. Richard Potter
Assistant Director
Central Michigan University
Institute for Personal and Career Development
Rowe 130
Mt. Pleasant, MI 48859
(517) 774-7133

PROGRAM DESCRIPTION/ OBJECTIVES:
Bachelor's program in Management and Supervision building on Chrysler's 2-year certificate program.

PROGRAM INITIATED:
1974

LENGTH OF STUDY FOR PARTICIPANT:
3–5 years

LENGTH OF CONTRACT:
Ongoing

LOCATION:
Chrysler Learning, Inc., Highland Park, MI

PARTICIPANTS:
Foremen and skilled trades workers from Chrysler and other Detroit area companies.

PROGRAM COSTS PROVIDED BY:
Sponsoring Company: 100%

PRINTED MATERIALS AVAILABLE FROM:
Institution

CIGNA
with
UNIVERSITY OF PENNSYLVANIA

PENN/CIGNA PROGRAM

COMPANY CONTACT:
Donald Levinson
Vice-President, Human Resources
CIGNA
1600 Arch Street
Philadelphia, PA 19101
(215) 241-1000

INSTITUTIONAL CONTACT:
Janet Theophano
Coordinator
College of General Studies, University of Pennsylvania
210 Logan Hall
Philadelphia, PA 19104
(215) 898-4847

PROGRAM DESCRIPTION/ OBJECTIVES:
To provide a liberal arts education at the work site for qualified employees of a major corporation

PROGRAM INITIATED:
1981

LENGTH OF STUDY FOR PARTICIPANT:
Students may take courses as long as they like for enrichment only or towards a BA degree.

LENGTH OF CONTRACT:
4 years plus

LOCATION:
CIGNA Headquarters

PARTICIPANTS:
Number: 150 currently accepted
Type: no limit on admissions for any permanent current employee

PROGRAM COSTS PROVIDED BY:
Institution: CIGNA $10,500 + professor's salaries
Company: $28,000 + individual tuition
Participant: Books

PRINTED MATERIALS AVAILABLE FROM:
Institution and Company

CITIBANK*
with
THE COLLEGE OF STATEN ISLAND

OUTREACH PROGRAMS

COMPANY CONTACT:
Eileen Sini
Citibank
399 Park Avenue
New York, NY 10022
(212) 559-0037

INSTITUTIONAL CONTACT:
Michael J. Pefrides
Associate Dean of Faculty
Outreach Centers
College of Staten Island
130 Stuyvesant Place
Staten Island, NY 10301
(212) 390-7551

PROGRAM DESCRIPTION/ OBJECTIVES:
Off campus credit courses applicable to AAS degrees with management empha-

sis. Non-credit occupational training programs.

PROGRAM INITIATED:
1974

LENGTH OF STUDY FOR PARTICIPANT:
Varies

LENGTH OF CONTRACT:
Varies

LOCATION:
In-plant

PARTICIPANTS:
Varies

PROGRAM COSTS PROVIDED BY:
Institution: 40%
Company: 40%
Participant: 20%

PRINTED MATERIALS AVAILABLE FROM:
Institution and Company

* Representative entry—complete list available from institutions.

CLEVELAND CLIFFS IRON COMPANY*
with
MICHIGAN TECHNOLOGICAL UNIVERSITY

COOPERATIVE FOR RESEARCH ON FOREST SOILS (CROFS)

COMPANY CONTACT:
Ray Haskings
Woodlands Manager
Forest Products Division
Cleveland Cliffs Iron Company
P.O. Box 338
Munifing, MI 49862
(906) 452-6221

INSTITUTIONAL CONTACT:
F.H. Erbisch
Acting Director of Research
Michigan Technological University
Houghton, MI 49931
(906) 487-2225

PROGRAM DESCRIPTION/OBJECTIVES:
The primary objective of the Cooperative for Research on Forest Soils (CROFS) is to encourage the development of technologies and resources necessary to increase forest productivity. This objective is to be accomplished through funding research and technology transfer activities. These functions will be performed in a cooperative venture between industry, university and public agency members.

PROGRAM INITIATED:
1977

LENGTH OF STUDY FOR PARTICIPANT:
1 month to several years

LENGTH OF CONTRACT:
Renewed annually by payment of dues

LOCATION:
Michigan Technological University

PARTICIPANTS:
Various numbers of forest research personnel annually

PROGRAM COSTS PROVIDED BY:
Institution: 25% of direct
Company: $2,000 per year (can be changed)

PRINTED MATERIALS AVAILABLE FROM:
Institution

* Representative entry—complete list available from institution.

CLEVELAND CLINIC FOUNDATION
with
KENT STATE UNIVERSITY

CAREER DEVELOPMENT PROGRAM

COMPANY CONTACT:
Fred Buck
Cleveland Clinic Foundation
9500 Euclid Avenue

Cleveland, OH 44106
(216) 444-2380

INSTITUTIONAL CONTACT:
Karen Rylander
Director, Continuing Education
Kent State University
327 Rockwell Hall
Kent, OH 44242
(216) 672-3100

PROGRAM DESCRIPTION/ OBJECTIVES:
Assists in identifying employees potential; provides information about options, career paths, and retraining; teaches a decision-making process to employees.

PROGRAM INITIATED:
1981

LENGTH OF STUDY FOR PARTICIPANT:
15 hours + 1 hour individual counseling

LENGTH OF CONTRACT:
15 hours + 1 hour individual counseling

LOCATION:
Cleveland Clinic Foundation

PARTICIPANTS:
63 clerical staff members

PROGRAM COSTS PROVIDED BY:
Company: 100%

PRINTED MATERIALS AVAILABLE FROM:
Institution

CLEVELAND STATE UNIVERSITY

MASTER OF EDUCATION IN POSTSECONDARY EDUCATION

COMPANY CONTACT:
Numerous placements*

INSTITUTIONAL CONTACT:
Laura A. Wilson
Coordinator
Postsecondary Education Program
Cleveland State University
Department of Educational Specialists
1419 Rhodes Tower
Cleveland, OH 44115
(216) 687-3704

PROGRAM DESCRIPTION/ OBJECTIVES:
Master's degree program designed for students planning to enter the field of training in the business sector.

PROGRAM INITIATED:
1981

LENGTH OF STUDY FOR PARTICIPANT:
Academic program with 6 month internship in business education

LENGTH OF CONTRACT:
Not available

LOCATION:
Varies

PARTICIPANTS:
100

PROGRAM COSTS PROVIDED BY:
Not reported

PRINTED MATERIALS AVAILABLE FROM:
Institution

* Representative entry—complete list available from institution.

COLLEGE AND UNIVERSITY PERSONNEL ASSOCIATION
with
CENTRAL MICHIGAN UNIVERSITY

CUPA/CMU DEGREE PROGRAM

COMPANY CONTACT:
Steve Miller
Executive Director
College and University Personnel
   Association
Suite 120
11 Dupont Circle
Washington, DC 20036
(202) 462-1038

INSTITUTIONAL CONTACT:
Lawrence R. Murphy
Director
Institute for Personal and Career
  Development
Central Michigan University
Mt. Pleasant, MI 48859
(517) 774-3865

PROGRAM DESCRIPTION/ OBJECTIVES:
To provide a graduate level program in Management and Supervision with a concentration in Personnel Administration.

PROGRAM INITIATED:
Not reported

LENGTH OF STUDY FOR PARTICIPANT:
36 months average

LENGTH OF CONTRACT:
Ongoing

LOCATION:
Varies in conjunction with national and regional meetings

PARTICIPANTS:
25 college and university personnel officers

PROGRAM COSTS PROVIDED BY:
Participant: 100%

PRINTED MATERIALS AVAILABLE FROM:
Institution

COLLEGE HOSPITAL OF THE UNIVERSITY OF MEDICINE AND DENTISTRY OF NEW JERSEY
with
RUTGERS, THE STATE UNIVERSITY OF NEW JERSEY

PRIMARY AFFILIATION

COMPANY CONTACT:
Hazel Williams
Director of Nursing
College Hospital
100 Bergen Street
Newark, NJ 07101
(201) 456-5669

INSTITUTIONAL CONTACT:
Lucille Joel
Associate Dean for Clinical Affairs
College of Nursing
Rutgers, The State University of New
  Jersey
University Avenue
Newark, NJ 07102
(201) 648-5298

PROGRAM DESCRIPTION/ OBJECTIVES:
Manpower sharing; continuing education institute; student placement.

PROGRAM INITIATED:
1980

LENGTH OF STUDY FOR PARTICIPANT:
Academic year

LENGTH OF CONTRACT:
10 months

LOCATION:
College Hospital and Rutgers

PARTICIPANTS:
9 clinical specialists and college faculty

PROGRAM COSTS PROVIDED BY:
Shared equally by exchange of time between company and institution

PRINTED MATERIALS AVAILABLE FROM:
Institution

COLONIAL HEIGHTS PACKAGING COMPANY
with
JOHN TYLER COMMUNITY COLLEGE

PRINTING APPRENTICESHIP PROGRAM

COMPANY CONTACT:
Mr. Ralph A. Short
Manufacturing Manager
Colonial Heights Packaging Company
P.O. Box 70
Colonial Heights, VA 23834
(804) 748-3319

INSTITUTIONAL CONTACT:
Dr. Samuel Lee Hancock
Director
Division of Continuing Education
John Tyler Community College
13101 Jefferson Davis Highway
Chester, VA 23831
(804) 796-4111

PROGRAM DESCRIPTION/OBJECTIVES:
To provide the means to train hourly personnel in the technology and art of Rotogravure printing beyond current on-the-job training.

PROGRAM INITIATED:
Fall, 1984

LENGTH OF STUDY FOR PARTICIPANT:
4 years

LENGTH OF CONTRACT:
24 bimonthly seminars of 8 hours each.

LOCATION:
On-site at Colonial Heights Packaging Company

PARTICIPANTS:
Number: 30–40
Type: Pressmen and Assistant Pressmen

PROGRAM COSTS PROVIDED BY:
Institution: Educational Leadership
Company: Printing, Tuition, Educational Resources
Participant: Time
Other Source: Virginia Apprentice Program—Instructors' Salaries

PRINTED MATERIALS AVAILABLE FROM:
Institution

COMPANIES IN NEW YORK AREA EMPLOYING 50+ WORKERS
with
THE COLLEGE OF NEW ROCHELLE

TUITION-AID BENEFITS SURVEY IN GREATER NEW YORK (part of "Workers as Students")

COMPANY CONTACT:
Not available

INSTITUTIONAL CONTACT:
Ronald W. Pollack
Director, Financial Aid
College of New Rochelle
New Rochelle, NY 10801
(914) 632-5300

PROGRAM DESCRIPTION/OBJECTIVES:
To compile a comprehensive directory of the tuition aid programs available to employees in New York, to help adults obtain financial aid.

PROGRAM INITIATED:
1980

LENGTH OF STUDY FOR PARTICIPANT:
2 years

LENGTH OF CONTRACT:
Not available

LOCATION:
College of New Rochelle

PARTICIPANTS:
No individual participants

PROGRAM COSTS PROVIDED BY:
Institution: $114,060
Other Source: $172,835 (grant from FIPSE)

PRINTED MATERIALS AVAILABLE FROM:
Institution

PRINTED MATERIALS AVAILABLE FROM:
Institution

* Representative entry—complete list available from institution.

VARIOUS FIRMS AND GOVERNMENT AGENCIES*
with
COLUMBIA COLLEGE

BUSINESS INTERNSHIPS

COMPANY CONTACT:
Specific company not identified

INSTITUTIONAL CONTACT:
James G. Bouknight
Chairman, Department of Business and Economics
Columbia College
Columbia, SC 29203
(803) 786-3724

PROGRAM DESCRIPTION/OBJECTIVES:
To provide senior business administration majors with the types of hands-on experiences necessary to apply their training to work situations.

PROGRAM INITIATED:
1982

LENGTH OF STUDY FOR PARTICIPANT:
7½ weeks

LENGTH OF CONTRACT:
7½ weeks

LOCATION:
Usually in the Columbia, SC area

PARTICIPANTS:
30 senior business administration and accounting majors

PROGRAM COSTS PROVIDED BY:
Institution: No direct
Company: Varies
Participant: Little

COMMONWEALTH OF PENNSYLVANIA JUVENILE COURT JUDGES COMMISSION
with
SHIPPENSBURG STATE COLLEGE

MASTER'S DEGREE—ADMINISTRATION OF JUSTICE

COMPANY CONTACT:
Ronald Fennell
Director
Center for Juvenile Justice Training and Research
JCJC
Shippensburg University, SrH 208
Shippensburg, PA 17257
(717) 532-1704

INSTITUTIONAL CONTACT:
Roosevelt E. Shepherd
Associate Professor/Chairperson
Criminal Justice (CRJ)
Shippensburg University
CEC 108
Shippensburg, PA 17257
(717) 532-1558

PROGRAM DESCRIPTION/OBJECTIVES:
Master's degree in Administration of Justice with a specialization in juvenile justice designed to train probation officers to deal more effectively with juveniles, especially in the development of preventive measures in order to cut down on juvenile crime.

PROGRAM INITIATED:
1982

LENGTH OF STUDY FOR PARTICIPANT:
2 years

LOCATION:
Weekend classes on Shippensburg State College campus

PARTICIPANTS:
60 chief probation officers throughout the Commonwealth

PROGRAM COSTS PROVIDED BY:
Institution: 34%
Company: 66%

PRINTED MATERIALS AVAILABLE FROM:
Not yet available

COMMUNITY CAREERS COUNCIL
with
MERRITT COLLEGE

INFORMATIONAL INTERVIEW REFERRAL

COMPANY CONTACT:
Frankie Arrington
Director, Clearinghouse
Community Careers Council
1730 Franklin Street
Oakland, CA 94612
(415) 763-4234

INSTITUTIONAL CONTACT:
Thressa Herzfeld
Student Services Specialist
Career Center
Merritt College
12500 Campus Drive
Oakland, CA 94519
(415) 436-2444

PROGRAM DESCRIPTION/ OBJECTIVES:
Local business and professional representatives volunteer to be interviewed by students interested in their occupation. Students request through college Career Center and are matched by Clearinghouse.

PROGRAM INITIATED:
1980

LENGTH OF STUDY FOR PARTICIPANT:
No prerequisite length

LENGTH OF CONTRACT:
Ongoing

LOCATION:
Merritt College

PARTICIPANTS:
150 students investigating a variety of occupations per semester

PROGRAM COSTS PROVIDED BY:
Costs of Clearinghouse shared by Peralta College District and New Oakland Committee

PRINTED MATERIALS AVAILABLE FROM:
Institution and Company

COMMUNITY NURSING SERVICE OF ESSEX AND WEST HUDSON
with
RUTGERS, THE STATE UNIVERSITY OF NEW JERSEY

PRIMARY AFFILIATION

COMPANY CONTACT:
Carolyn Smith
Associate Director
Community Nursing Service of Essex and West Hudson
451 Lincoln Avenue
Orange, NJ 07050
(201) 673-0158

INSTITUTIONAL CONTACT:
Lucille Joel
Associate Dean for Clinical Affairs
College of Nursing
Rutgers, The State University of New Jersey
University Avenue
Newark, NJ 07102
(201) 648-5298

PROGRAM DESCRIPTION/ OBJECTIVES:
Manpower sharing; student placement.

PROGRAM INITIATED:
1981

LENGTH OF STUDY FOR PARTICIPANT:
Academic year

LENGTH OF CONTRACT:
10 months

LOCATION:
Community Nursing Service and Rutgers

PARTICIPANTS:
2

PROGRAM COSTS PROVIDED BY:
Shared equally by exchange of time between company and institution

PRINTED MATERIALS AVAILABLE FROM:
Institution

LENGTH OF STUDY FOR PARTICIPANT:
Varies

LENGTH OF CONTRACT:
Varies

LOCATION:
In-plant

PARTICIPANTS:
Varies

PROGRAM COSTS PROVIDED BY:
Institution: 40%
Company: 40%
Participant: 20%

PRINTED MATERIALS AVAILABLE FROM:
Institution and Company

* Representative entry—complete list available from institution.

CON EDISON*
with
THE COLLEGE OF STATEN ISLAND

OUTREACH PROGRAMS

COMPANY CONTACT:
Judith Warner
Con Edison
708 1st Avenue
New York, NY 10017
(212) 576-3186

INSTITUTIONAL CONTACT:
Michael J. Pefrides
Associate Dean of Faculty
Outreach Centers
College of Staten Island
130 Stuyvesant Place
Staten Island, NY 10301
(212) 390-7551

PROGRAM DESCRIPTION/ OBJECTIVES:
Off campus credit courses applicable to AAS degrees with a technical emphasis. Non-credit occupational training programs.

PROGRAM INITIATED:
1974

CONCRETE INDUSTRY BOARD, INC.
with
NEW YORK TECHNICAL COLLEGE, DIVISION OF CONTINUING EDUCATION

FIELD TESTING OF FRESH CONCRETE

COMPANY CONTACT:
Ernest E. Trolio
Managing Director
The Concrete Industry Board, Inc.
95 Madison Avenue
New York, NY 10016
(212) 684-2323

INSTITUTIONAL CONTACT:
James Goldman
Program Coordinator
Division of Continuing Education and Extension Services
New York City Technical College
300 Jay Street
Brooklyn, NY 11201
(718) 643-4560

PROGRAM DESCRIPTION/ OBJECTIVES:
A 4 week 16-hour cycle course specified in the ACI Trainer Manual (CP-3) which prepares a technician for ACI Certification as Concrete Field Testing Technician-Grade 1.

LENGTH OF STUDY FOR PARTICIPANT:
16 hours each cycle-4 cycles total

LENGTH OF CONTRACT:
16 weeks

LOCATION:
Jay Building, Room 404

PARTICIPANTS:
Number: 20 each cycle-total 80
Type: Concrete laboratory technicians

PROGRAM COSTS PROVIDED BY:
Company: 100%

PRINTED MATERIALS AVAILABLE FROM:
Institution and Company

CONNECTICUT NATURAL GAS
with
UNIVERSITY OF HARTFORD

ON-SITE UNDERGRADUATE CREDIT

COMPANY CONTACT:
Michael J. Keppler
Industrial Relations Administrator
Connecticut Natural Gas Company
P.O. Box 1500
Hartford, CT 06144
(203) 727-3000

INSTITUTIONAL CONTACT:
William T. George
Program Development Consultant
Division of Adult Educational Services
University of Hartford
200 Bloomfield Avenue
West Hartford, CT 06117
(203) 243-4507/4381

PROGRAM DESCRIPTION/ OBJECTIVES:
Undergraduate business courses.

PROGRAM INITIATED:
1981

LENGTH OF STUDY FOR PARTICIPANT:
1 semester

LENGTH OF CONTRACT:
Indefinite

LOCATION:
Connecticut Natural Gas

PARTICIPANTS:
7 qualified employees per semester

PROGRAM COST PROVIDED BY:
Company: 100%

PRINTED MATERIALS AVAILABLE FROM:
Not available

CONTAINER CORPORATION
with
FLORIDA JUNIOR COLLEGE AT JACKSONVILLE

MULTI-CRAFT TRAINING

COMPANY CONTACT:
Terry Barnum
Training Director
Personnel
Container Corporation
Post Office Box 2000
Fernandina Beach, FL 32034
(904) 261-5551

INSTITUTIONAL CONTACT:
Dr. James R. Myers
Instructional Dean
Occupational Education
Florida Junior College at Jacksonville
101 West State Street
Jacksonville, FL 32202
(904) 633-8284

PROGRAM DESCRIPTION/ OBJECTIVES:
Cross-training of maintenance personnel to familiarize them with at least 3 crafts.

PROGRAM INITIATED:
1984

LENGTH OF STUDY FOR PARTICIPANT:
3 years

LENGTH OF CONTRACT:
Open-ended

LOCATION:
On-site

PARTICIPANTS:
Number: 168
Type: Employees

PROGRAM COSTS PROVIDED BY:
Company: 100%

PRINTED MATERIALS AVAILABLE FROM:
Institution and Company

CONTINENTAL PIPELINE COMPANY
with
OKLAHOMA STATE TECH

DIGITAL PRINCIPLES, INTRODUCTION TO MICROPROCESSORS

COMPANY CONTACT:
R.C. Ashlock
Superintendent of Terminals
Continental Pipeline Company
3025 East Skelly Drive
Suite 420
Tulsa, OK 74105
(918) 743-8803

INSTITUTIONAL CONTACT:
Bill J. Lyons
Department Head
Electrical-Electronics Technology
Oklahoma State Tech
4th and Mission
Okmulgee, OK 74447
(918) 765-6211, X252

PROGRAM DESCRIPTION/ OBJECTIVES:
To provide instrumentation technicians with current state-of the-art with increased awareness of microprocessor capabilities.

PROGRAM INITIATED:
1982

LENGTH OF STUDY FOR PARTICIPANT:
Not reported

LENGTH OF CONTRACT:
Not reported

LOCATION:
Not reported

PARTICIPANTS:
24 employees annually

PROGRAM COSTS PROVIDED BY:
Company: 100%

PRINTED MATERIALS AVAILABLE FROM:
Not available

VARIOUS NEW YORK CITY AREA COMPANIES
with
LEHMAN COLLEGE/CUNY

COOPERATIVE EDUCATION PROGRAMS

COMPANY CONTACT:
Various

INSTITUTIONAL CONTACT:
Joseph Enright
Director of Cooperative Education/ Internships
Lehman College/CUNY
Bronx, NY 10468
(212) 960-8366

PROGRAM DESCRIPTION/OBJECTIVES:
To provide a high quality liberal arts education by creatively combining work experience with theoretical learning. To improve the career opportunities of students. To provide employers with higher quality workers and potential recruits.

PROGRAM INITIATED:
1980

LENGTH OF STUDY FOR PARTICIPANTS:
1 semester or 1 semester plus summer.

LENGTH OF CONTRACT:
1 semester with renewal option

LOCATION:
Various

PARTICIPANTS:
Number: 300 sophomore, junior, and senior students
Type: Annually

PROGRAM COSTS PROVIDED BY:
Institution: 100% except salaries and benefits provided by participating companies.

PRINTED MATERIALS AVAILABLE FROM:
Institution

COORS
with
COLORADO SCHOOL OF MINES

WELLNESS PROGRAM

COMPANY CONTACT:
Ben Mason
Director
Coors Company
Golden, CO 80401
(303) 277-3838

INSTITUTIONAL CONTACT:
Diana Doyle
Director
Student Development Center
Colorado School of Mines
Golden, CO 80401
(303) 273-3377

PROGRAM DESCRIPTION/OBJECTIVES:
Increase C.S.M. students' and Coors employees' knowledge of wellness, physical health and mental health, increase opportunities for involvement in health/fitness related activities, decrease alcohol abuse.

PROGRAM INITIATED:
1981

LENGTH OF STUDY FOR PARTICIPANT:
Variable

LENGTH OF CONTRACT:
Indefinite

LOCATION:
On campus/Coors

PARTICIPANTS:
500–800 students annually

PROGRAM COSTS PROVIDED BY:
Institution: salaries, maintenance
Company: equipment, supplies (approx. $12,000)

PRINTED MATERIALS AVAILABLE FROM:
Institution

COPELAND ASSOCIATES*
with
GORDON COLLEGE

COOPERATIVE EDUCATION

COMPANY CONTACT:
Russell W. Copeland
President
Copeland Associate
129 Dodge Street
Beverly, MA 01915
(617) 922-3702

INSTITUTIONAL CONTACT:
Mary Jane Knudson
Director, Cooperative Education and Career Development
Gordon College
255 Grapevine Road
Wenham, MA 01984
(617) 927-2300, X4077

PROGRAM DESCRIPTION/OBJECTIVES:
An educational program for liberal arts students to explore careers and apply theory to practice. It allows employers to examine a pool of qualified recruits as well as fill seasonal and regular personnel needs.

PROGRAM INITIATED:
1978

LENGTH OF STUDY FOR PARTICIPANT:
6 months per co-op placement; 3 placements total

LENGTH OF CONTRACT:
6 months, ongoing

LOCATION:
Various employer sites

PARTICIPANTS:
100 liberal arts students annually

PROGRAM COSTS PROVIDED BY:
Institution: $107,000
Company: Student salaries
Other Source: $57,000 (Title VIII grant)

PRINTED MATERIALS AVAILABLE FROM:
Institution

* Representative entry—complete list available from institution.

COPELAND CORPORATION
with
EDISON STATE COMMUNITY COLLEGE

SUPERVISORY TRAINING: SMALL GROUP COMMUNICATION

COMPANY CONTACT:
Susan Way
Corporate Manager
Employee Relations
Copeland Corporation
Campbell Road
Sidney, OH 45365
(513) 498-3353

INSTITUTIONAL CONTACT:
Gary W. Wilson
Assistant Dean for Continuing Education
Edison State Community College
1973 Edison Drive
Piqua, OH 45356
(513) 778-8600

PROGRAM DESCRIPTION/OBJECTIVES:
Improve employee relations, better trained workers, more efficient work performance and decrease in the frequency of misunderstandings between employees.

PROGRAM INITIATED:
1981

LENGTH OF STUDY FOR PARTICIPANT:
26 hours

LENGTH OF CONTRACT:
1 month with renewal options

LOCATION:
Hueston Woods State Park

PARTICIPANTS:
10 first-line supervisors

PROGRAM COSTS PROVIDED BY:
Institution: $913.00
Company: $2,414.80
Other Source: $273.00

PRINTED MATERIALS AVAILABLE FROM:
Institution

PRINTED MATERIALS AVAILABLE FROM:
Institution and Company

* Representative entry—complete list available from institution.

CRANE NAVAL WEAPON SUPPORT CENTER*
with
UNIVERSITY OF EVANSVILLE

COOPERATIVE EDUCATION

COMPANY CONTACT:
Mary Swarn
Personnel Department
Crane Naval Weapons Support Center
Crane, IN 47522
(812) 854-1606

INSTITUTIONAL CONTACT:
Donna Norris
Director of Cooperative Education
University of Evansville
P.O. Box 329
Evansville, IN 47711
(812) 479-2652

PROGRAM DESCRIPTION/ OBJECTIVES:
Combine classroom education with work experience in industry.

PROGRAM INITIATED:
1947

LENGTH OF STUDY FOR PARTICIPANT:
4 to 6 quarterly work periods.

LENGTH OF CONTRACT:
Not reported

LOCATION:
Industrial work site

PARTICIPANTS:
120 electrical, mechanical, civil and computer engineering and computer science students

PROGRAM COSTS PROVIDED BY:
Participant: 100%

CUMMINS
with
CHARLESTON H.Ed. CONSORTIUM AND COUNTY SCHOOL DISTRICT

SUMMER PROGRAM FOR PRINCIPALS

COMPANY CONTACT:
Alumax: Harry Hoppman
 (803) 572-0550
Cummins: John Reed (803) 554-6700
Lockheed-Georgia: Don Duckworth
 (803) 747-6331
Medical University of South Carolina:
 Steve Jones (803) 792-2211

INSTITUTIONAL CONTACT:
Ann Baker
Associate Director
Charleston Higher Education
 Consortium
171 Ashley Avenue
Charleston, S.C. 29425
(803) 792-3627

PROGRAM DESCRIPTION/ OBJECTIVES:
Graduate course to improve management capabilities of public school principals. Course combines seminars with work exposure to upper level management in each of four companies/institutions.

LENGTH OF STUDY FOR PARTICIPANT:
5 weeks

LENGTH OF CONTRACT:
year by year

LOCATION:
Charleston, S.C.

PARTICIPANTS:
Number: 7
Type: principals

PROGRAM COSTS PROVIDED BY:
School District: $200 tuition/principal
Company: 30%
Other Sources: Chas. Higher Educ. Consort.: all administrative support

PRINTED MATERIALS AVAILABLE FROM:
Institution

DAN RIVER, INC.
with
DANVILLE COMMUNITY COLLEGE

SUPERVISION FOR DAN RIVER, INC.

COMPANY CONTACT:
Ed Carroll
Director, Industrial Relations
Dan River, Inc.
West Main Street
Danville, VA 24541
(804) 799-7368

INSTITUTIONAL CONTACT:
Max R. Glass
Director, Continuing Education
Danville Community College
1008 South Main Street
Danville, VA 24541
(804) 797-3553

PROGRAM DESCRIPTION/ OBJECTIVES:
To train hourly employees to assume positions in supervision.

PROGRAM INITIATED:
1978

LENGTH OF STUDY FOR PARTICIPANT:
3 quarters on a part-time basis

LENGTH OF CONTRACT:
9 months with continual option

LOCATION:
Danville Community College

PARTICIPANTS:
20 hourly employees per class

PROGRAM COSTS PROVIDED BY:
Institution: $3,000 per class
Company: $5,350 per class

PRINTED MATERIALS AVAILABLE FROM:
Institution

DATA GENERAL*
with
WORCESTER STATE COLLEGE

EDUCATION AT YOUR DOORSTEP

COMPANY CONTACT:
Steven Widen
Training Specialist
Data General
4400 Computer Drive
Westboro, MA 01581
(617) 366-8911

INSTITUTIONAL CONTACT:
William O'Neill
Dean, Division of Graduate and Continuing Education
Worcester State College
486 Chandler Street
Worcester, MA 01602
(617) 793-8100

PROGRAM DESCRIPTION/ OBJECTIVES:
To meet the educational needs of Westboro area company employees, to facilitate employee training and development in areas of high need, high quality credit-bearing training at a convenient time and location.

PROGRAM INITIATED:
1981

LENGTH OF STUDY FOR PARTICIPANT:
Not reported

LENGTH OF CONTRACT:
None

LOCATION:
Westboro High School

PARTICIPANTS:
90 employees per semester

PROGRAM COSTS PROVIDED BY:
Institution: $130 per course
Company: $130 per course

PRINTED MATERIALS AVAILABLE FROM:
Institution

* Representative entry—complete list available from institution.

DAVEY LANDSCAPE
with
KENT STATE UNIVERSITY

MANAGEMENT DEVELOPMENT SEMINAR

COMPANY CONTACT:
Gordon Ober
Davey Landscape
117 South Water Street
Kent, OH 44240
(216) 673-9511

INSTITUTIONAL CONTACT:
Karen Rylander
Director, Continuing Education
Kent State University
327 Rockwell Hall
Kent, OH 44242
(216) 672-3100

PROGRAM DESCRIPTION/OBJECTIVES:
Designed to develop an understanding of leadership activities that build individual motivation, group support, improve quality of decisions and their implementation.

PROGRAM INITIATED:
1980

LENGTH OF STUDY FOR PARTICIPANT:
4 hours

LENGTH OF CONTRACT:
4 hours

LOCATION:
Kent State University

PARTICIPANTS:
16 district managers

PROGRAM COSTS PROVIDED BY:
Company: 100%

PRINTED MATERIALS AVAILABLE FROM:
Institution

DAVEY TREE EXPERT COMPANY
with
KENT STATE UNIVERSITY

LEADERSHIP, EMPLOYEE BEHAVIOR AND PRODUCTIVITY

COMPANY CONTACT:
Harry Taylor
Davey Tree Expert Company
117 South Water Street
Kent, OH 44240
(216) 673-9511

INSTITUTIONAL CONTACT:
Karen Rylander
Director, Continuing Education
Kent State University
327 Rockwell Hall
Kent, OH 44242
(216) 672-3100

PROGRAM DESCRIPTION/OBJECTIVES:
Designed to explore the supervisor's leadership role and to identify and develop activities and skills in communication, motivation, problem solving and decision making that build productive units. Related skills, such as performance evaluation, training and development are also covered.

PROGRAM INITIATED:
1981

LENGTH OF STUDY FOR PARTICIPANT:
16 hours + 2 hour follow-up session

LENGTH OF CONTRACT:
16 hours + 2 hour follow-up session

LOCATION:
Davey Tree Expert Company

PARTICIPANTS:
25 first-line supervisors

PROGRAM COSTS PROVIDED BY:
Company: 100%

PRINTED MATERIALS AVAILABLE FROM:
Institution

DAYTONA BEACH AREA BUSINESS COMMUNITY
with
BETHUNE-COOKMAN COLLEGE

PARTNERS-IN-PROGRESS

COMPANY CONTACT:
R.G. Mulligan
Former Visiting Professor at Bethune-Cookman College
NASA Headquarters
Code NS
Washington, DC 20546
(202) 755-3140

INSTITUTIONAL CONTACT:
Shirley Lee
Director of Planning and Development
Business Division
Bethune-Cookman College
640 Second Avenue
Daytona Beach, FL 32015
(904) 255-1401, X355

PROGRAM DESCRIPTION/ OBJECTIVES:
To develop closer links with the community through seminars on contemporary business management topics designed by campus faculty in an effort to create more intern or cooperative experiences for students.

PROGRAM INITIATED:
1981

LENGTH OF STUDY FOR PARTICIPANT:
Varied

LENGTH OF CONTRACT:
1 year

LOCATION:
Campus and community

PARTICIPANTS:
50–100 local businessmen

PROGRAM COSTS PROVIDED BY:
Institution: $5,000 (administrative)
Company: NASA—salary

PRINTED MATERIALS AVAILABLE FROM:
Institution

DEARBORN CHEMICAL
with
COLLEGE OF LAKE COUNTY

IMPROVING SUPERVISORY SKILLS

COMPANY CONTACT:
Neil Everett
Plant Manager
Dearborn Chemical
300 Genesee
Lake Zurich, IL 60047
(312) 438-8241

INSTITUTIONAL CONTACT:
Keri Thiessen
Business/Industry Training Coordinator
Open Campus
College of Lake County
Grayslake, IL 60030
(312) 223-3616

PROGRAM DESCRIPTION/ OBJECTIVES:
To improve, develop, and introduce skills and techniques necessary for effective supervision.

PROGRAM INITIATED:
1981

LENGTH OF STUDY FOR PARTICIPANT:
11 weeks

LENGTH OF CONTRACT:
11 weeks

LOCATION:
Dearborn Chemical

PARTICIPANTS:
14 supervisors of various departments

PROGRAM COSTS PROVIDED BY:
Company: $1,683

PRINTED MATERIALS AVAILABLE FROM:
Institution

DEERE & COMPANY
with
GLENDALE COMMUNITY COLLEGE

JOHN DEERE SERVICE MANAGERS TRAINING

COMPANY CONTACT:
Mr. Joe DeMeyer
Service Training Coordinator
Service Training
Deere & Company
John Deere Road
Moline, IL 61265
(309) 752-6698

INSTITUTIONAL CONTACT:
Stanley J. Grossman
Director
The Institute for Business, Industry and Technology
Glendale Community College
6000 W. Olive Avenue
Glendale, AZ 85302
(602) 934-2211

PROGRAM DESCRIPTION/ OBJECTIVES:
Intensive 8-week service training program for John Deere Service Managers.

PROGRAM INITIATED:
1984

LENGTH OF STUDY FOR PARTICIPANT:
1 week

LENGTH OF CONTRACT:
10 weeks

LOCATION:
College

PARTICIPANTS:
Number: 250
Type: John Deere employees

PROGRAM COSTS PROVIDED BY:
Institution: Facilities, security, etc.
Company: Monetary and equipment donations
Participant: 100% company paid

PRINTED MATERIALS AVAILABLE FROM:
None available

DEFENSE CONTRACT AUDIT AGENCY
with
CENTRAL MICHIGAN UNIVERSITY

COMPANY CONTACT:
Mr. Robert DeTienne
Defense Contract Audit Agency
Room 4A
130 Cameron Station
Alexandria, VA 22314
(202) 274-6439

INSTITUTIONAL CONTACT:
Dr. Richard Potter
Assistant Director
Central Michigan University
Institute for Personal and Career Development
Rowe 130
Mt. Pleasant, MI 48859
(517) 774-7133

PROGRAM DESCRIPTION/ OBJECTIVES:
To provide selected managers of DCAA with a professional development program. Participants may at their option earn a Master of Science in Administration degree as a result of their participation.

PROGRAM INITIATED:
1978

LENGTH OF STUDY FOR PARTICIPANT:
30 months

LENGTH OF CONTRACT:
Ongoing

LOCATION:
DCAA Institute, Memphis, Tennessee

PARTICIPANTS:
30 high performance managers selected by DCAA

PROGRAM COSTS PROVIDED BY:
DCAA: 100%

PRINTED MATERIALS AVAILABLE FROM:
Institution

DEFENSE MAPPING AGENCY
with
PANAMA CANAL COLLEGE

ASSOCIATE DEGREE IN EARTH SCIENCES

COMPANY CONTACT:
Jack E. Staples
Director
Defense Mapping Agency
InterAmerican Geodetic Survey
Cartographic School
Drawer 936
APO Miami, FL 34004

INSTITUTIONAL CONTACT:
Jack E. Staples
Dean
Panama Canal College
DODDS, Panama Region
APO Miami, FL 34002

PROGRAM DESCRIPTION/ OBJECTIVES:
Provide academic degree program for military and governmental employees in Earth Sciences area.

PROGRAM INITIATED:
1982

LENGTH OF STUDY FOR PARTICIPANT:
4 semesters

LENGTH OF CONTRACT:
Memorandum of understanding

LOCATION:
Panama Canal College

PARTICIPANTS:
40 Panama Canal employees annually

PROGRAM COSTS PROVIDED BY:
Institution: 40%

PRINTED MATERIALS AVAILABLE FROM:
Not reported

DEL MONTE CORPORATION
WALNUT CREEK, CA
with
IOWA STATE UNIVERSITY

TEXTURE OF CANNED VEGETABLES

COMPANY CONTACT:
Dr. Kenneth Goodnight
Director Applications Research
Del Monte Research Center
205 N. Wiget Lane, Box 9004
Walnut Creek, CA 94598
(415) 933-8000, Ext. 345

INSTITUTIONAL CONTACT:
Mark H. Love, Ph.D.
Associate Professor
Food and Nutrition Department
Iowa State University
110 MacKay Hall

Ames, IA 50011
(515) 294-4432

PROGRAM DESCRIPTION/ OBJECTIVES:
Improve quality of thermally processed vegetables. Initially, focus on green bean texture to ascertain if texture of processed product is related to quantity and types of pectin in varieties commonly processed for consumer market, and if rate of softening can be reduced.

PROGRAM INITIATED:
1985

LENGTH OF CONTRACT:
24 months

LOCATION:
On campus and at Del Monte's Plover, Wisconsin Research Farm.

PARTICIPANTS:
NA

PROGRAM SUPPORT PROVIDED BY:
Institution: $36,000
Company: $49,750

PRINTED MATERIALS AVAILABLE FROM:
Iowa State University

DELCO REMY DIVISION OF GENERAL MOTORS
with
MERIDIAN JUNIOR COLLEGE

APPRENTICESHIP TRAINING PROGRAM FOR MAINTENANCE PERSONNEL

COMPANY CONTACT:
Leroy Johnston
Personnel Manager
Delco Remy
Highway 11 South
P.O. Box 4396
Meridian, MS 39301
(601) 485-5122

INSTITUTIONAL CONTACT:
Jack Shank
Dean, Continuing Education
Meridian Junior College
5500 Highway 19 North
Meridian, MS 39301
(601) 483-8241, X112

PROGRAM DESCRIPTION/ OBJECTIVES:
To provide classroom training to accompany apprenticeship program for Delco Remy for personnel training as maintenance mechanics and/or electricians.

PROGRAM INITIATED:
1978

LENGTH OF STUDY FOR PARTICIPANT:
4 years, part-time

LENGTH OF CONTRACT:
Ongoing

LOCATION:
Meridian Junior College

PARTICIPANTS:
15 mechanics and electricians annually

PROGRAM COSTS PROVIDED BY:
Institution: $5,000
Company: $24,000 (participants receive hourly wage rate paid for regular work while attending classes)

PRINTED MATERIALS AVAILABLE FROM:
Not available

DELOITTE, HASKINS AND SELLS
with
CENTENARY COLLEGE

ACCOUNTING DEGREE DESIGNED BY ACCOUNTANTS

COMPANY CONTACT:
Guy Budinsack
Manager, Accounting
Deloitte, Haskins & Sells
111 Madison Avenue

Morristown, NJ 07960
(201) 540-0940
INSTITUTIONAL CONTACT:
Dan Sherwood
Dean of External Affairs Development
Centenary College
400 Jefferson Street
Hackettstown, NJ 07840
(201) 852-1400
PROGRAM DESCRIPTION/ OBJECTIVES:
Design an accounting degree with total input from the accounting representatives. Skill tests given to measure value of program. All text books reviewed and chapters eliminated that are unnecessary. Supply instructors also.
PROGRAM INITIATED:
1980
LENGTH OF STUDY FOR PARTICIPANT:
4 year degree program
LENGTH OF CONTRACT:
4 years
LOCATION:
Centenary College
PARTICIPANTS:
25 business majors/accounting majors annually
PROGRAM COSTS PROVIDED BY:
Institution: Total
Company: In-kind
PRINTED MATERIALS AVAILABLE FROM:
Institution

DEPARTMENT OF DEFENSE
with
MARYMOUNT COLLEGE

MBA PROGRAM FOR MILITARY AND DEPARTMENT OF DEFENSE PERSONNEL
COMPANY CONTACT:
Mr. Philip F. Strauss
Director, Pentagon Education Center
Department of the Army
Washington, DC 20310
INSTITUTIONAL CONTACT:
Dr. Richard Ross
Dean, School of Business Administration
Marymount College of Virginia
Arlington, VA 22207
LENGTH OF STUDY FOR PARTICIPANT:
1–2 years
LENGTH OF CONTRACT:
On-going
PROGRAM COSTS PROVIDED BY:
Institution: Costs of instruction and support services not covered by tuition
Company: Cost of tuition for participants

DIGITAL CORPORATION
with
JOHNSON STATE COLLEGE

AB/BA DEGREE AT DIGITAL CORPORATION
COMPANY CONTACT:
Jack Burnham
Training and Development Manager
Digital Corporation
Burlington, VT 05401
(802) 863-1611
INSTITUTIONAL CONTACT:
William A. Cook
Academic Dean
Johnson State College
Johnson, VT 05656
(802) 635-2356, X220
PROGRAM DESCRIPTION/ OBJECTIVES:
Associate of Science and Bachelor of Arts degree program in general business offered on location for employees at Digital Corporation. Objectives: provide convenient and complete degree program related to employee needs and business needs.
PROGRAM INITIATED:
1981

LENGTH OF STUDY FOR PARTICIPANT:
5 years

LENGTH OF CONTRACT:
5 years

LOCATION:
Burlington, VT

PARTICIPANTS:
70+ Digital employees per semester

PROGRAM COSTS PROVIDED BY:
Company: 100%
Participant: (If a student drops out or makes less than C, student must pay back company)

PRINTED MATERIALS AVAILABLE FROM:
Institution

DIGITAL EQUIPMENT CORPORATION
with
PRINCE GEORGE'S COMMUNITY COLLEGE

PRE-SUPERVISORY TRAINING

COMPANY CONTACT:
Phil Pons
Director of Training
Digital Equipment Corporation
8301 Professional Place
Landover, MD 20785
(301) 459-7900

INSTITUTIONAL CONTACT:
Veronica Norwood
Director, Contract Services
Prince George's Community College
301 Largo Road
Largo, MD 20772
(301) 322-0726

PROGRAM DESCRIPTION/OBJECTIVES:
To provide training in effective communication skills, individual and group dynamics, decision-making techniques, and fundamentals of management to employees designated for promotion to a supervisory position.

PROGRAM INITIATED:
1981

LENGTH OF STUDY FOR PARTICIPANT:
53 hours

LENGTH OF CONTRACT:
1 month

LOCATION:
The Sheraton Hotel, Lanham, MD

PARTICIPANTS:
15 employees designated for promotion to a supervisory position

PROGAM COSTS PROVIDED BY:
Company: 58%
Other Source: 42% (state funding)

PRINTED MATERIALS AVAILABLE FROM:
Institution

DREW CHEMICAL; EXXON
with
DREW UNIVERSITY

COOPERATIVE EDUCATION IN CHEMISTRY

COMPANY CONTACT:
Drew Chem
Mr. Al Teller
Analytical
Drew Chemical Co.
Boonton, NJ
  and
Exxon
Paul Smith
Public Affairs Dept.
Exxon
Clinton, NJ

INSTITUTIONAL CONTACT:
James M. Miller
Co-op Coordinator
Dept. Chemistry
Drew University
Madison, NJ 07940
(201) 377-3000

PROGRAM DESCRIPTION/ OBJECTIVES:
An elective co-op program for chemistry majors with non-alternating work periods. Some college credit given for work; program completed in 4 years.

PROGRAM INITIATED:
1980

LENGTH OF STUDY FOR PARTICIPANT:
2 work periods: 1 of 3 months and 1 of 8 months.

LENGTH OF CONTRACT:
2 years

LOCATION:
Chemical and pharmaceutical companies, most in the northern NJ region

PARTICIPANTS:
Number: Approximately 2 per year
Type: Juniors and seniors

PROGRAM COSTS PROVIDED BY:
Company: Salary

PRINTED MATERIALS AVAILABLE FROM:
Institution

VARIOUS SMALL TYPESETTING BUSINESSES IN THE BALTIMORE-METRO AREA
with
DUNDALK COMMUNITY COLLEGE

ON-SITE PHOTOTYPESETTING TRAINING

COMPANY CONTACT:
The company contact is generally the owner of the business. Names of companies and owners are available upon request.

INSTITUTIONAL CONTACT:
Michael Galiazzo
Director, Community Development and Retraining
Continuing Education
Dundalk Community College
7200 Sollers Point Road
Dundalk, MD 21222
(301) 522-5867

PROGRAM DESCRIPTION/ OBJECTIVES:
Customized on-site phototypesetting training—non-credit

PROGRAM INITIATED:
January 1985

LENGTH OF STUDY FOR PARTICIPANT:
Varies

LENGTH OF CONTRACT:
Varies

LOCATION:
Business sites

PARTICIPANTS:
Number: Up to 5 people
Type: New and experienced typesetters

PROGRAM COSTS PROVIDED BY:
Company: pays tuition

PRINTED MATERIALS AVAILABLE FROM:
Institution

DUPONT
with
UNIVERSITY OF MARYLAND-BALTIMORE COUNTY

DUPONT-UMBC PROJECT TO EXPRESS INTERFERON

COMPANY CONTACT:
Bruce Korant
Research Supervisor of Molecular Genetics
Dupont Experimental Station
Building 328
Wilmington, DE 19898
(302) 772-4823

INSTITUTIONAL CONTACT:
P. Lovett
Professor of Biological Sciences

University of Maryland-Baltimore
  County
Catonsville, MD 21228
(301) 455-2249

PROGRAM DESCRIPTION/ OBJECTIVES:
Production of human interferon in *B. subtilis*.

PROGRAM INITIATED:
1981

LENGTH OF STUDY FOR PARTICIPANT:
2 years

LENGTH OF CONTRACT:
2 years

LOCATION:
On campus

PARTICIPANTS:
5 Ph.D. level special research assistants

PROGRAM COSTS PROVIDED BY:
Company: $500,000

PRINTED MATERIALS AVAILABLE FROM:
Not reported

E.G. & G.
with
SALEM STATE COLLEGE

PRE-RETIREMENT PLANNING SEMINAR

COMPANY CONTACT:
Dot McKeen
Senior Personnel Administrator
Industrial Relations
E.G. & G.
35 Congress Street
Salem, MA 01970
(617) 745-3200

INSTITUTIONAL CONTACT:
Maureen Johnson
Director
Resource Center for Business
Salem State College

Alumni House
Salem State College
(617) 745-0556

PROGRAM DESCRIPTION/ OBJECTIVES:
Topic Areas: Pre-retirement Planning/ Framework for Planning, Government Benefits, Financial Planning, Company Benefits, Consumer Education, Health and Safety, Housing Options, Attitude and Role Adjustment, Meaningful Use of Leisure Time

LENGTH OF STUDY FOR PARTICIPANT:
8 hours

LENGTH OF CONTRACT:
2 months

LOCATION:
Salem State College

PARTICIPANTS:
Number: 85
Type: Open to all employees and spouses over age 55

PROGRAM COSTS PROVIDED BY:
Institution: $1,500
Company: $4,000

PRINTED MATERIALS AVAILABLE FROM:
Institution

E.I. DUPONT DE NEMOURS, COMPANY
with
PATRICK HENRY COMMUNITY COLLEGE

COMPUTER LANGUAGE TRAINING FOR MANAGEMENT

COMPANY CONTACT:
Wayne Watson
Chairman of Management Training
E.I. DuPont De Nemours, Company
Martinsville, VA 24112
(703) 632-9761

INSTITUTIONAL CONTACT:
Steve Maradian
Director
Continuing Education-Community
 Service
Patrick Henry Community College
P.O. Drawer 5311
Martinsville, VA 24115
(705) 635-8777

PROGRAM DESCRIPTION/ OBJECTIVES:
Provide language training in "fortran" and "basic" for management personnel.

PROGRAM INITIATED:
1982

LENGTH OF STUDY FOR PARTICIPANT:
12 weeks

LENGTH OF CONTRACT:
12 weeks with renewal and/or new training options

LOCATION:
DuPont, Martinsville

PARTICIPANTS:
60 mid- and upper-management personnel

PROGRAM COSTS PROVIDED BY:
Company: $16,000

PRINTED MATERIALS AVAILABLE FROM:
Institution

CITY OF EL MIRAGE
with
GLENDALE COMMUNITY COLLEGE

PUEBLO EL MIRAGE RV RESORT AND COUNTRY CLUB TRAINING PROJECT

COMPANY CONTACT:
Dr. Joseph A. Martinez
Director of Special Services
P.O. Box 26
El Mirage, AZ 85335
(602) 972-8116

INSTITUTIONAL CONTACT:
Stanley J. Grossman
Director
The Institute for Business, Industry &
 Technology
Glendale Community College
6000 W. Olive Avenue
Glendale, AZ 85302
(602) 934-2211

PROGRAM DESCRIPTION/ OBJECTIVES:
A program to train entry level office operation, recreational vehicle and turf and groundskeepers for the city's new RV Park and Country Club.

PROGRAM INITIATED:
1984

LENGTH OF STUDY FOR PARTICIPANT:
10 weeks

LENGTH OF CONTRACT:
10 weeks

LOCATION:
College/City of El Mirage/business training sites

PARTICIPANTS:
Number: 50
Type: Unemployed

PROGRAM COSTS PROVIDED BY:
Institution: In kind
Company: Equipment donations/budget
 funds
Participant: Tuition

PRINTED MATERIALS AVAILABLE FROM:
Institution

EL PASO ELECTRIC COMPANY
with
EL PASO COMMUNITY COLLEGE DISTRICT

MID-MANAGEMENT DEVELOPMENT PROGRAM

COMPANY CONTACT:
Jack Duffey
Director of Training
El Paso Electric Company
P.O. Box 982
El Paso, TX 79960
(915) 543-5711

INSTITUTIONAL CONTACT:
Gregory F. Linden
Associate Dean
Community Services/Continuing Education
El Paso Community College
P.O. Box 20500
El Paso, TX 79998
(915) 594-2597

PROGRAM DESCRIPTION/OBJECTIVES:
To provide mid-management skills development training.

PROGRAM INITIATED:
1976

LENGTH OF STUDY FOR PARTICIPANT:
64 hours in half or full day increments

LENGTH OF CONTRACT:
12 months renewed annually

LOCATION:
El Paso Electric Company

PARTICIPANTS:
120 mid-management personnel annually

PROGRAM COSTS PROVIDED BY:
Company: $5,500

PRINTED MATERIALS AVAILABLE FROM:
Institution

ELECTRICAL PRODUCTS CORPORATION*
with
MERRITT COLLEGE

COOPERATIVE EDUCATION

COMPANY CONTACT:
Harry Inn
Electrical Products Corporation
P.O. Box 23444
Oakland, CA 94623
(415) 655-9300

INSTITUTIONAL CONTACT:
Wesley Ingram
Counselor, Cooperative and Occupational Education
Career Center
Merritt College
12500 Campus Drive
Oakland, CA 94619
(415) 436-2446

PROGRAM DESCRIPTION/OBJECTIVES:
Provides students with learning in a work situation, generally relating work to college studies. Provides opportunity for career exploration or upgrading on the job. Provides employer with back-up services/training for employee.

PROGRAM INITIATED:
1970

LENGTH OF STUDY FOR PARTICIPANT:
Usually at least 2 semesters

LENGTH OF CONTRACT:
At least 1 semester

LOCATION:
Merritt College

PARTICIPANTS:
400 students in all college disciplines per semester

PROGRAM COSTS PROVIDED BY:
Institution: Staff salaries
Company: Student salaries
Other Source: $10,000 (federal and state grants)

PRINTED MATERIALS AVAILABLE FROM:
Institution

* Representative entry—complete list available from institution.

EPISCOPAL HOSPITAL
with
WIDENER UNIVERSITY

ASSOCIATE IN SCIENCE DEGREE ON-SITE FOR RADIOLOGIC TECHNOLOGISTS

COMPANY CONTACT:
Jane Leggieri
Program Director
School of Radiography
Episcopal Hospital
Front Street and Lehigh Avenue
Philadelphia, PA 19125
(215) 427-7000

INSTITUTIONAL CONTACT:
Michael P. Murphy
Associate Dean
University College
Widener University
P.O. Box 7139, Concord Pike
Wilmington, DE 19803
(302) 478-3000, X332

PROGRAM DESCRIPTION/ OBJECTIVES:
To provide the requirements on-site for completing an Associate's degree in radiologic technology at University College.

PROGRAM INITIATED:
1982

LENGTH OF STUDY FOR PARTICIPANT:
3–5 semesters of part-time study

LENGTH OF CONTRACT:
12 months with renewal option

LOCATION:
Episcopal Hospital

PARTICIPANTS:
15–25 students in radiologic technology programs, or technicians already in the field

PROGRAM COSTS PROVIDED BY:
Participant: $95 per credit hour

PRINTED MATERIALS AVAILABLE FROM:
Institution

EQUITABLE LIFE ASSURANCE SOCIETY OF THE UNITED STATES
with
MANHATTAN COLLEGE

EQUITABLE/MANHATTAN COLLEGE MIDTOWN PROGRAM IN HIGHER EDUCATION

COMPANY CONTACT:
Peter A. Lipuma
Vice President
General Studies
Equitable Life Assurance Society
1285 Avenue of the Americas
New York, NY 10019
(212) 554-3476

INSTITUTIONAL CONTACT:
Thomas E. Chambers
Dean
School of General Studies
Manhattan College
Manhattan College Parkway
Riverdale, NY 10471
(212) 920-0341

PROGRAM DESCRIPTION/ OBJECTIVES:
A cooperative higher education program which coordinates the financial and the physical facility resources of a major international insurance carrier with the academic and teaching resources of a private independent college.

PROGRAM INITIATED:
Not reported

DIRECTORY OF CAMPUS-BUSINESS LINKAGES

LENGTH OF STUDY FOR PARTICIPANT:
1 semester

LENGTH OF CONTRACT:
12 months continuous program for classrooms, yearly lease for office

LOCATION:
Conference Center at the Equitable Headquarters Building

PARTICIPANTS:
Approximately 90 high school, college and graduate students per year

PROGRAM COSTS PROVIDED BY:
Institution: $20,000
Company: $32,000
Participant: $90

PRINTED MATERIALS AVAILABLE FROM:
Institution and Company

ERIE INSURANCE GROUP
with
VILLA MARIA COLLEGE

BUSINESS INTERNSHIP

COMPANY CONTACT:
Martin P. Eisert
Director, Human Resources
Erie Insurance Group
144 East 6th Street
Erie, PA 16530
(814) 452-6831

INSTITUTIONAL CONTACT:
Ruth F. Hahn
Chairperson, Business Department
Villa Maria College
2551 West Lake Road
Erie, PA 16505
(814) 838-1966, X242

PROGRAM DESCRIPTION/ OBJECTIVES:
Educationally directed internship in an institution in which the student learns by observation and participation in the functioning of a particular department within a business or industry.

PROGRAM INITIATED:
1978

LENGTH OF STUDY FOR PARTICIPANT:
1 semester usually; can be up to 4 months during summer

LENGTH OF CONTRACT:
Dependent on student availability

LOCATION:
Villa Maria College

PARTICIPANTS:
1 senior business major

PROGRAM COSTS PROVIDED BY:
Company: Approximately $850
Participant: Travel costs

PRINTED MATERIALS AVAILABLE FROM:
Institution

ERNEST AND WHINNEY*
with
CASE WESTERN RESERVE UNIVERSITY

INDUSTRIAL SOCIAL WORK

COMPANY CONTACT:
Kenneth Macjen
National Director
Personnel Assistance Program
Ernst and Whinney
2000 National City Center
Cleveland, OH 44115
(216) 566-7333

INSTITUTIONAL CONTACT:
Holly Krailo
Director
Industrial Social Work Program
School of Applied Social Sciences
Case Western Reserve University
2035 Abington Road
Cleveland, OH 44106
(216) 368-2135

PROGRAM DESCRIPTION/ OBJECTIVES:
To demonstrate the scope and potential of social work practice in business and labor settings through the use of graduate internships.

PROGRAM INITIATED:
1981

LENGTH OF CONTRACT:
1 academic year

LOCATION:
Ernst and Whinney

PARTICIPANTS:
1 graduate social work student**

PROGRAM COSTS PROVIDED BY:
Institution: 50%
Company: 50%

PRINTED MATERIALS AVAILABLE FROM:
Institution

* Representative entry—complete list available from institution.
** Figures given reflect the entire program.

ESCAN
with
BAY DE NOC COMMUNITY COLLEGE

CONTRACTING WITH BUSINESS AND INDUSTRY (CWB&I)

COMPANY CONTACT:
Paul Parker
Escan Corporation
Danforth Road
Escanaba, MI 49829
(906) 786-3997

INSTITUTIONAL CONTACT:
Chuck Gold
Program Director
Bay de Noc Community College
College Avenue
Escanaba, MI 49829
(906) 786-5802

PROGRAM DESCRIPTION/ OBJECTIVES:
CWB&I is a method of specialized individual career orientation, training, and opportunities. It utilizes the local business and industrial complex of the community as a training laboratory. Students can acquire job skills in interests and capabilities under realistic settings.

PROGRAM INITIATED:
1976

LENGTH OF STUDY FOR PARTICIPANT:
2 semesters

LENGTH OF CONTRACT:
2 semesters

LOCATION:
Bay College/local businesses

PARTICIPANTS:
90 annually

PROGRAM COSTS PROVIDED BY:
Participant: $560.00

PRINTED MATERIALS AVAILABLE FROM:
Institution

EQUITABLE LIFE ASSURANCE SOCIETY OF THE UNITED STATES
with
MANHATTAN COLLEGE

EQUITABLE/MANHATTAN COLLEGE MIDTOWN PROGRAM IN HIGHER EDUCATION

COMPANY CONTACT:
William T. McCaffrey
Senior Vice President
Corporate Operations
Equitable Life Assurance Society
1285 Avenue of the Americas
New York, NY 10019
(212) 554-3476

INSTITUTIONAL CONTACT:
Thomas E. Chambers
Dean

School of General Studies
Manhattan College
Manhattan College Parkway
Riverdale, NY 10471
(212) 920-0341

PROGRAM DESCRIPTION/ OBJECTIVES:
A cooperative higher education program which coordinates the financial and the physical facility resources of a major international insurance carrier with the academic and teaching resources of a private independent college.

PROGRAM INITIATED:
January 1978

LENGTH OF STUDY FOR PARTICIPANT:
Yearly academic and continuing education programs

LENGTH OF CONTRACT:
Facilities assigned by Corporation

LOCATION:
Conference rooms at the Equitable Headquarters Building

PARTICIPANTS:
Number: Approximately 100 (per year)
Type: High school, college, and graduate students

PROGRAM COSTS PROVIDED BY:
Institution: Approximately $31,000
Company: Approximately $27,000
Participant: Approximately 100

PRINTED MATERIALS AVAILABLE FROM:
Institution and company

EXOLON COMPANY
with
STATE UNIVERSITY COLLEGE AT BUFFALO

EVALUATION STUDY OF WORKER ATTITUDES

COMPANY CONTACT:
Robert F. Taylor
Works Manager
Personnel Department
Exolon Company
1000 East Niagara Street
Tonowanda, NY 14150
(716) 693-4550

INSTITUTIONAL CONTACT:
William T. Ganley
Director, Center for Applied Research
State University College at Buffalo
1300 Elmwood Avenue, GC 409
Buffalo, NY 14222
(716) 878-4110

PROGRAM DESCRIPTION/ OBJECTIVES:
Tabulate raw data, analyze data, determine for similar and dissimilar reaction, submit a written report identifying the implications.

PROGRAM INITIATED:
1981

LENGTH OF STUDY FOR PARTICIPANT:
4 months

LENGTH OF CONTRACT:
4 months

LOCATION:
Exolon in-house

PARTICIPANTS:
29 managers-supervisors, employees

PROGRAM COSTS PROVIDED BY:
Institution: $1,900
Company: $3,400

PRINTED MATERIALS AVAILABLE FROM:
Not reported

EXXON*
with
DREW UNIVERSITY

COOPERATIVE EDUCATION IN CHEMISTRY

COMPANY CONTACT:
Paul Smith
Public Affairs Department
Exxon
P.O. Box 101
Florham Park, NJ 07932
(201) 765-6622

INSTITUTIONAL CONTACT:
James M. Miller
Chairman
Department of Chemistry
Drew University
Madison, NJ 07940
(201) 377-3000

PROGRAM DESCRIPTION/ OBJECTIVES:
An optional co-op program for chemistry majors with non-alternating work periods. Some college credit given for work; program completed in 4 years.

PROGRAM INITIATED:
1980

LENGTH OF STUDY FOR PARTICIPANT:
2 work periods: 1 of 3 months and 1 of 8 months

LENGTH OF CONTRACT:
2 years

LOCATION:
Various chemical and pharmaceutical companies

PARTICIPANTS:
Approximately 2 junior and senior chemistry majors annually

PROGRAM COSTS PROVIDED BY:
Company: Salary

PRINTED MATERIALS AVAILABLE FROM:
Institution

* Representative entry—complete list available from institution.

EXXON*
with
DREW UNIVERSITY

RESEARCH INSTITUTE FOR SCIENTISTS EMERITII (RISE)

COMPANY CONTACT:
Paul Smith
Public Affairs Department
Exxon
P.O. Box 101
Florham Park, NJ 07932
(201) 765-6622

INSTITUTIONAL CONTACT:
George deStevens
Director
Charles A. Dana Research Institute for Scientists Emerti
Chemistry Department
Drew University
Madison, NJ 07940
(201) 377-3000

PROGRAM DESCRIPTION/ OBJECTIVES:
Retirees (including early retirees) from industry are provided space and facilities at the university in return for their help in directing the research of undergraduate students. Students receive better education and an improved image of industry.

PROGRAM INITIATED:
1977

LENGTH OF STUDY FOR PARTICIPANT:
2 to 3 years renewable

LENGTH OF CONTRACT:
3 years, renewable

LOCATION:
Drew University

PARTICIPANTS:
5 expanding to 12; currently chemistry retirees but expanding to all sciences and math

PROGRAM COSTS PROVIDED BY:
Institution: minimal

PRINTED MATERIALS AVAILABLE FROM:
Institution

* Representative entry—complete list available from institution.

FAIRCHILD INDUSTRIES
with
UNIVERSITY OF MARYLAND

FAIRCHILD SCHOLARS AND DOCTORAL FELLOWS PROGRAM

COMPANY CONTACT:
Frank Schmidt
Vice President
Employee Relations and Administrative Services
Fairchild Industries
Fairchild Space and Electric Company
20301 Century Blvd.
Germantown, MD 20767
(301) 428-6495

INSTITUTIONAL CONTACT:
Anthony Ephremides
Professor and Program Director
Electrical Engineering Department
University of Maryland
College Park, MD 20742
(301) 454-6871

PROGRAM DESCRIPTION/OBJECTIVES:
To provide MS or Ph.D. training at full salary to outstanding electrical engineering graduates at a time of great need for postgraduate engineers. Students work 3 days per week, and study 2 days per week working on their degrees. They specialize in communication and computer engineering.

PROGRAM INITIATED:
1980

LENGTH OF STUDY FOR PARTICIPANT:
2 years for MS, 3 additional years for Ph.D. at 2 full days per week

LENGTH OF CONTRACT:
Minimum 3 years, renewable

LOCATION:
University of Maryland

PARTICIPANTS:
30 MS candidates and 9 Ph.D. candidates in electrical engineering annually

PROGRAM COSTS PROVIDED BY:
Company: $240,000 per year

PRINTED MATERIALS AVAILABLE FROM:
Institution

FEDERAL LAW ENFORCEMENT TRAINING CENTER
with
ALABAMA STATE UNIVERSITY*

CRIMINAL JUSTICE INTERN PROGRAM

COMPANY CONTACT:
Peter W. Phillips
Education Advisor
Office of the Director
Federal Law Enforcement Training Center
Glynco, GA 31524
(912) 267-2336

INSTITUTIONAL CONTACT:
Nicholas Astone
Criminal Justice Director
Alabama State University
P.O. Box 282
Montgomery, AL 36195
(205) 293-4285

PROGRAM DESCRIPTION/ OBJECTIVES:
To provide quality internship experiences for graduate and undergraduate criminal justice majors.

PROGRAM INITIATED:
1978

LENGTH OF STUDY FOR PARTICIPANT:
1 academic quarter or semester

LENGTH OF CONTRACT:
Not available

LOCATION:
Federal Law Enforcement Training Center

PARTICIPANTS:
Usually 4 graduates and undergraduates per term

PROGRAM COSTS PROVIDED BY:
Company: Provides lodging at nominal cost
Participant: 100%

PRINTED MATERIALS AVAILABLE FROM:
Company

*Representative entry—complete list available from institution.

FIRST NATIONAL BANK OF CHICAGO*
with
VANDERBILT UNIVERSITY

THE VANDERBILT INSTITUTE FOR THE ADVANCED STUDY OF CORPORATE LEARNING ENVIRONMENTS

COMPANY CONTACT:
Richard Wood
Senior Vice President
First National Bank of Chicago
Chicago, IL 60670
(312) 732-4000

INSTITUTIONAL CONTACT:
John C. Glidewell
Director, Vanderbilt Institute for the Advanced Study of Corporate Learning Environments
Peabody College
Vanderbilt University
Box 321
Nashville, TN 37203
(615) 322-8414

PROGRAM DESCRIPTION/ OBJECTIVES:
Established by Peabody College, Vanderbilt's school of education and human development, the Institute seeks to contribute to the enhancement of learning in corporations through research, program evaluation and the conduct of various types of educational activities. The Institute offers joint research programs on a contractual basis to corporations interested in assessing the impact of corporate learning environments on the development of productivity in the corporation. Specific information about each joint venture is available on request.

PROGRAM INITIATED:
1982

LENGTH OF STUDY FOR PARTICIPANT:
6 months to 6 years

LENGTH OF CONTRACT:
6 months to 6 years

LOCATION:
On campus, at corporate site, or both

PARTICIPANTS:
12 research associates who are faculty members who represent several colleges within the university.

PROGRAM COSTS PROVIDED BY:
Institution: Varies with contract but usually less than 40%
Company: Varies with contract but usually exceeds 60%

PRINTED MATERIALS AVAILABLE FROM:
Institution

* Representative entry—complete list available from institution

FISHER-SCIENTIFIC
with
INDIANA UNIVERSITY OF PENNSYLVANIA

PLANNING FOR PROSPERITY

COMPANY CONTACT:
James Cename
Plant Manager
Fisher-Scientific
Indiana, PA 15701
(412) 463-0253

INSTITUTIONAL CONTACT:
C.A. Altimus, Jr.
Dean, School of Business
Indiana University of Pennsylvania
109 McElhany Hall
Indiana, PA 15705
(412) 357-2520

PROGRAM DESCRIPTION/ OBJECTIVES:
Provide a positive atmosphere in plant for upgrading of worker skills and equipment.

PROGRAM INITIATED:
1981

LENGTH OF STUDY FOR PARTICIPANT:
½ year

LENGTH OF CONTRACT:
1 year

LOCATION:
Indiana, PA

PARTICIPANTS:
300 employees

PROGRAM COSTS PROVIDED BY:
Company: 75%
Participant: 25%
Other Source: Union funds for members

PRINTED MATERIALS AVAILABLE FROM:
Institution

FOGELSON GROUP
with
TRITON COLLEGE

PROJECT BUILD

COMPANY CONTACT:
Jerry Fogelson
President
Fogelson Group
867 N. Dearborn
Chicago, IL 60606

INSTITUTIONAL CONTACT:
LaMont Veenendaal
Project Coordinator
Construction Technology
Triton College
2000 5th Avenue
River Grove, IL
(312) 456-0300

PROGRAM DESCRIPTION/ OBJECTIVES:
Actual construction of a single-family home on a local site. All construction is done by Triton students, financing is arranged by the college and the finished product is sold by students as well.

PROGRAM INITIATED:
Summer 1985

LENGTH OF STUDY FOR PARTICIPANT:
1 year

LENGTH OF CONTRACT:
2 years

LOCATION:
In district

PARTICIPANTS:
16

PROGRAM COSTS PROVIDED BY:
Institution $75,000

PRINTED MATERIALS AVAILABLE FROM:
Institution

FOOD LION STORES, INC.
with
JOHN TYLER COMMUNITY COLLEGE

WAREHOUSE MANAGEMENT CAREER STUDIES CERTIFICATE

COMPANY CONTACT:
Mr. William Meath
Personnel Specialist
Personnel
Food Lion Stores, Inc.
P.O. Box 250
Prince George, VA 23875
(804) 861-8960

INSTITUTIONAL CONTACT:
Dr. Samuel Lee Hancock
Director
Division of Continuing Education
John Tyler Community College
13101 Jefferson Davis Highway
Chester, VA 23831
(804) 796-4111

PROGRAM DESCRIPTION/OBJECTIVES:
Program is designed to promote understanding of the warehouse supervisors' duties and skills which will lead to effective supervisory leadership.

PROGRAM INITIATED:
Spring, 1984

LENGTH OF STUDY FOR PARTICIPANT:
2½ years.

LENGTH OF CONTRACT:
30 instructional hours each 3 months.

LOCATION:
On-site at the Food Lion Distribution Center, Prince George

PARTICIPANTS:
Number: 18
Type: Current or potential warehouse supervisors

PROGRAM COSTS PROVIDED BY:
Institution: Administrative leadership, instructors' salaries
Company: Tuition, textbooks
Participant: Time
Other Source: N/A

PRINTED MATERIALS AVAILABLE FROM:
Institution

FORD MOTOR CO.
with
UNIVERSITY OF CINCINNATI

STATISTICAL EDUCATION OF FORD EMPLOYEES

COMPANY CONTACT:
Carlos Spicer
Statistical Process Control Facilitator
Quality Control
Ford Motor Co.-Sharonville
  Transmission Plant
3000 Sharon Road
Sharonville, OH 45241
(513) 782-7116

INSTITUTIONAL CONTACT:
Ralph Widmer
Program Coordinator
Division of Continuing Education
University of Cincinnati
Cincinnati, OH 45221-0146
(513) 475-6836

PROGRAM DESCRIPTION/OBJECTIVES:
To provide Ford employees knowledge and statistical methods to enhance analysis and problem solving consistent with Ford's goal of never-ending improvement in manufacturing processes and resultant products.

PROGRAM INITIATED:
September, 1983

LENGTH OF STUDY FOR PARTICIPANT:
10 weeks per course-Statistical Methods I & II

LENGTH OF CONTRACT:
Indefinite

LOCATION:
Plant (3000 Sharon Rd.)

PARTICIPANTS:
Number: 141 to date
Type: salaried and hourly employees

PROGRAM COSTS PROVIDED BY:
Company: Ford Motor Co.

PRINTED MATERIALS AVAILABLE FROM:
Institution

FORD/UAW-COUNCIL FOR ADVANCEMENT OF EXPERIENTIAL LEARNING
with
NORTHERN KENTUCKY UNIVERSITY

COLLEGE AND UNIVERSITY OPTIONS PROGRAM

COMPANY CONTACT:
Diana Bamford-Reese
Associate Director
College & University Options Project
C.A.E.L.
10598 Marble Faun Court
Columbia, MD 21044
(301) 997-3535

INSTITUTIONAL CONTACT:
Dr. Susan Kemper
Director
Credit Continuing Education
Northern Kentucky University
1401 Dixie Highway
Covington, Kentucky 41011
(606) 572-5601

PROGRAM DESCRIPTION/OBJECTIVES:
Provides training and evaluation of prior learning for Ford auto workers

LENGTH OF STUDY FOR PARTICIPANT:
Varies in length

LENGTH OF CONTRACT:
Ongoing beginning Fall 1985

LOCATION:
NKU

PARTICIPANTS:
Type: Undergraduates

PROGRAM COSTS PROVIDED BY:
Participant: Reimbursed by Ford

FORT LOGAN MENTAL HEALTH CENTER
with
ARAPAHOE JPTA

CAREER EMPLOYMENT EXPERIENCE AND WORK EXPERIENCE

COMPANY CONTACT:
Boris Gertz
Coordinator of Training
Fort Logan Mental Health Center
3920 West Oxford Avenue
Denver, CO 80237
(303) 761-0220

INSTITUTIONAL CONTACT:
Arlia Schildmeier
Counselor
Arapahoe JPTA
311 South Broadway
Englewood, CO 80110
(303) 761-7673

PROGRAM DESCRIPTION/OBJECTIVES:
To provide trainees with job and/or work experience; opportunities to "shadow" hospital staff as part of career explorations.

PROGRAM INITIATED:
1977

LENGTH OF STUDY FOR PARTICIPANT:
Variable, 3 months, 6 months, 1 year

LENGTH OF CONTRACT:
12 months renewable

LOCATION:
Fort Logan Mental Health Center

PARTICIPANTS:
Approximately 14 18-year-olds

PROGRAM COSTS PROVIDED BY:
Institution: $3.50 per hour to trainees

PRINTED MATERIALS AVAILABLE FROM:
Institution

GALLAUDET COLLEGE
with
PRINCE GEORGE'S COMMUNITY COLLEGE

CERTIFIED PROFESSIONAL SECRETARIAL PROGRAM

COMPANY CONTACT:
Irene Pruitt
Manager, Personnel
Gallaudet College
Kendall Green
Washington, DC 20002
(202) 651-5517

INSTITUTIONAL CONTACT:
Veronica S. Norwood
Director, Contract Services
Prince George's Community College
301 Largo Road
Largo, MD 20772
(301) 322-0726

PROGRAM DESCRIPTION/ OBJECTIVES:
To prepare participants to successfully complete the Certified Professional Secretary Examination and to enhance present skills and abilities, leading to positions of greater responsibility.

PROGRAM INITIATED:
1980

LENGTH OF STUDY FOR PARTICIPANT:
5 1-semester credit classes and 3 18–30 hour noncredit classes offered over a 24-month period

LENGTH OF CONTRACT:
Renewable each semester

LOCATION:
Gallaudet College

PARTICIPANTS:
16 clerk-typists and secretaries

PROGRAM COSTS PROVIDED BY:
Company: 50%
Other Source: 50% (state funding)

PRINTED MATERIALS AVAILABLE FROM:
Institution

GENERAL BUSINESS SERVICES, INC.
with
MONTGOMERY COMMUNITY COLLEGE

TAX PREPARATIONS CERTIFICATION

COMPANY CONTACT:
Andy Rains
Vice President
Tax Services
General Business Services, Inc.
51 Monroe Street
Rockville, MD 20850
(301) 424-1040

INSTITUTIONAL CONTACT:
Thomas W. Fuhr
Coordinator
Off-Campus Credit Program
Montgomery Community College
51 Mannakee Street
Rockville, MD 20850
(301) 279-5254

PROGRAM DESCRIPTION/ OBJECTIVES:
To meet need of prospective tax preparers to pass an IRS special enrollment exam.

PROGRAM INITIATED:
1981

LENGTH OF STUDY FOR PARTICIPANT:
1 semester

LENGTH OF CONTRACT:
Open-ended

LOCATION:
GBS facility

PARTICIPANTS:
44 adult students

PROGRAM COSTS PROVIDED BY:
Company: $5,227

PRINTED MATERIALS AVAILABLE FROM:
Company

GENERAL DYNAMICS-ELECTRIC BOAT DIVISION
with
COMMUNITY COLLEGE OF RHODE ISLAND

GENERAL DYNAMICS/ COMMUNITY COLLEGE OF R.I. ASSOCIATE DEGREE APPRENTICESHIP PROGRAM

COMPANY CONTACT:
Frank McCann
Supervisor of Trade Training
Training
Electric Boat Division, General Dynamics Corp. Quonset Point Facility,
North Kingstown, RI 02852
(401) 268-2682

INSTITUTIONAL CONTACT:
Richard P. Anderson
Coordinator
Business and Industry
Community College of Rhode Island
Flanagan Campus
Louis Quisset Pike
Lincoln, RI 02865
(401) 333-7127

PROGRAM DESCRIPTION/ OBJECTIVES:
4-year apprenticeship/Associate degree program. Upon successful completion of program apprentice receives journeyman's status from company and the Associate in Applied Science-Technical Studies from the community college.

PROGRAM INITIATED:
1983

LENGTH OF STUDY FOR PARTICIPANT:
4 years

LENGTH OF CONTRACT:
Continuing

LOCATION:
General Dynamics, Electric Boat Division
Quonset Point, Rhode Island

PARTICIPANTS:
Number: 150
Type: Apprentices

PROGRAM COSTS PROVIDED BY:
Company: 100%

PRINTED MATERIALS AVAILABLE FROM:
Institution

GENERAL ELECTRIC COMPANY
with
SALEM STATE COLLEGE

EDUCATORS IN INDUSTRY

COMPANY CONTACT:
Ms. Pat Dincecco
Manager Employee Publication
Lynn Relations Operation
General Electric Company
1000 Western Avenue

Lynn, MA 01902
(617) 594-2245

INSTITUTIONAL CONTACT:
Dr. Leonard Zani
Professor, Psychology
Psychology
Salem State College
Salem, MA 01970
(617) 745-0556

PROGRAM DESCRIPTION/ OBJECTIVES:
To provide our educators with first-level knowledge about industrial careers by participating in a 12-week on-site classroom and industrial setting experiences.

LENGTH OF STUDY FOR PARTICIPANT:
12 weeks

LENGTH OF CONTRACT:
12 weeks

LOCATION:
Salem State/General Electric

PARTICIPANTS:
Number: 29
Type: Educators

PROGRAM COSTS PROVIDED BY:
Institution: $1,000.00
Company: $5,000.00

PRINTED MATERIALS AVAILABLE FROM:
Institution and company

GENERAL ELECTRIC EDUCATION FOUNDATION
with
CHARLESTON HIGHER EDUCATION CONSORTIUM

SUMMER WORK-EDUCATION PROGRAM

COMPANY CONTACT:
Richard Yarborough
General Electric Co.
P.O. Box 10167
Charleston, SC 29411
(803) 553-8500

INSTITUTIONAL CONTACT:
Ann Baker
Associate Director
Charleston Higher Education
  Consortium
171 Ashley Avenue
Charleston, SC 29425
(803) 792-3627

PROGRAM DESCRIPTION/ OBJECTIVES:
To provide entry level work experience to teachers and counselors and help them relate work experience to educational policies and practices in context of a graduate level course.

LENGTH OF STUDY FOR PARTICIPANT:
6 weeks

LENGTH OF CONTRACT:
Renewed each summer for past 8 years

LOCATION:
Charleston, SC

PARTICIPANTS:
Number: 15-25 per year
Type: Teachers and counselors from public schools in three counties

PROGRAM COSTS PROVIDED BY:
Institution: All administrative support
Company: $4,600-GE
Other Sources: Approximately $950/person from local private companies

PRINTED MATERIALS AVAILABLE FROM:
Institution

GENERAL MOTORS CORPORATION
with
COLLEGE OF ALAMEDA

GENERAL MOTORS TRAINING CENTER PROGRAM

COMPANY CONTACT:
A.H. Warner
Manager
Training Department
General Motors
1444 Marina Blvd.
San Francisco, CA 94577
(415) 357-7200

INSTITUTIONAL CONTACT:
John Price
Division Chairperson
Business Transportation Department
College of Alameda
555 Atlantic Avenue
Alameda, CA 94501
(415) 522-7221

PROGRAM DESCRIPTION/ OBJECTIVES:
Provide product service training for General Motors dealer technicians under the auspices of the General Motors Training Center.

PROGRAM INITIATED:
1981

LENGTH OF STUDY FOR PARTICIPANT:
185 total days of training plus 10 instructor training days in Michigan

LENGTH OF CONTRACT:
1 academic year

LOCATION:
General Motors Training Center, San Leandro, CA

PARTICIPANTS:
3 instructors in Auto Mechanics

PROGRAM COSTS PROVIDED BY:
Company: $51,747.53

PRINTED MATERIALS AVAILABLE FROM:
Company

GENERAL MOTORS
with
GLENDALE COMMUNITY COLLEGE

GENERAL MOTORS AUTOMOTIVE SERVICE EDUCATION PROGRAM

COMPANY CONTACT:
John J. Choulochas
Manager
National College Coordinator
Service Development Center
3051 Van Dyke Avenue
Warren, MI 48090-2008

INSTITUTIONAL CONTACT:
Phil Randolph
Dean of Occupational Education Administration
Glendale Community College
6000 West Olive Avenue
Glendale, AZ 85302
(602) 934-2211

PROGRAM DESCRIPTION/ OBJECTIVES:
The Automotive Service Education Program is a comprehensive 2-year automotive program. This program provides classroom and laboratory training, as well as on-the-job experience at a GM dealership.

PROGRAM INITIATED:
1982

LENGTH OF STUDY FOR PARTICIPANT:
2 years

LENGTH OF CONTRACT:
On-going

LOCATION:
College/Dealership

PRINTED MATERIALS AVAILABLE FROM:
Institution and company

GENERAL MOTORS CORPORATION
with
GOLDEN WEST COLLEGE

GMC/GWC AUTOMOTIVE— DIESEL CONTRACT INSTRUCTION

COMPANY CONTACT:
Ed Banett
Region Training Supervisor
General Motors Corporation
1105 Riverside Drive
Burbank, CA 91506
(213) 849-5544

INSTITUTIONAL CONTACT:
Gene L. Tardy
Director of Community and Corporate Relations
Public Information Department
Golden West College
15744 Golden West Street
Huntington Beach, CA 92647
(714) 892-7711

PROGRAM DESCRIPTION/ OBJECTIVES:
To provide "state-of-the-art" instruction to dealer/agency employees of General Motors Corporation.

PROGRAM INITIATED:
1981

LENGTH OF STUDY FOR PARTICIPANT:
8–16 hours

LENGTH OF CONTRACT:
12 months, 170 teaching days

LOCATION:
Golden West College

PARTICIPANTS:
12–20 dealership employees per class

PROGRAM COSTS PROVIDED BY:
Institution: 5%
Company: 95%

PRINTED MATERIALS AVAILABLE FROM:
Institution

GENERAL MOTORS CORPORATION
with
MACOMB COMMUNITY COLLEGE

COOPERATIVE TRAINING PROGRAM

COMPANY CONTACT:
Calvin H. Cook
Manager
General Motors Training Center
General Motors Corporation
30901 Van Dyke
Warren, MI 48090
(313) 575-0246

INSTITUTIONAL CONTACT:
Edward J. Lynch
Dean
Occupational Education Technology
Macomb Community College
14500 Twelve Mile Road
Warren, MI 48093
(313) 445-7432

PROGRAM DESCRIPTION/ OBJECTIVES:
To provide product service training for General Motors dealer technicians under the auspices of the General Motors Training Center.

PROGRAM INITIATED:
1981

LENGTH OF STUDY FOR PARTICIPANT:
Varies

LENGTH OF CONTRACT:
Annually

LOCATION:
General Motors Training Center

PARTICIPANTS:
Varying number of G.M. dealer technicians

PROGRAM COSTS PROVIDED BY:
Not reported

PRINTED MATERIALS AVAILABLE FROM:
Not reported

GENERAL MOTORS ASSEMBLY DIVISION-LEEDS (KANSAS CITY, MO)
with
PIONEER COMMUNITY COLLEGE

BASIC SKILLS TRAINING (PRE-APPRENTICESHIP TYPE TRAINING FOR PLANT MAINTENANCE)

COMPANY CONTACT:
Floyd Luker
Coordinator, Apprentice Committee
Personnel
General Motors
68117 Stadium Drive
Kansas City, MO 64129
(913) 281-7315

INSTITUTIONAL CONTACT:
Roland Morreale
Program Coordinator
Adult Distributive Education; Director, The Management Institute
Pioneer Community College
6217 Prospect Avenue
Kansas City, MO 64119
(816) 444-4600

PROGRAM DESCRIPTION/ OBJECTIVES:
To encourage female and minority employees to apply for openings in the plant maintenance department by receiving the necessary pre-training.

PROGRAM INITIATED:
April 1, 1985

LENGTH OF STUDY FOR PARTICIPANT:
60 clock hours (8 weeks)

LENGTH OF CONTRACT:
April and May, 1985.

LOCATION:
5501 Cleveland, Kansas City, MO. The W.E.B. DuBois Center (a minority, non-profit community organization)

PARTICIPANTS:
Number: 46
Type: GM employees presently working on the assembly line. Approximately half are women or minorities.

PROGRAM COSTS PROVIDED BY:
Institution: 60%
Company: 25%
Other Source: 15% (State Exemplary Programs—Dept. of Elementary & Secondary Education, for Sex Equity)

PRINTED MATERIALS AVAILABLE FROM:
Institution and company

GENERAL MOTORS CORPORATION
with
TRITON COLLEGE

GENERAL MOTORS MECHANICS TRAINING PROGRAM

COMPANY CONTACT:
Jeff Watts
Director
Training Center
General Motors Corporation
336 Ogden Avenue
Hinsdale, IL 60521
(312) 323-6000

INSTITUTIONAL CONTACT:
Tom Bondi
Dean

Industrial Technology
Triton College
2000 5th Avenue
River Grove, IL 60171
(312) 456-0300

PROGRAM DESCRIPTION/ OBJECTIVES:
General Motors dealership mechanics and service managers receive intensive training in Triton's automotive laboratories.

PROGRAM INITIATED:
1984

LENGTH OF STUDY FOR PARTICIPANT:
2 years

LENGTH OF CONTRACT:
NA

LOCATION:
Triton College

PARTICIPANTS:
NA

PROGRAM COSTS PROVIDED BY:
Participant: Equipment costs

PRINTED MATERIALS AVAILABLE FROM:
Institution and company

GENERAL MOTORS
CORPORATION
with
OKLAHOMA STATE TECH

OKLAHOMA STATE TECH/
GENERAL MOTORS
CORPORATION COOPERATIVE
EDUCATION PROGRAM

COMPANY CONTACT:
Jim Collier
Manager
General Motors Corporation
12101 N.E. Expressway, RR #1
Oklahoma City, OK 73131
(405) 733-6011

INSTITUTIONAL CONTACT:
W.E. Bailey
Automotive Center Coordinator
Oklahoma State Tech
4th and Mission
Okmulgee, OK 74447
(918) 756-6211, X279

PROGRAM DESCRIPTION/ OBJECTIVES:
Provide technical instruction for General Motors dealer technicians to service and repair components and systems of new model vehicles with particular emphasis on computerized control and diesel engines.

PROGRAM INITIATED:
1981

LENGTH OF STUDY FOR PARTICIPANT:
Not reported

LENGTH OF CONTRACT:
Not reported

LOCATION:
Not reported

PARTICIPANTS:
1,450 dealers technicians

PROGRAM COSTS PROVIDED BY:
Company: 100%

PRINTED MATERIALS AVAILABLE FROM:
Institution

GULFSTREAM AEROSPACE
with
GEORGIA INSTITUTE OF
TECHNOLOGY

TECHNICAL MANAGEMENT
SKILL DEVELOPMENT

COMPANY CONTACT:
Mr. Cotton Hope
Training Manager
Training
Gulfstream Aerospace Corporation

P.O. Box 2206
Savannah, GA 31402
(912) 964-3413

INSTITUTIONAL CONTACT:
Dr. H. Ben Roberson
Director
Industrial Education
Georgia Institute of Technology
225 North Avenue, NW
Atlanta, GA 30332
(404) 894-3950

PROGRAM DESCRIPTION/OBJECTIVES:
To increase the management and human relations skills of technical supervisors.

LENGTH OF STUDY FOR PARTICIPANT:
30 hours

LENGTH OF CONTRACT:
6 weeks

LOCATION:
Gulfstream Training Department

PARTICIPANTS:
Number: 25
Type: Middle managers

PROGRAM COSTS PROVIDED BY:
Institution: $2,408.00
Company: $3,612.00

PRINTED MATERIALS AVAILABLE FROM:
Institution

**INDUSTRIAL MANUFACTURING COMPANY
with
GEORGIA INSTITUTE OF TECHNOLOGY**

MOTIVATION FOR SUPERVISORS

COMPANY CONTACT:
Dr. H. Ben Roberson
Director, Industrial Education
   Department
Georgia Institute of Technology
Atlanta, GA 30332
(404) 894-3950

INSTITUTIONAL CONTACT:
Dr. H. Ben Roberson
Director, Industrial Education
   Department
Georgia Institute of Technology
Atlanta, GA 30332
(404) 894-3950

PROGRAM DESCRIPTION/OBJECTIVES:
To provide supervisors with motivational tools they can use with employees and to train them in the use of motivational tools and implementation in the work place.

PROGRAM INITIATED:
Not reported

LENGTH OF STUDY FOR PARTICIPANT:
16 hours

LENGTH OF CONTRACT:
2 weeks

LOCATION:
In-plant

PARTICIPANTS:
50 supervisors

PROGRAM COSTS PROVIDED BY:
Institution: 50%
Company: 50%

PRINTED MATERIALS AVAILABLE FROM:
Institution

**GIANT FOOD, INC.
with
PRINCE GEORGE'S COMMUNITY COLLEGE**

BASIC INSTRUMENT REPAIR

COMPANY CONTACT:
Chuck Moon
Manager, Maintenance
Giant Food, Inc.

6300 Sheriff Road
Landover, MD 20785
(301) 386-0525

INSTITUTIONAL CONTACT:
Veronica Norwood
Director, Contract Services
Prince George's Community College
301 Largo Road
Largo, MD 20772
(301) 322-0726

PROGRAM DESCRIPTION/ OBJECTIVES:
To provide instruction in basic analog and digital electronics to enable participants to troubleshoot computerized store equipment.

PROGRAM INITIATED:
1982

LENGTH OF STUDY FOR PARTICIPANT:
32 hours (1 2-hour class per week)

LENGTH OF CONTRACT:
32 weeks with renewal

LOCATION:
Prince George's Community College

PARTICIPANTS:
11 first-level technicians per session

PROGRAM COSTS PROVIDED BY:
Company: 61%
Other Source: 39% (state funding)

PRINTED MATERIALS AVAILABLE FROM:
Institution

GLIE FARMS, INC.
with
BRONX COMMUNITY COLLEGE

GREENHOUSE TRANSITION PROGRAM

COMPANY CONTACT:
Gary Waldron
President
Glie Farms, Inc.
1818 Bathgate Avenue
Bronx, NY 10457
(212) 731-2130

INSTITUTIONAL CONTACT:
Rafael Infante
Director, Contracts & Training
Continuing Education
Bronx Community College
University Avenue & 181 Street
Bronx, NY 10453
(212) 220-6424

PROGRAM DESCRIPTION/ OBJECTIVES:
To facilitate the transition from the old greenhouse to a new hydroponic facility; to train greenhouse manager/supervisors in optimum cultural practices.

LENGTH OF STUDY FOR PARTICIPANT:
5 months

LENGTH OF CONTRACT:
5 months

LOCATION:
Glie Farms

PARTICIPANTS:
Number: 25

PROGRAM COSTS PROVIDED BY:
Company: $26,617
Other Sources: $23,700

PRINTED MATERIALS AVAILABLE FROM:
Institution

GODDARD SPACE FLIGHT CENTER
with
PRINCE GEORGE'S COMMUNITY COLLEGE

CERTIFIED PROFESSIONAL SECRETARIAL PROGRAM

COMPANY CONTACT:
Bonnie Kaiser
Employee Development Specialist

Goddard Space Flight Center
Greenbelt, MD 20770
(301) 344-8930

INSTITUTIONAL CONTACT:
Veronica Norwood
Director, Contract Services
Prince George's Community College
301 Largo Road
Largo, MD 20772
(301) 322-0726

PROGRAM DESCRIPTION/ OBJECTIVES:
To prepare participants to successfully complete the Certified Professional Secretary Examination and to enhance present skills and abilities, leading to positions of greater responsibility.

PROGRAM INITIATED:
1978

LENGTH OF STUDY FOR PARTICIPANT:
5 1-semester credit classes and 3 18–30 hour noncredit classes offered over a 24-month period

LENGTH OF CONTRACT:
Renewable each semester

LOCATION:
Goddard Space Flight Center

PARTICIPANTS:
16 clerks-typists and secretaries

PROGRAM COSTS PROVIDED BY:
Company: 50%
Other Source: 50% (state funding)

PRINTED MATERIALS AVAILABLE FROM:
Institution

GOMBERT VOLKSWAGON-MAZDA*
with
SPARTANBURG TECHNICAL COLLEGE

RETURN-TO-INDUSTRY PROGRAM

COMPANY CONTACT:
Howard Gombert
Gombert Volkswagon-Mazda
402 McCrary Drive
Spartanburg, SC 29303
(803) 585-2492

INSTITUTIONAL CONTACT:
Jane Reece
Director of Grants and Staff Development
Spartanburg Technical College
P.O. Drawer 4386
Spartanburg, SC 29303
(803) 576-5770

PROGRAM DESCRIPTION/ OBJECTIVES:
Program provides faculty with information on rapidly changing technology and procedures by placing instructors in business, industry, or health care facilities for "hands-on" experience in new trends and technology. For periods of 2–15 weeks, instructors have worked in 50 industries in the past 3 years. The current information is inserted immediately into classrooms and labs resulting in 72 curriculum revisions and the development of 8 custom-designed courses. Benefits are obvious to students, instructors, the company involved and the industrial community as a whole.

PROGRAM INITIATED:
1978

LENGTH OF STUDY FOR PARTICIPANT:
2–15 weeks

LENGTH OF CONTRACT:
Ongoing

LOCATION:
Spartanburg County businesses

PARTICIPANTS:
Approximately 30 faculty members

PROGAM COSTS PROVIDED BY:
Institution: $3,000

PRINTED MATERIALS AVAILABLE FROM:
Institution

* Representative entry—complete list available from institution.

LENGTH OF CONTRACT:
16 hours + 4-hour follow-up sessions

LOCATION:
Local hotel

PARTICIPANTS:
96 persons with technical and engineering backgrounds

PROGRAM COSTS PROVIDED BY:
Company: 100%

PRINTED MATERIALS AVAILABLE FROM:
Institution

GOODYEAR AEROSPACE
with
KENT STATE UNIVERSITY

PRINCIPLES OF MANAGEMENT

COMPANY CONTACT:
Rod Harris
Goodyear Aerospace
1210 Massilon Road
Akron, OH 44315
(216) 794-3270

INSTITUTIONAL CONTACT:
Karen Rylander
Director, Continuing Education
Kent State University
327 Rockwell Hall
Kent, OH 44242
(216) 672-3100

PROGRAM DESCRIPTION/ OBJECTIVES:
Principles covered include motivation, problem-solving, leadership, communications, and discipline. Subordinates are surveyed to obtain information on the general work environment. Program culminates in development of an action plan.

PROGRAM INITIATED:
1980

LENGTH OF STUDY FOR PARTICIPANT:
16 hours + 4-hour follow-up sessions

GOODYEAR TIRE AND RUBBER COMPANY
with
KENT STATE UNIVERSITY

MANAGEMENT SEMINAR

COMPANY CONTACT:
Dan Lyons
         and
Jack Hathaway
Goodyear Tire and Rubber Company
1144 East Market
Akron, OH 44310
(216) 796-2837
(216) 796-6332

INSTITUTIONAL CONTACT:
Karen Rylander
Director, Continuing Education
Kent State University
327 Rockwell Hall
Kent, OH 44242
(216) 672-3100

PROGRAM DESCRIPTION/ OBJECTIVES:
Designed to develop understanding of concepts and skills in the areas of cost effectiveness, profit control, fiscal discipline, return on investment, and managing a business in an inflationary environment. An exploration of corporate strategy is also conducted.

PROGRAM INITIATED:
1980

LENGTH OF STUDY FOR PARTICIPANT:
84 hours

LENGTH OF CONTRACT:
84 hours

LOCATION:
Kent State University

PARTICIPANTS:
60 upper and middle managers

PROGRAM COSTS PROVIDED BY:
Company: 100%

PRINTED MATERIALS AVAILABLE FROM:
Institution

GRAPHIC CENTER
with
UNIVERSITY OF HARTFORD

MANAGEMENT AND SALES TRAINING

COMPANY CONTACT:
Robert Charbeneau
President
The Graphic Center
26 Tobey Road
Bloomfield, CT 06002
(203) 522-2223

INSTITUTIONAL CONTACT:
William T. George
Program Development Consultant
Division of Adult Educational Services
University of Hartford
200 Bloomfield Avenue
West Hartford, CT 06117
(203) 243-4507/4381

PROGRAM DESCRIPTION/OBJECTIVES:
First and second line management programs and sale skills.

PROGRAM INITIATED:
1979

LENGTH OF STUDY FOR PARTICIPANT:
5 to 6 weeks (12.5 hours per program)

LENGTH OF CONTRACT:
4 programs

LOCATION:
The Graphic Center

PARTICIPANTS:
12 first and second line managers

PROGRAM COSTS PROVIDED BY:
Company: 100%

PRINTED MATERIALS AVAILABLE FROM:
Institution

GREATER CLEVELAND CHAPTER OF ASTD
with
CLEVELAND STATE UNIVERSITY, COLLEGE OF EDUCATION

MASTER OF EDUCATION IN POSTSECONDARY EDUCATION: HUMAN RESOURCE DEVELOPMENT INTERNSHIP PROGRAM

COMPANY CONTACT:
Kenneth J. Kovach
President, Greater Cleveland Chapter, American Society for Training and Development
CIVAC
2800 Euclid Avenue
Cleveland, OH 44115
(216) 696-4613

INSTITUTIONAL CONTACT:
Ernest M. Schuttenberg
Associate Professor of Education/Coordinator Postsecondary Masters Program
Educational Specialists
Cleveland State University, College of Education
Euclid Ave. at E. 24th Street

Cleveland, OH 44115
(216) 687-4613

PROGRAM DESCRIPTION/OBJECTIVES:
Master's degree program designed for students planning careers in training and development in business organizations. Internship is 6 months in duration.

PROGRAM INITIATED:
1981 for Master's Program; 1984 for Internship

LENGTH OF STUDY FOR PARTICIPANT:
52 quarter hours of coursework, including a 6-month internship in a business organization.

LENGTH OF CONTRACT:
N/A

LOCATION:
Interns work in a variety of business organizations in Northeast Ohio

PARTICIPANTS:
Number: 30–50
Type: Graduate students

PROGRAM COSTS PROVIDED BY:
Participant: 100%

PRINTED MATERIALS AVAILABLE FROM:
Institution

GREENEVILLE/GREENE COMPANY CHAMBER OF COMMERCE
with
TUSCULUM COLLEGE

MANAGEMENT DEVELOPMENT PROGRAM

COMPANY CONTACT:
Ruth Reynolds
Executive Director
Greeneville/Greene Company Chamber of Commerce
Greeneville, TN 37743
(615) 638-4111

INSTITUTIONAL CONTACT:
John Reiners
Director of Planning and Budget
Tusculum College
Tusculum Station
Greeneville, TN 37743
(615) 639-9471

PROGRAM DESCRIPTION/OBJECTIVES:
To provide working personnel with a training program in basic skills of management; course work in management principles, accounting, human reactions, computer usage, communications, and economics. Offered in the evenings; upon completion of the 6 one-credit courses participants receive certificate.

PROGRAM INITIATED:
1981

LENGTH OF STUDY FOR PARTICIPANT:
Completion of 6 courses each lasting 6 weeks

LENGTH OF CONTRACT:
Ongoing

LOCATION:
Tusculum College

PARTICIPANTS:
20 ranging from unemployed to senior engineers in first cycle

PROGRAM COSTS PROVIDED BY:
Institution: $5,000
Company: Option to reimburse employee
Participant: $30 per course

PRINTED MATERIALS AVAILABLE FROM:
Institution

GRENADIER REALTY CORP.
with
NEW YORK CITY TECHNICAL COLLEGE

DIFFERENTIAL VACUUM STEAM HEATING

COMPANY CONTACT:
Vernon Douglas
Assistant Vice President to Personnel
Personnel Dept.
Grenadier Realty Corp.
155 Elmira Loop
Brooklyn, NY 11239
(718) 642-2550

INSTITUTIONAL CONTACT:
Beverly LaPuma
Coordinator, Continuing Education and Extension Services
Continuing Education
New York City Technical College
300 Jay Street
Brooklyn, NY 11201
(718) 643-5570

PROGRAM DESCRIPTION/OBJECTIVES:
Complete "walk through" of the Dunham-Bush in the basement of a typical hi-rise residential building, viewing the actual operation system and stressing the critical items to be monitored and adjusted.

LENGTH OF STUDY FOR PARTICIPANT:
2 days

LENGTH OF CONTRACT:
1 day

LOCATION:
Off campus—Jefferson Towers

PARTICIPANTS:
Number: 21
Type: Superintendents, building managers

PROGRAM COSTS PROVIDED BY:
Company: 100%

PRINTED MATERIALS AVAILABLE FROM:
Institution

GRENADIER REALTY CORP.
with
NEW YORK CITY TECHNICAL COLLEGE

HEATING/HOT WATER SYSTEMS IN MULTI-FAMILY BUILDINGS

COMPANY CONTACT:
Vernon Douglas
Assistant Vice President to Personnel
Personnel
Grenadier Realty Corp.
155 Elmira Loop
Brooklyn, NY 11239
(718) 642-2550

INSTITUTIONAL CONTACT:
Beverly LaPuma
Coordinator, Continuing Education and Extension Services
Continuing Education
New York City Technical College
300 Jay Street
Brooklyn, NY 11201
(718) 643-5570

PROGRAM DESCRIPTION/OBJECTIVES:
Explanation of fuels and combustion, operation of boilers, description of air pollution, pumps, fans, valves, and pipe systems. Heat timers, thermostats, controls, and instrumentations are also discussed.

LENGTH OF STUDY FOR PARTICIPANT:
30 hours

LENGTH OF CONTRACT:
10 weeks

LOCATION:
Voorhees, 417

PARTICIPANTS:
Number: 18
Type: superintendents, building managers

PROGRAM COSTS PROVIDED BY:
Company: 100%

PRINTED MATERIALS
AVAILABLE FROM:
Institution

GRENADIER REALTY CORP.
with
NEW YORK CITY TECHNICAL
COLLEGE

OIL BURNER #2
DEMONSTRATION

COMPANY CONTACT:
Vernon Douglas
Assistant Vice President to Personnel
Personnel Dept.
Grenadier Realty Corp.
155 Elmira Loop
Brooklyn, NY 11239
(718) 642-2550

INSTITUTIONAL CONTACT:
Beverly LaPuma
Coordinator of Continuing Education
  and Extension Services
Continuing Education
New York City Technical College
300 Jay Street
Brooklyn, NY 11201
(718) 643-5570

PROGRAM DESCRIPTION/
OBJECTIVES:
Oil Burner No. 2 Demonstration—including on-site lecture, walk through, and demonstration of the problems of #2 Oil Burner.

LENGTH OF STUDY FOR
PARTICIPANT:
7 hours

LENGTH OF CONTRACT:
1 day

LOCATION:
Off campus—Poly Clinic, 345 W. 50 Street, New York City.

PARTICIPANTS:
Number: 4
Type: Building managers, superintendents

PROGRAM COSTS PROVIDED BY:
Company: 100%

PRINTED MATERIALS
AVAILABLE FROM:
Institution

GRENADIER REALTY CORP.
with
NEW YORK CITY TECHNICAL
COLLEGE

TROUBLESHOOTING HEATING/
HOT WATER SYSTEMS

COMPANY CONTACT:
Vernon Douglas
Assistant Vice President to Personnel
Personnel Department
Grenadier Realty Corp.
155 Elmira Loop
Brooklyn, NY 11239
(718) 642-2550

INSTITUTIONAL CONTACT:
Beverly LaPuma
Coordinator of Continuing Education
  and Extension Services
Continuing Education
New York City Technical College
300 Jay Street
Brooklyn, NY 11201
(718) 643-5570

PROGRAM DESCRIPTION/
OBJECTIVES:
Follow-up of the Fall 1984 contract course with Grenadier Realty entitled, "Heating and Hot Water Systems for Multifamily Dwellings," which started on October 1, 1984 and ended December 1, 1984. This follow up course is designed

to discuss and explain consumption rates, heating problems, and energy conservation.

LENGTH OF STUDY FOR PARTICIPANT:
6 hours

LENGTH OF CONTRACT:
1 day

LOCATION:
Voorhees, Room 506

PARTICIPANTS:
Number: 3
Type: Building managers and superintendents

PROGRAM COSTS PROVIDED BY:
Company: 100%

PRINTED MATERIALS AVAILBLE FROM:
Institution

GRENADIER REALTY CORP.
with
NEW YORK TECHNICAL COLLEGE

VACUUM STEAM HEATING SYSTEM

COMPANY CONTACT:
Vernon Douglas
Assistant Vice President to Personnel
Personnel Dept.
Grenadier Realty Corp.
155 Elmira Loop
Brooklyn, NY 11239
(718) 642-2550

INSTITUTIONAL CONTACT:
Beverly LaPuma
Coordinator, Continuing Education and Extension Services
Continuing Education
New York City Technical College, Division of Continuing Education
300 Jay Street
Brooklyn, NY 11201
(718) 643-5570

PROGRAM DESCRIPTION/ OBJECTIVES:
Lecture/laboratory demonstration seminar for building superintendents and others in multi-dwelling housing. This seminar will provide technical assistance in the operation, maintenance, and trouble-shooting of the vacuum steam heating system, and the Dunham-Bush system will be examined in detail. One maintenance manual will be distributed to each participant.

LENGTH OF STUDY FOR PARTICIPANT:
4 hours

LENGTH OF CONTRACT:
1 day

LOCATION:
Voorhees, 411

PARTICIPANTS:
Number: 24
Type: Superintendents, housing managers

PROGRAM COSTS PROVIDED BY:
Company: 100%

PRINTED MATERIALS AVAILABLE FROM:
Institution

H&R BLOCK, INC.
with
PIONEER COMMUNITY COLLEGE

H&R BLOCK TAX PREPARATION

COMPANY CONTACT:
Bernie Smith
Regional Director
H&R Block, Inc.
3600 South Noland Road
Independence, MO 64055
(816) 461-6345

INSTITUTIONAL CONTACT:
Roland A. Morreale
Program Coordinator

Adult Distributive Education
Pioneer Community College
6217 Prospect
Kansas City, MO 64130
(816) 444-4600

PROGRAM DESCRIPTION/ OBJECTIVES:
To provide cooperative programming and accreditation for tax preparation courses offered by H&R Block to the public and to its employees.

PROGRAM INITIATED:
1979

LENGTH OF STUDY FOR PARTICIPANT:
Varies — 13 weeks to 2 days

LENGTH OF CONTRACT:
Open-ended

LOCATION:
H&R Block offices

PARTICIPANTS:
Approximately 400 general public and Block employees annually

PROGRAM COSTS PROVIDED BY:
Institution: 25%
Company: 24%
Other Source: 51% (state aid and vocational reimbursement)

PRINTED MATERIALS AVAILABLE FROM:
Company

HANCOCK MUTUAL LIFE INSURANCE COMPANY
with
SIMMONS COLLEGE

SIMMONS/HANCOCK PROGRAM
COMPANY CONTACT:
Corporate Education
John Hancock Mutual Life Insurance
John Hancock Place
Boston, MA 02117
(617) 421-4718

INSTITUTIONAL CONTACT:
Louise Comeau
Director of Special Program
Continuing Education
Simmons College
300 The Fenway
Boston, MA 02115
(617) 738-2141

PROGRAM DESCRIPTION/ OBJECTIVES:
A series of credit courses offered to John Hancock employees to assist in professional development and encourage further education.

PROGRAM INITIATED:
1981

LENGTH OF STUDY FOR PARTICIPANT:
12 months

LENGTH OF CONTRACT:
Annual length of contract

LOCATION:
The Hancock Tower, Boston, MA

PARTICIPANTS:
200 John Hancock employees

PROGRAM COSTS PROVIDED BY:
Company: Absorbs all costs

PRINTED MATERIALS AVAILABLE FROM:
Institution and company

HARTFORD HOSPITAL
with
UNIVERSITY OF HARTFORD

CAREER FATIGUE AND BURNOUT
COMPANY CONTACT:
Jack Lylis
Director of Education
Hartford Hospital
Hartford, CT 06115
(203) 524-3011

INSTITUTIONAL CONTACT:
Gilbert J. Maffeo
Program Development Consultant

Division of Adult Educational Services
University of Hartford
200 Bloomfield Avenue
West Hartford, CT 06117
(203) 243-4350/4381

PROGRAM DESCRIPTION/ OBJECTIVES:
To provide information and skills training concerning the prevention of burnout.

PROGRAM INITIATED:
1981

LENGTH OF STUDY FOR PARTICIPANT:
1-3 days

LENGTH OF CONTRACT:
1-3 days ongoing

LOCATION:
On-site

PARTICIPANTS:
15-25 employees

PROGRAM COSTS PROVIDED BY:
Company: 100%

PRINTED MATERIALS AVAILABLE FROM:
Institution and company

HARTFORD HOSPITAL
with
UNIVERSITY OF HARTFORD

SEMINAR IN GROUP DECISION MAKING

COMPANY CONTACT:
Jack Lylis
Director of Education
Hartford Hospital
Hartford, CT 06115
(203) 524-3011

INSTITUTIONAL CONTACT:
Gilbert J. Maffeo
Program Development Consultant
Division of Adult Educational Services
University of Hartford

200 Bloomfield Avenue
West Hartford, CT 06117
(203) 243-4350/4381

PROGRAM DESCRIPTION/ OBJECTIVES:
To provide skills training in decision making, conflict resolution, and small group processes.

PROGRAM INITIATED:
1981

LENGTH OF STUDY FOR PARTICIPANT:
1-3 days

LENGTH OF CONTRACT:
1-3 days ongoing

LOCATION:
On-site

PARTICIPANTS:
15-25 employees per program

PROGRAM COSTS PROVIDED BY:
Company: 100%

PRINTED MATERIALS AVAILABLE FROM:
Institution and company

HERCULES, INC.
with
BRIGHAM YOUNG UNIVERSITY

MANAGEMENT TRAINING FOR SUPERVISORS

COMPANY CONTACT:
Weldon Daines
Training Coordinator
Product Engineering
Hercules, Inc. Bacchus Works
Magna, UT 84044
(801) 250-5911, X3205

INSTITUTIONAL CONTACT:
Richard L. White
Coordinator of Management Programs, Conferences and Workshops
Brigham Young University

156 HCEB
Provo, UT 84602

PROGRAM DESCRIPTION/ OBJECTIVES:
To teach management skills to engineers who have been promoted to be supervisors.

PROGRAM INITIATED:
1982

LENGTH OF STUDY FOR PARTICIPANT:
2 full days of training

LENGTH OF CONTRACT:
Trained 3 groups within 2-month time period

LOCATION:
Hercules plant

PARTICIPANTS:
75 engineering supervisors and their department managers

PROGRAM COSTS PROVIDED BY:
Company: 100%

PRINTED MATERIALS AVAILABLE FROM:
Institution

HEWLETT-PACKARD*
with
EVERGREEN VALLEY COLLEGE

TRANSITION TO TECHNOLOGY

COMPANY CONTACT:
Sylvia Gerst
Affirmative Action Officer
Hewlett-Packard
3000 Hanover Street
Palo Alto, CA 94304
(415) 857-1501, X3716

INSTITUTIONAL CONTACT:
Andrew McFarlin
Engineering Instructor and Coordinator
Evergreen Valley College
3095 Yerba Buena Road
San Jose, CA 95135
(408) 274-7900, X6570

PROGRAM DESCRIPTION/ OBJECTIVES:
To provide those with no prior understanding of technical fields of employment with a realistic exposure to several such fields so that an intelligent approach might be made in determining a suitable training program.

PROGRAM INITIATED:
1977

LENGTH OF STUDY FOR PARTICIPANT:
135 hours during semester (9 hours per week)

LENGTH OF CONTRACT:
Agreements with individual company personnel to teach

LOCATION:
Evergreen Valley College

PARTICIPANTS:
80-100 unemployed women

PROGRAM COSTS PROVIDED BY:
Institution: 100% subsequent years
Other Source: 100% first year from Women's Equity Grant

PRINTED MATERIALS AVAILABLE FROM:
Institution

* Representative entry—complete list available from institution.

HEWLETT-PACKARD
with
MERRITT COLLEGE

ELECTRONICS INSTRUCTOR/ ENGINEER EXCHANGE

COMPANY CONTACT:
Edward Butts
Engineer
Hewlett-Packard
c/o Merritt College
12500 Campus Drive
Oakland, CA 95619
(415) 436-2427

Directory of Campus-Business Linkages

INSTITUTIONAL CONTACT:
Jim Albritton
Chair, Electronics Department
Merritt College
12500 Campus Drive
Oakland, CA 95619
(415) 436-2427

PROGRAM DESCRIPTION/ OBJECTIVES:
Instructors are exchanged with engineers from firm for 1 year to maintain currency with industry.

PROGRAM INITIATED:
1980

LENGTH OF STUDY FOR PARTICIPANT:
1 year

LENGTH OF CONTRACT:
Open-ended

LOCATION:
Merritt College

PARTICIPANTS:
1 electronics engineer per year

PROGRAM COSTS PROVIDED BY:
Institution: None (exchange program)
Company: None (exchange program)

PRINTED MATERIALS AVAILABLE FROM:
Institution

HEWLETT PACKARD*
with
PALOMAR COMMUNITY COLLEGE

WORKSITE TRAINING/ ELECTRONICS TECHNOLOGY

COMPANY CONTACT:
Robert E. Schultz
Technical Training Manager
Hewlett-Packard
16399 West Bernardo Drive
San Diego, CA 92128
(714) 487-4100, X239

INSTITUTIONAL CONTACT:
Thomas C. Dolan
Director
or Linda M. Repsher
Coordinator
Worksite Training/Vocational
  Education
Palomar Community College
1140 West Mission Road
San Marcos, CA 92069
(714) 744-1150, X2567

PROGRAM DESCRIPTION/ OBJECTIVES:
Provide an electronics training program to employees with inadequate or obsolete skills at their worksite. This enables employees to upgrade their skills/knowledge in a highly technical and rapidly changing field.

PROGRAM INITIATED:
1979

LENGTH OF STUDY FOR PARTICIPANT:
General electronics technology, 18 months; microelectronics technology, 12 months

LENGTH OF CONTRACT:
Ongoing

LOCATION:
Palomar Community College

PARTICIPANTS:
400 entry-level technicians annually

PROGRAM COSTS PROVIDED BY:
Institution: $27,390 per program annually
Company: $150,000 annually

PRINTED MATERIALS AVAILABLE FROM:
Institution and company

* Representative entry—complete list available from institution.

HONEYWELL INFORMATION SYSTEMS, INC.
with
REGIS COLLEGE

REGIS COLLEGE/HONEYWELL BAY STATE SKILLS TRAINING PROGRAM IN COMPUTER PROGRAMMING

COMPANY CONTACT:
Timothy W. Kilduff
Manager
Community Relations and Public Affairs
Honeywell Information Systems, Inc.
200 Smith Street
Waltham, MA 02154
(617) 895-3201

INSTITUTIONAL CONTACT:
Edward Mulholland
Academic Dean
Regis College
235 Wellesley Street
Weston, MA 02193
(617) 893-1820, X293

PROGRAM DESCRIPTION/ OBJECTIVES:
To retrain professional adults to be computer programmers (entry level skills).

PROGRAM INITIATED:
1981

LENGTH OF STUDY FOR PARTICIPANT:
Pilot: 20 weeks; expanded program, 30 weeks

LENGTH OF CONTRACT:
Pilot: 6 months; expanded program, 9 months

LOCATION:
Regis College, Weston, MA, and Honeywell, Waltham, MA

PARTICIPANTS:
Pilot, 30; expanded program: 35 adult professionals

PROGRAM COSTS PROVIDED BY:
Institution: $11,967
Company: $120, 764
Participant: $8,250
Other Source: $50,165 (state funds)

PRINTED MATERIALS AVAILABLE FROM:
Not reported

HOSPITAL COUNCIL UNILATERAL COMMITTEE
with
SAN DIEGO COMMUNITY COLLEGE

LVN TO RN APPRENTICESHIP PROGRAM

COMPANY CONTACT:
Marlene Ruiz
Staff Development Director
Chairperson, Unilateral Committee
Kaiser Foundation Hospital
4647 Zion
San Diego, CA 92120
(714) 563-2554

INSTITUTIONAL CONTACT:
Maryann Gellis
Program Dean
Nursing
San Diego Community College
1313 Twelfth Avenue
San Diego, CA 92101
(714) 230-2439

PROGRAM DESCRIPTION/ OBJECTIVES:
Upgrade licensed LVN to RN; assist personal development; financial support while continuing education.

PROGRAM INITIATED:
1981

LENGTH OF STUDY FOR PARTICIPANT:
1 year

LENGTH OF CONTRACT:
Ongoing; optional with some area hospitals

LOCATION:
Supporting hospital

PARTICIPANTS:
40 LVN

PROGRAM COSTS PROVIDED BY:
Company: 10 hours/week
Participant: 6 hours/week
Other Source: CETA 6 hours/week

PRINTED MATERIALS AVAILABLE FROM:
Institution

HONEYWELL
with
GLENDALE COMMUNITY COLLEGE

AAS PRODUCTION MANAGEMENT

COMPANY CONTACT:
Educational Director
Honeywell Large Information Systems
  Division
13430 N. Black Canyon Highway
Phoenix, AZ 85029
(602) 862-8000

INSTITUTIONAL CONTACT:
Dr. LaRue Hubbard
Business Professor
Business
Glendale Community College
6000 W. Olive Avenue
Glendale, AZ 85302
(602) 934-2211

PROGRAM DESCRIPTION/OBJECTIVES:
This program will provide a formal education path leading from the Honeywell required MM course to the AAS degree in Production Management at Glendale Community College.

PROGRAM INITIATED:
1982

LENGTH OF STUDY FOR PARTICIPANT:
2 years

LENGTH OF CONTRACT:
On-going

LOCATION:
College/Honeywell facility

PARTICIPANTS:
Number: 50 students per semester
Type: Honeywell employees

PROGRAM COSTS PROVIDED BY:
Institution: Faculty salaries
Company: Facilities usage
Participant: Tuition

PRINTED MATERIALS AVAILABLE FROM:
Institution and company

HUMBER COLLEGE OF APPLIED ARTS AND TECHNOLOGY
with
CENTRAL MICHIGAN UNIVERSITY

COMPANY CONTACT:
Dr. Ruth McClain
Humber College of Applied Arts and
  Technology
205 Humber College Boulevard
Rexdale, Ontario
Canada M9W 5L7
(416) 675-3111

INSTITUTIONAL CONTACT:
Dr. Richard Potter
Assistant Director
Central Michigan University
Institute for Personal and Career
  Development
Rowe 130
Mt. Pleasant, MI 48859
(517) 774-7133

PROGRAM DESCRIPTION/OBJECTIVES:
To provide graduate level professional development programs to selected faculty members of Humber CAAT.

PROGRAM INITIATED:
Spring, 1984

LENGTH OF STUDY FOR PARTICIPANT:
30 months

LENGTH OF CONTRACT:
36 months

LOCATION:
Humber College Campus, Rexdale, Ontario

PARTICIPANTS:
30 faculty members from Humber CAAT

PROGRAM COSTS PROVIDED BY:
Humber College: 100%

PRINTED MATERIALS AVAILABLE FROM:
Institution

OVER 250 SEPARATE COMPANIES
with
INDIANA UNIVERSITY OF PENNSYLVANIA

SAFETY SCIENCES DEPARTMENTAL INTERNSHIP AND COOP PROGRAMS

COMPANY CONTACT:
Numerous, available upon request

INSTITUTIONAL CONTACT:
R.E. McClay
Associate Professor
Safety Sciences Department
Indiana University of Pennsylvania
Indiana, PA 15705
(412) 357-3019

PROGRAM DESCRIPTION/ OBJECTIVES:
To reinforce the education of safety science students with closely related experience in an industrial environment.

LENGTH OF STUDY FOR PARTICIPANT:
Internship-1 semester; coops-2 semesters

LENGTH OF CONTRACT:
4–6 months

PARTICIPANTS:
Number: 40 annually
Type: Internships-senior; Coops-sophomores

PROGRAM COSTS PROVIDED BY:
Various arrangements possible.

PRINTED MATERIALS AVAILABLE FROM:
Institution

INSTA PRO INTERNATIONAL, LTD.
with
IOWA STATE UNIVERSITY

DEVELOPMENT OF EXTRUDED FOOD SYSTEMS

COMPANY CONTACT:
Dr. LeRoy J. Hanson
President
10301 Dennis Drive
Des Moines, IA 50322
(515) 276-4524, Telex: 478375

INSTITUTIONAL CONTACT:
Mark H. Love, Ph.D.
Associate Professor
Food and Nutrition Department
Iowa State University
Ames, IA 50011
(515) 294-4432

PROGRAM DESCRIPTION/ OBJECTIVES:
Research into the application of autogenous extruders for processing of food ingredients for developing countries; evaluation of ingredients in traditional foods and novel food concepts.

PROGRAM INITIATED:
1980

LENGTH OF CONTRACT:
Varies with each project

LOCATION:
Iowa State University and Insta Pro Processing Plant, Des Moines, IA

PARTICIPANTS:
N/A

PROGRAM COSTS PROVIDED:
Institution: 30%
Company: 70% + In-Kind
Other Sources: Occasionally

PRINTED MATERIALS AVAILABLE FROM:
Company and institution

INSTITUTE FOR MOTOR FLEET TRAINING
with
UNIVERSITY OF HARTFORD

MAINTENANCE OF COMMERCIAL VEHICLES— PHASE I

COMPANY CONTACT:
Mr. William Simons
Fleet Training Specialist
Institute for Motor Fleet Training
The Pennsylvania State University
University Park, PA 16802
(814) 865-2581

INSTITUTIONAL CONTACT:
M. Brady
Director, Continuing Education
Division of Adult Educational Services
University of Hartford
200 Bloomfield Avenue
West Hartford, CT 06117
(203) 243-4387

PROGRAM DESCRIPTION/ OBJECTIVES:
Technical training in motor fleet maintenance designed for maintenance supervisors of common carriers, etc. Curriculum developed by the Institute for Motor Fleet Training at Pennsylvania State University.

PROGRAM INITIATED:
1981

LENGTH OF STUDY FOR PARTICIPANT:
3 days (18 contact hours)

LENGTH OF CONTRACT:
This will be an annual offering

LOCATION:
Hartford, CT

PARTICIPANTS:
18 supervisors, fleet owners

PROGRAM COSTS PROVIDED BY:
Company: 100%

PRINTED MATERIALS AVAILABLE FROM:
Institution

INSURANCE COMPANY OF NORTH AMERICA
with
UNIVERSITY OF PENNSYLVANIA

PENN/INA PROGRAM

COMPANY CONTACT:
John Hurley
Director of Training, Education and Development
Insurance Company of North America
1600 Arch Street
Philadelphia, PA 19101
(215) 241-1000

INSTITUTIONAL CONTACT:
Katherine Pollak
Vice Dean
College of General Studies
University of Pennsylvania
210 Logan Hall
Philadelphia, PA 19104
(215) 243-4847

PROGRAM DESCRIPTION/ OBJECTIVES:
To provide a liberal arts education at the work site for qualified employees of a major corporation.

PROGRAM INITIATED:
1981

LENGTH OF STUDY FOR PARTICIPANT:
Students may take courses as long as they like for enrichment only or towards a BA degree

LENGTH OF CONTRACT:
4 years plus

LOCATION:
INA Headquarters

PARTICIPANTS:
150 currently accepted, no current limit on admissions for any permanent INA employee

PROGRAM COSTS PROVIDED BY:
Institution: $10,500 + professors' salaries
Company: $28,000 + individual tuition
Participant: Books

PRINTED MATERIALS AVAILABLE FROM:
Institution and company

INTERNAL REVENUE SERVICE
with
NEW YORK CITY TECHNICAL COLLEGE

I.R.S. BUSINESS WRITING

COMPANY CONTACT:
Lonnie Berkowitz
Employee Development Specialist
Training and Development
Internal Revenue Service
120 Church Street
New York, NY 10008
(212) 264-2080

INSTITUTIONAL CONTACT:
Barbara Ritchin
Director of Contract Programs
Continuing Education
New York City Technical College
450 West 41st Street, Room 501
New York, NY 10036
(212) 239-1664

PROGRAM DESCRIPTION/OBJECTIVES:
Business Writing class offered to I.R.S. first and second level supervisory personnel. Course objective is to assist students to write effective office memos and business letters employing correct capitalization, punctuation, grammar, sentence structure, and paragraph organization skills.

LENGTH OF STUDY FOR PARTICIPANT:
30 hours

LENGTH OF CONTRACT:
New contract for each cycle

LOCATION:
On site at I.R.S.

PARTICIPANTS:
Number: 16
Type: First and second level supervisory

PROGRAM COSTS PROVIDED BY:
Company: 100%

PRINTED MATERIALS AVAILABLE FROM:
Institution and company

NORTHERN KENTUCKY UNIVERSITY
with
INTERNAL REVENUE SERVICE

IRS CERTIFICATE PROGRAM

COMPANY CONTACT:
Paulette Duennis
Education Director
Education
IRS Service Center
Covington, KY 41011
(606) 292-5627

INSTITUTIONAL CONTACT:
Susan Kemper
Director
Credit Continuing Education
Northern Kentucky University
1401 Dixie Highway
Covington, KY 41001
(606) 572-5601

PROGRAM DESCRIPTION/OBJECTIVES:
Provides credit courses which can be applied toward certificate.

LENGTH OF STUDY FOR PARTICIPANT:
Individual rate

LENGTH OF CONTRACT:
Ongoing

LOCATION:
IRS Covington Branch

PARTICIPANTS:
Number: 60 per semester

PRINTED MATERIALS AVAILABLE FROM:
Institution

INTERNAL REVENUE SERVICE*
with
UNIVERSITY OF NORTH FLORIDA

COOPERATIVE EDUCATION

COMPANY CONTACT:
Diane Holifield
Recruiting Coordinator
P.O. Box 35045
Internal Revenue Service
Jacksonville, FL 32202
(904) 791-2966

INSTITUTIONAL CONTACT:
Carol Ann Boyles
Director, Career Planning Student Affairs
University of North Florida
4567 St. Johns Bluff Road South
Jacksonville, FL 32216
(904) 646-2955

PROGRAM DESCRIPTION/OBJECTIVES:
To provide students with opportunities to blend academic theory with real life work experiences.

PROGRAM INITIATED:
1977

LENGTH OF STUDY FOR PARTICIPANT:
2 semesters minimum

LENGTH OF CONTRACT:
2 semesters minimum

LOCATION:
Jacksonville, FL

PARTICIPANTS:
40 juniors, seniors and graduate students per semester

PROGRAM COSTS PROVIDED BY:
Institution: 100% of staff salaries
Company: 100% of student salaries

PRINTED MATERIALS AVAILABLE FROM:
Institution

* Representative entry—complete list available from institution.

INTERNATIONAL BROTHERHOOD OF ELECTRICAL WORKERS
with
FLORIDA JUNIOR COLLEGE

ADVANCED MOTOR CONTROLS CLASS JOURNEYMEN ELECTRICIANS

COMPANY CONTACT:
Thomas Gilmore
Director
Electrical Local I.B.E.W.
2941 Dawn Road
Jacksonville, FL 32216
(904) 737-7533

INSTITUTIONAL CONTACT:
James R. Myers
Dean, Occupational Education
Florida Junior College
101 West State Street
Jacksonville, FL 32202
(904) 633-8284

PROGRAM DESCRIPTION/OBJECTIVES:
To update/upgrade Journeymen Electricians to optimize their effectiveness in maintaining the state of the art of electrical/electronic systems.

PROGRAM INITIATED:
1982

LENGTH OF STUDY FOR PARTICIPANT:
1 semester

LENGTH OF CONTRACT:
Continuing

LOCATION:
Florida Junior College, Downtown

PARTICIPANTS:
25 I.B.E.W. Journeymen

PROGRAM COSTS PROVIDED BY:
Participant: 100%

PRINTED MATERIALS AVAILABLE FROM:
Institution

IBM COMPUTER CENTER
with
EVERGREEN VALLEY COLLEGE

MECHANICAL DESIGNER TRAINING PROGRAM

COMPANY CONTACT:
John Smoot
Special Education
Department 276
IBM Corporation
5600 Cottle Road
San Jose, CA 95193
(408) 997-4016

INSTITUTIONAL CONTACT:
Andrew McFarlin
Engineering Instructor and Coordinator
Evergreen Valley College
3095 Yerba Buena Road
San Jose, CA 95135
(408) 274-7900, X 6570

PROGRAM DESCRIPTION/ OBJECTIVES:
To provide a group of courses to develop an understanding and appreciation of a variety of theoretical concepts necessary in the competent execution of mechanical design problems and projects.

PROGRAM INITIATED:
1978

LENGTH OF STUDY FOR PARTICIPANT:
2 years (15 courses, 2–4 classes offered per quarter)

LENGTH OF CONTRACT:
1 year with annual renewal

LOCATION:
IBM Corporation

PARTICIPANTS:
Approximately 20 mechanical designers, drafters and technical personnel per quarter

PROGRAM COSTS PROVIDED BY:
Company: 100%

PRINTED MATERIALS AVAILABLE FROM:
Institution and company

IBM
with
HAMPTON INSTITUTE

IBM FACULTY LOAN PROGRAM

COMPANY CONTACT:
John C. Steers
Program Manager
Affirmative Action
IBM
Armonk, NY 10504
(914) 765-1900

INSTITUTIONAL CONTACT:
Dr. Willis Sheftall
Dean, School of Business
Hampton Institute
Hampton, VA 23668
(804) 727-5361

PROGRAM DESCRIPTION/ OBJECTIVES:
To expose faculty and students to interaction with business executives.

PROGRAM INITIATED:
1970

LENGTH OF STUDY FOR PARTICIPANT:
1 academic year

LENGTH OF CONTRACT:
Yearly, with renewal

LOCATION:
Hampton Institute

PARTICIPANTS:
1 IBM executive is on loan to the educational institution; fills the role of visiting faculty

PROGRAM COSTS PROVIDED BY:
Company: 100%

PRINTED MATERIALS AVAILABLE FROM:
Not available

INTERNATIONAL BUSINESS MACHINES
with
MEDGAR EVERS COLLEGE

COOPERATIVE EDUCATION

COMPANY CONTACT:
Craig Esslinger
Customer Engineering Manager
International Business Machines
330 Madison Avenue
New York, NY 10017
(212) 972-4523

INSTITUTIONAL CONTACT:
Brenda J. Barley
Director, Student Services
Medgar Evers College
1150 Carroll Street
Brooklyn, NY 11225
(212) 735-1776

PROGRAM DESCRIPTION/ OBJECTIVES:
To provide skills in customer service through repair of company products leading to possible management training and development.

PROGRAM INITIATED:
1981

LENGTH OF STUDY FOR PARTICIPANT:
Alternate semesters

LENGTH OF CONTRACT:
Unlimited

LOCATION:
International Business Machines

PARTICIPANTS:
15 undergraduates per semester

PROGRAM COSTS PROVIDED BY:
Institution: $6,472
Company: $53,100

PRINTED MATERIALS AVAILABLE FROM:
Institution

IBM WORLD TRADE ORGANIZATION*
with
AMERICAN UNIVERSITY

COOPERATIVE EDUCATION PROGRAM

COMPANY CONTACT:
Edward B. Wilber
Manager, Export Regulation Services
Office of Export Regulation
IBM World Trade Organization
1801 K Street, NW
Washington, DC 20016-1397
(202) 833-6738

INSTITUTIONAL CONTACT:
Barbara J. Taylor
Director
Career Center-Cooperative Education
American University
4400 Mass. Avenue, NW
Washington, DC 20016
(202) 885-1804

PROGRAM DESCRIPTION/ OBJECTIVES:
To provide opportunities for liberal arts undergraduate and graduate students to test career goals and earn academic credit by working in preprofessional positions in private business, non-profit or government organization.

PROGRAM INITIATED:
1974

LENGTH OF STUDY FOR PARTICIPANT:
4 or 6 months

LENGTH OF CONTRACT:
4 or 6 months

LOCATION:
The majority of the placement, although not restricted to, are in the metropolitan Washington, DC, area.

PARTICIPANTS:
500 degree-seeking undergraduate and graduate students from all academic programs per year

PROGRAM COSTS PROVIDED BY:
Company: 100% of student salaries
Participant: Tuition for academic credit earned through this program

PRINTED MATERIALS AVAILABLE FROM:
Institution

* Representative entry—complete list available from institution.

INTERNATIONAL FENCE INDUSTRY ASSOCIATION
with
PRINCE GEORGE'S COMMUNITY COLLEGE

LEGAL CONSIDERATIONS OF CONSTRUCTION CONTRACTS

COMPANY CONTACT:
Paul Champion
Champion Fence Company
P.O. Box 573
Bowie, MD 20715
(301) 262-8008

INSTITUTIONAL CONTACT:
Veronica Norwood
Director, Contract Services
Prince George's Community College
301 Largo Road
Largo, MD 20772
(301) 322-0726

PROGRAM DESCRIPTION/OBJECTIVES:
This course addresses issues relating to the legal ramifications of standard clauses in construction agreements, both general and sub-contracts.

PROGRAM INITIATED:
1982

LENGTH OF STUDY FOR PARTICIPANTS:
7 hours

LENGTH OF CONTRACT:
7 hours

LOCATION:
Prince George's Community College

PARTICIPANTS:
20 fence company owners and associates

PROGRAM COSTS PROVIDED BY:
Company: 75%
Other Source: 25% (state funds)

PRINTED MATERIALS AVAILABLE FROM:
Institution

INTERNATIONAL MINERALS AND CHEMICALS
with
INDIANA STATE UNIVERSITY

COOPERATIVE PROFESSIONAL PRACTICE PROGRAM

COMPANY CONTACT:
Pete Ray
Assistant Director of Personnel
International Minerals and Chemicals, Inc.
1331 South First Street
Terre Haute, IN 47802
(812) 232-0121

INSTITUTIONAL CONTACT:
Jack A. Brewer
Coordinator, Cooperative Professional Practice Program
Indiana State University

Alumni Center 247
Terre Haute, IN 47809
(812) 232-6311, X2582

PROGRAM DESCRIPTION/ OBJECTIVES:
To help provide students with research experience in chemistry at an international chemical corporation.

PROGRAM INITIATED:
1980

LENGTH OF STUDY FOR PARTICIPANT:
Student works 20 hours per week during the semester

LENGTH OF CONTRACT:
Not available

LOCATION:
Terre Haute, IN

PARTICIPANTS:
8 junior and senior chemistry students

PROGRAM COSTS PROVIDED BY:
Company: $5.00 per hour

PRINTED MATERIALS AVAILABLE FROM:
Institution and company

INTERNATIONAL MANAGEMENT COUNCIL
with
JOHN TYLER COMMUNITY COLLEGE

CERTIFIED PROFESSIONAL MANAGERS CERTIFICATE

COMPANY CONTACT:
Ms. Cindy Arterbery
Education Committee Chairman
International Management Council
c/o Philip Morris, U.S.A.
P.O. Box 26603
Richmond, VA 23261
(804) 274-3579

INSTITUTIONAL CONTACT:
Dr. Samuel Lee Hancock
Director
Division of Continuing Education
John Tyler Community College
13101 Jefferson Davis Highway
Chester, VA 23831
(804) 796-4111

PROGRAM DESCRIPTION/ OBJECTIVES:
Program is to assist those considered a manager to gain professional development skills in the areas of controlling, communicating, organizing, planning, budgeting, and motivating. The manager learns how to hire/fire and to take responsibility for directing the activities of others.

PROGRAM INITIATED:
Fall, 1982

LENGTH OF STUDY FOR PARTICIPANT:
1 academic year.

LENGTH OF CONTRACT:
30 instructional hours per 3-month period.

LOCATION:
Philip Morris Training Center, Richmond, Virginia

PARTICIPANTS:
Number: 25
Type: Managers of local businesses and industries who are members of the International Management Council

PROGRAM COSTS PROVIDED BY:
Institution: Administrative leadership, instructors' salaries
Company: Coordination leadership
Participant: Time, examination fees
Other Source: Businesses and industries: tuition, textbooks

PRINTED MATERIALS AVAILABLE FROM:
Institution and company

VARIOUS COMPANIES
with
IOWA STATE UNIVERSITY

TRAINING WORKSHOPS

COMPANY CONTACT:
Various Research and Technical Development

INSTITUTIONAL CONTACT:
A.H. Epstein
Professor and Chairman
Plant Pathology, Seed and Weed Sciences
Iowa State University
351 Bessey
Iowa State University
Ames, IA 50011
(515) 294-1741

PROGRAM DESCRIPTION/OBJECTIVES:
Updates for technical personnel in the areas of Plant Pathology, Weed Science, Seed Testing and Seed Conditioning

LENGTH OF STUDY FOR PARTICIPANTS:
From 3 days to 2 weeks

LOCATION:
Ames campus

PARTICIPANTS:
20+

PROGRAM COSTS PROVIDED BY:
Participant: Fees

PRINTED MATERIALS AVAILABLE FROM:
Institution

IOWA DEVELOPMENT COMMISSION
with
IOWA STATE UNIVERSITY

FOREIGN STUDENT CONTACT PROGRAM

COMPANY CONTACT:
Mr. Max Olson
Marketing Manager
International Trade Division
Iowa Development Commission
600 East Court Street
Des Moines, Iowa 50309
(515) 281-3138

INSTITUTIONAL CONTACT:
Dean Stebbins
Foreign Student Contact Program Coordinator
International Educational Services
Iowa State University
Ames, Iowa 50011
(515) 294-1120

PROGRAM DESCRIPTION/OBJECTIVES:
Arrange plant visits for foreign nationals at Iowa State University with export-oriented Iowa manufacturers to explore mutual international trade interests and expose visitors to the private sector in the state. Exchange of valuable cross-cultural information to overcome barriers to successful international trade relations. Co-sponsored by Center for Industrial Research and Service at ISU and Des Moines Regional Office, Department of Commerce.

PROGRAM INITIATED:
1975

LENGTH OF STUDY FOR PARTICIPANT:
1 to 3 days.

LENGTH OF CONTRACT:
Ongoing program

LOCATION:
Throughout Iowa.

PARTICIPANTS:
Number: 250 students, 52 Iowa firms
Type: International trade oriented foreign students and visiting faculty; Iowa firms.

PROGRAM COSTS PROVIDED BY:
Institution: All correspondence, orientation for participants.
Company: Local travel to firm, meals, overnight expenses paid by host firms.

Participant: Prepared talks on home country culture.

PRINTED MATERIALS AVAILABLE FROM:
Institution and company

SPECIFIC COMPANY NOT IDENTIFIED
with
IOWA STATE UNIVERSITY

MICROELECTRONICS RESEARCH CENTER

INSTITUTIONAL CONTACT:
Kenneth M. Lakin
Chairman, Microelectronics Research Center
EMRRI
125 Applied Sciences Center
Iowa State University
Ames, Iowa 50011
(515) 294-7732

PROGRAM DESCRIPTION/OBJECTIVES:
The Microelectronics Research Center is uniquely concerned with the development and characterization of materials and specialized devices including thin film piezoelectric devices, integrated communications circuits, solar cells, and amorphous semiconductor materials. The center is also initiating the first research effort in the United States to evaluate a promising new technique, Ionized Cluster Beam (ICB) thin film deposition in ultrahigh vacuum.

PROGRAM INITIATED:
1984

LENGTH OF STUDY FOR PARTICIPANT:
Ongoing

LENGTH OF CONTRACT:
Ongoing

LOCATION:
At Applied Sciences Center

PARTICIPANTS:
Various companies

PROGRAM COSTS PROVIDED BY:
Various industrial organizations and federal and state agencies

PRINTED MATERIALS AVAILABLE FROM:
Institution and company

ITT*
with
BREVARD COMMUNITY COLLEGE

COMMUNICATION AND ELECTRONIC ASSEMBLERS

COMPANY CONTACT:
Al Perry
Plant Manager
HW AIA
ITT Communications Systems
Cape Canaveral, FL 32920
(305) 783-6911

INSTITUTIONAL CONTACT:
Maurice F. Buckner
Dean, Continuing Education
Brevard Community College
1519 Clearlake Road
Cocoa, FL 32922
(305) 632-1111, X360

PROGRAM DESCRIPTION/OBJECTIVES:
Technical training for unemployed individuals (40% women, 30% minorities).

PROGRAM INITIATED:
1982

LENGTH OF STUDY FOR PARTICIPANT:
80 hours

LENGTH OF CONTRACT:
Ongoing, on request

LOCATION:
Brevard Community College

PARTICIPANTS:
47 on-line employees

PROGRAM COSTS PROVIDED BY:
Institution: 16%
Company: 16%
Other Source: 68% (Industrial Services grant from Florida Department of Education)

PRINTED MATERIALS AVAILABLE FROM:
Not available

* Representative entry—complete list available from institution.

ITT RAYONIER
with
FLORIDA JUNIOR COLLEGE AT JACKSONVILLE

MULTI-CRAFT TRAINING

COMPANY CONTACT:
Jerry Arceneaux
Training Director
Personnel
ITT Rayonier
P.O. Box 2002
Fernandina Beach, FL 32034
(904) 261-3611

INSTITUTIONAL CONTACT:
Dr. James R. Myers
Instructional Dean
Occupational Education
Florida Junior College at Jacksonville
101 West State Street
Jacksonville, FL 32202
(904) 633-8284

PROGRAM DESCRIPTION/ OBJECTIVES:
Cross-training of maintenance personnel to familiarize them with at least 3 crafts.

PROGRAM INITIATED:
1982

LENGTH OF STUDY FOR PARTICIPANT:
180 hours per employee

LENGTH OF CONTRACT:
Open-ended

LOCATION:
On-site

PARTICIPANTS:
Number: 104
Type: Employees

PROGRAM COSTS PROVIDED BY:
Company: 100%

PRINTED MATERIALS AVAILABLE FROM:
Institution and company

MANUFACTURERS ASSOCIATION OF THE JAMESTOWN AREA
with
JAMESTOWN COMMUNITY COLLEGE

FLUID ENERGY-HYDRAULIC, PNEUMATIC AND LUBRICATION MAINTENANCE PROGRAM

COMPANY CONTACT:
Charles Turcotte
Executive Director
Manufacturers Association of the Jamestown Area
101 West Fifth Street
Jamestown, NY 14701
(716) 484-1101

INSTITUTIONAL CONTACT:
Rose M. Scott
Director, Development Center for Business
Office for Continuing Education
Jamestown Community College
525 Falconer Street
Jamestown, NY 14701
(716) 665-5220

PROGRAM DESCRIPTION/ OBJECTIVES:
Offered to local industrial maintenance people to assist individuals to learn and to eventually correct problems regarding fluid energy in their respective plants.

PROGRAM INITIATED:
Fall 1985

LENGTH OF STUDY FOR PARTICIPANT:
17 weeks

LENGTH OF CONTRACT:
On-going

LOCATION:
Jamestown Community College Campus, Cummins Engine Company

PARTICIPANTS:
Number: 18
Type: Maintenance Employees

PROGRAM COSTS PROVIDED BY:
Institution: 20%
Company: 80%

JACKSONVILLE ELECTRIC AUTHORITY
with
FLORIDA JUNIOR COLLEGE AT JACKSONVILLE

ELECTRICAL TRADES

COMPANY CONTACT:
Andy Sabol
Training Director
Personnel
Jacksonville Electric Authority
129 King Street
Jacksonville, FL 32204
(904) 389-4104

INSTITUTIONAL CONTACT:
Dr. James R. Myers
Instructional Dean
Occupational Education
Florida Junior College at Jacksonville
101 West State Street
Jacksonville, FL 32202
(904) 633-8284

PROGRAM DESCRIPTION/OBJECTIVES:
To upgrade skills of present employees.

PROGRAM INITIATED:
1980

LENGTH OF STUDY FOR PARTICIPANT:
10 weeks–2 years

LENGTH OF CONTRACT:
Open-ended

LOCATION:
Florida Junior College—Downtown Campus

PARTICIPANTS:
Number: 20–60
Type: Employees

PROGRAM COSTS PROVIDED BY:
Company: 100%

PRINTED MATERIALS AVAILABLE FROM:
Institution

JACKSONVILLE SHIPYARDS, INC.
with
FLORIDA JUNIOR COLLEGE AT JACKSONVILLE

METAL TRADES

COMPANY CONTACT:
Hank Morgan
Assistant Training Director
Personnel
Jacksonville Shipyards, Inc.
P.O. Box 2347
Jacksonville, FL 32203
(904) 355-1711 Ext. 293

INSTITUTIONAL CONTACT:
Dr. James R. Myers
Instructional Dean
Occupational Education
Florida Junior College at Jacksonville
101 West State Street
Jacksonville, FL 32202
(904) 633-8284

PROGRAM DESCRIPTION/OBJECTIVES:
To upgrade skills of present employees.

PROGRAM INITIATED:
1973

LENGTH OF STUDY FOR PARTICIPANT:
10 weeks–1 year

LENGTH OF CONTRACT:
Open-ended

LOCATION:
Florida Junior College—Downtown Campus

PARTICIPANTS:
Number: 40–100 per term
Type: Employees

PROGRAM COSTS PROVIDED BY:
Company: 100%

PRINTED MATERIALS AVAILABLE FROM:
Institution and company

JEWISH HOSPITAL OF ST. LOUIS
with
WEBSTER COLLEGE

DIMENSION III

COMPANY CONTACT:
Henry Langer
Director of Education
Jewish Hospital
216 South Kingshighway
St. Louis, MO 63110
(314) 454-8663

INSTITUTIONAL CONTACT:
Chris Cogger
Corporate Based Education
Webster College
470 East Lockwood
St. Louis, MO 63119
(314) 968-6913

PROGRAM DESCRIPTION/OBJECTIVES:
Program designed to provide 12 hours of college credit in the basic liberal arts through a 3-way approach of closed-circuit TV, weekend sessions and a weekly class.

PROGRAM INITIATED:
1982

LENGTH OF STUDY FOR PARTICIPANT:
1 semester

LENGTH OF CONTRACT:
Ongoing

LOCATION:
Jewish Hospital

PARTICIPANTS:
24 employees from all levels

PROGRAM COSTS PROVIDED BY:
Company: Tuition reimbursement (80% upon completion of course, 100% upon completion of degree)

PRINTED MATERIALS AVAILABLE FROM:
Institution

JOHNNY APPLESEED, INC.*
with
GORDON COLLEGE

COOPERATIVE EDUCATION

COMPANY CONTACT:
Russell W. Copeland
Vice President
Johnny Appleseed, Inc.
54 Dodge Street
Beverly, MA 01915
(617) 922-2040

INSTITUTIONAL CONTACT:
Mary Jane Knudson
Director, Cooperative Education and Career Development
Gordon College
255 Grapevine Road
Wenham, MA 01984
(617) 927-2300, X327

PROGRAM DESCRIPTION/OBJECTIVES:
An educational program for liberal arts students to explore careers and apply theory to practice. It allows employers to examine a pool of qualified recruits as well as fill seasonal and regular personnel needs.

PROGRAM INITIATED:
1978

LENGTH OF STUDY FOR PARTICIPANT:
6 months per co-op placement; 3 placements total

LENGTH OF CONTRACT:
6 months, ongoing

LOCATION:
Various employer sites

PARTICIPANTS:
100 liberal arts students annually

PROGRAM COSTS PROVIDED BY:
Institution: $38,000
Company: Student salaries
Other Source: $57,000 (Title VIII grant)

PRINTED MATERIALS AVAILABLE FROM:
Institution

* Representative entry—complete list available from institution

**JOHNSON MEMORIAL HOSPITAL
with
UNIVERSITY OF HARTFORD**

EFFECTIVE MANAGERIAL SKILLS TRAINING

COMPANY CONTACT:
Peter McGee
Director, Human Resources
Johnson Memorial Hospital
Stafford Springs, CT 06076
(203) 684-4251

INSTITUTIONAL CONTACT:
Gilbert J. Maffeo
Program Development Consultant
Division of Adult Educational Services
University of Hartford
200 Bloomfield Avenue
West Hartford, CT 06117
(203) 243-4350/4381

PROGRAM DESCRIPTION/OBJECTIVES:
To provide basic managerial skills training to hospital supervisors.

PROGRAM INITIATED:
1981

LENGTH OF STUDY FOR PARTICIPANT:
10–12 weeks

LENGTH OF CONTRACT:
10–12 weeks ongoing

LOCATION:
Johnson Memorial Hospital

PARTICIPANTS:
15–25 different levels of management personnel

PROGRAM COSTS PROVIDED BY:
Company: 100%

PRINTED MATERIALS AVAILABLE FROM:
Institution and company

**MULTIPLE COMPANIES*
with
KANSAS CITY ART INSTITUTE**

INTERNSHIP

COMPANY CONTACT:
Specific company not identified

INSTITUTIONAL CONTACT:
Ronald B. Kemnitzer
Associate Professor
Design
Kansas City Art Institute
4415 Warwick Blvd.
Kansas City, MO 64111
(816) 561-4852

PROGRAM DESCRIPTION/OBJECTIVES:
To provide practical experience for students on various aspects of design as it relates to their formal classroom education.

PROGRAM INITIATED:
1975

LENGTH OF STUDY FOR PARTICIPANT:
1 semester

LENGTH OF CONTRACT:
Not available

LOCATION:
Kansas City Art Institute

PARTICIPANTS:
20 juniors and seniors annually

PROGRAM COSTS PROVIDED BY:
Not available

PRINTED MATERIALS AVAILABLE FROM:
Institute

* Representative entry—complete list available from institution.

W.K. KELLOGG FOUNDATION
with
WESTERN MICHIGAN UNIVERSITY

SOUTHWEST MICHIGAN GROUNDWATER SURVEY AND MONITORING PROGRAM

COMPANY CONTACT:
William J. Grove, M.D.
Program Director
W.K. Kellogg Foundation
400 North Avenue
Battle Creek, MI 49017
(616) 968-1611

INSTITUTIONAL CONTACT:
Dr. Jack S. Wood, Director, WESTOPS
Dr. Donald J. Brown, Director, Science for Citizens Center
Western Michigan University
Kalamazoo, MI 49008
(616) 383-0077

PROGRAM DESCRIPTION/OBJECTIVES:
Develop computer-based groundwater data system on location, quantity, quality, and movement as well as related subsurface geology for business and industry for siting, effluent discharge, and resource evaluation decisions.

PROGRAM INITIATED:
January 1, 1985

LENGTH OF STUDY FOR PARTICIPANT:
3 years

LENGTH OF CONTRACT:
3 years

LOCATION:
Western Michigan University

PARTICIPANTS:
25 agencies, firms and local governmental units.

PROGRAM COSTS PROVIDED BY:
Western Michigan University: (in kind) $303,621
W.K. Kellogg Foundation: $418,571
County, State and Federal Agencies: (in kind) $137,050

PRINTED MATERIALS AVAILABLE FROM:
Institution

KENTON COUNTY FISCAL COURT
with
GSI-NORTHERN KENTUCKY UNIVERSITY

COMPREHENSIVE PACKAGE OF SERVICES FOR KENTON COUNTY JAIL

COMPANY CONTACT:
John Nienaber
Director of Administration
Kenton County Fiscal Court
Kenton County
P.O. Box 792
Covington, KY 41012
(606) 491-2801

INSTITUTIONAL CONTACT:
Jon Pierce
Director
Governmental Services Institute
Northern Kentucky University
University College, Northern Kentucky University
1401 Dixie Highway
Covington, KY 41011
(606) 572-5583

PROGRAM DESCRIPTION/OBJECTIVES:
To provide a package of comprehensive services to the Kenton County Jail Facility, i.e., intake, psychological counseling, recreation, physical education, nutrition.

LENGTH OF CONTRACT:
12 months with renewal option
LOCATION:
Kenton County Jail/NKU
PROGRAM COSTS PROVIDED BY:
Company: $25,560

KENTUCKY CABINET FOR HUMAN RESOURCES
with
UNIVERSITY COLLEGE, NORTHERN KENTUCKY UNIVERSITY

RE-EMPLOYMENT CENTER

COMPANY CONTACT:
Kathy McDonald
Branch Manager
Contracts and Compliance
Department of Employment Services
275 E. Main Street
Frankfort, KY 41011
(502) 564-6646

INSTITUTIONAL CONTACT:
E. Jean Rodgers
Director
Re-Employment Center, University College
University College, NKU
West Building, Rm. 7
1401 Dixie Highway
Covington, KY 41011
(606) 572-5654

PROGRAM DESCRIPTION/OBJECTIVES:
To assist workers in the eight counties of Northern Kentucky who face dislocation in a job market unable to absorb them without retraining and access skills. The Center provides a Job Search Workshop, Professional Counseling, Retraining, OJT and Job Development.

LENGTH OF STUDY FOR PARTICIPANT:
Services provided until placed on job.

LENGTH OF CONTRACT:
12 months
LOCATION:
University College, Northern Kentucky University
PARTICIPANTS:
Number: 97
Type: Dislocated Workers
PRINTED MATERIALS AVAILABLE FROM:
Institution

KOHLER COMPANY
with
LAKESHORE TECHNICAL INSTITUTE

GEOMETRIC TOLERANCING AND TRUE POSITION DIMENSIONING

COMPANY CONTACT:
Lloyd Everard
Training Coordinator
Kohler Company
Kohler, WI 53044
(414) 457-4441

INSTITUTIONAL CONTACT:
Steve Smith
Economic Development/Industrial Training
Lakeshore Technical Institute
1290 North Avenue
Cleveland, WI 53015
(414) 684-4408, X247

PROGRAM DESCRIPTION/OBJECTIVES:
Designed to serve industry by training entire employee group in new drafting method of dimensioning.

PROGRAM INITIATED:
1982
LENGTH OF STUDY FOR PARTICIPANT:
30 hours
LENGTH OF CONTRACT:
3 years

LOCATION:
Kohler Company

PARTICIPANTS:
300 engineers, draftsmen, assembly supervisors, and office personnel

PROGRAM COSTS PROVIDED BY:
Company: $16.30 per participant

PRINTED MATERIALS AVAILABLE FROM:
Institution

KOHLER COMPANY
with
LAKESHORE TECHNICAL INSTITUTE

KOHLER SMALL ENGINE SERVICING SCHOOL

COMPANY CONTACT:
Lloyd Everard
Training Coordinator
Kohler Company
Kohler, WI 53044
(414) 457-4441

INSTITUTIONAL CONTACT:
Steve Smith
Economic Development/Industrial Training
Lakeshore Technical Institute
1290 North Avenue
Cleveland, WI 53015
(414) 684-4408, X247

PROGRAM DESCRIPTION/ OBJECTIVES:
Designed to serve industry by providing quality education for dealers through courses presenting information on increased product knowledge and productivity.

PROGRAM INITIATED:
1979

LENGTH OF STUDY FOR PARTICIPANT:
40 hours

LENGTH OF CONTRACT:
1 year

LOCATION:
Lakeshore Technical Institute

PARTICIPANTS:
200 service representatives and dealers (nationwide)

PROGRAM COSTS PROVIDED BY:
Company: $16.30 per participant

PRINTED MATERIALS AVAILABLE FROM:
Institutions

LA CROSSE TELEPHONE CORPORATION
with
WESTERN WISCONSIN TECHNICAL INSTITUTE

SELLING PERSONALITY

COMPANY CONTACT:
Rebecca Faas
Division Staff Personnel Manager
La Crosse Telephone Corporation
206 5th Avenue South
La Crosse, WI 54601
(608) 782-9980

INSTITUTIONAL CONTACT:
Harold P. Erickson
Corporate Campus Administrator
Adult and Continuing Education
Western Wisconsin Technical Institute
Sixth and Vine Streets
La Crosse, WI 54601
(608) 785-9232

PROGRAM DESCRIPTION/ OBJECTIVES:
To increase sales awareness and awareness of profitability principles for every employee of the Telephone Corporation.

PROGRAM INITIATED:
1982

LENGTH OF STUDY FOR PARTICIPANT:
1 quarter

LENGTH OF CONTRACT:
Not available

LOCATION:
Western Wisconsin Technical Institute

PARTICIPANTS:
283 Telephone Company employees

PROGRAM COSTS PROVIDED BY:
Institution: $4,200
Company: $7,641
Other Source: State funds

PRINTED MATERIALS AVAILABLE FROM:
Not reported

LAND O'LAKES CORPORATION
with
IOWA STATE UNIVERSITY

CONSTRUCTION OF IMPROVED STRAINS OF RHIZOBIUM JAPONICUM

COMPANY CONTACT:
Drew Ivers
Research Geneticist
Land O'Lakes Corporation, Inc.
Research Farm, R. R. #2
Webster City, IA 50595

INSTITUTIONAL CONTACT:
Alan G. Atherly
Professor & Chairman
Department of Genetics
8 Curtiss Hall, Iowa State University
Ames, IA 50011
(515) 294-7133

PROGRAM DESCRIPTION/OBJECTIVES:
By understanding the molecular genetics of *Rhizobium japonicum* we hope to eventually construct better bacterial strains with improved nitrogen fixing capabilities with a variety of soybean cultivars.

PROGRAM INITIATED:
April 1, 1983

LENGTH OF STUDY FOR PARTICIPANT:
3 years

LENGTH OF CONTRACT:
6 years

LOCATION:
Iowa State University, Department of Genetics, Ames, IA

PARTICIPANTS:
Number: 6
Type: graduate students and post-doctoral students

PROGRAM COSTS PROVIDED BY:
Institution: In kind
Company: $150,000
Participant: In kind
Other Source: $300,000

LANDS' END YACHT STORES, INC.
with
NORTHEAST IOWA TECHNICAL INSTITUTE

NEW AND EXPANDING BUSINESS AND INDUSTRY TRAINING

COMPANY CONTACT:
Earl Glemp
Vice President of Manufacturing
Lands' End Yacht Stores, Inc.
116 Franklin
West Union, IA 52175
(319) 422-6051

INSTITUTIONAL CONTACT:
Ken Vande Berg
Coordinator of Community Education
Northeast Iowa Technical Institute
P.O. Box 400
Calmar, IA 52132
(319) 562-3263

PROGRAM DESCRIPTION/OBJECTIVES:
To develop a training plan and specific training for industrial sewing machine

operators. To provide funding for expansion within the local industry.

PROGRAM INITIATED:
1982

LENGTH OF STUDY FOR PARTICIPANT:
1 quarter

LENGTH OF CONTRACT:
9 months

LOCATION:
Lands' End Yacht Stores, Inc.

PARTICIPANTS:
64 operators annually

PROGRAM COSTS PROVIDED BY:
Institution: $500
Other Source: $23,509.70 (State of Iowa, Department of Public Instruction)

PRINTED MATERIALS AVAILABLE FROM:
Not available

LEATHER INDUSTRY ANNUAL DISPLAY AND DEMONSTRATION
with
OKLAHOMA STATE TECH

LEATHER INDUSTRY ANNUAL DISPLAY AND DEMONSTRATION OF NEW EQUIPMENT AND METHODS

COMPANY CONTACT:
W.C. Gatlin
Southern Leather and Shoe Company
706 West California
Oklahoma City, OK 73102
(405) 235-0373

INSTITUTIONAL CONTACT:
Earl Bain
Supervisor, Shoe-Boot-Saddle Program
Small Business Trades Department
Oklahoma State Tech
4th and Mission
Okmulgee, OK 74447
(918) 756-6211, X256

PROGRAM DESCRIPTION/ OBJECTIVES:
Provides members of the industry and students with an opportunity to stay current with the field; provides contact opportunities between students and potential employers; provides public awareness of programs in shoe repair, bootmaking, and saddlemaking.

PROGRAM INITIATED:
1978

LENGTH OF STUDY FOR PARTICIPANT:
Not reported

LENGTH OF CONTRACT:
Not reported

LOCATION:
Not reported

PARTICIPANTS:
125

PROGRAM COSTS PROVIDED BY:
Institution: 33%
Company: 67%

PRINTED MATERIALS AVAILABLE FROM:
Not available

LIFE INSURANCE MARKETING AND RESEARCH ASSOCIATION
with
UNIVERSITY OF HARTFORD

EFFECTIVE ORAL PRESENTATION

COMPANY CONTACT:
Peter S. Roberts
Vice President
Life Insurance Marketing and Research Association
8 Farm Sprints
Farmington, CT 06032
(203) 677-0033

INSTITUTIONAL CONTACT:
M. Brady/G. Maffeo
Director, Continuing Education

Division of Adult Educational Services
University of Hartford
200 Bloomfield Avenue
West Hartford, CT 06117
(203) 243-4387

PROGRAM DESCRIPTION/ OBJECTIVES:
Six-week seminar on planning, preparing and delivering oral presentations before both large and small audiences. Training included didactic material as well as speaking practicum and feedback.

PROGRAM INITIATED:
1982

LENGTH OF STUDY FOR PARTICIPANT:
6 half days (24 contact hours)

LENGTH OF CONTRACT:
1 time (for 6 weeks)

LOCATION:
Farmington, CT

PARTICIPANTS:
14 professionals

PROGRAM COSTS PROVIDED BY:
Company: 100%

PRINTED MATERIALS AVAILABLE FROM:
Institution

LOCKHEED MISSILES AND SPACE CORPORATION*
with
EVERGREEN VALLEY COLLEGE

TRANSITION INTO ELECTRONICS

COMPANY CONTACT:
Carol Trammell
Lockheed Missiles and Space
  Corporation
6105 Castleknoll Drive
San Jose, CA 95129
(408) 742-2080
          and
Clara Brock
Lockheed Missiles and Space
  Corporation
19930 Oakmont Drive
Los Gatos, CA 95030
(408) 742-5413

INSTITUTIONAL CONTACT:
Andrew McFarlin
Engineering Instructor and Coordinator
Evergreen Valley College
3095 Yerba Buena Road
San Jose, CA 95135
(408) 274-7900, X6570

PROGRAM DESCRIPTION/ OBJECTIVES:
To provide those with no prior understanding of technical fields of employment in the electronics industry with a realistic exposure to several such fields so that intelligent approach might be made in determining a suitable training program.

PROGRAM INITIATED:
1980

LENGTH OF STUDY FOR PARTICIPANT:
10 weeks

LENGTH OF CONTRACT:
Varies with individual company personnel to teach

LOCATION:
Evergreen Valley College

PARTICIPANTS:
12–24 primarily displaced homemakers, reentry students per semester

PROGRAM COSTS PROVIDED BY:
Institution: 100% the following years
Other Source: 100% the first year from
    Displaced Homemakers Act

PRINTED MATERIALS AVAILABLE FROM:
Institution

* Representative entry—complete list available from institution.

LUCAS CAV*
with
GREENVILLE TECHNICAL COLLEGE

TECHNICAL SCHOLARSHIP PROGRAM

COMPANY CONTACT:
Peter Elliman
Vice President and General Mgr.
Lucas CAV
P.O. Box 5755, Station B
Greenville, SC 29606
(803) 297-1700

INSTITUTIONAL CONTACT:
Marty Jensen
Director, Technical Scholarship Program
Greenville Technical College
P.O. Box 5616, Station B
Greenville, SC 29606
(803) 242-3170

PROGRAM DESCRIPTION/OBJECTIVES:
To equip Greenville people for jobs in area industries by providing classroom theory at Greenville TEC and on-the-job application of this theory at work.

PROGRAM INITIATED:
1979

LENGTH OF STUDY FOR PARTICIPANT:
6 to 11 quarters

LENGTH OF CONTRACT:
No contract

LOCATION:
Greenville Technical College

PARTICIPANTS:
In Fall 1981, 95 associate degree engineering technology and business division students

PROGRAM COSTS PROVIDED BY:
Institution: $29,000
Company: $88,000
Other Source: $89,000 (Title VIII)

PRINTED MATERIALS AVAILABLE FROM:
Institution

* Representative entry—complete list available from institution.

MAIL-WELL ENVELOPE COMPANY*
with
OREGON STATE UNIVERSITY

PRODUCTIVITY BY OBJECTIVES

COMPANY CONTACT:
Pete Gartshore
Vice President
Mail-Well Envelope Company
2515 SW Mail-Well Drive
Milwaukie, OR 97222
(503) 654-3141

INSTITUTIONAL CONTACT:
Jim Riggs
Director, Oregon Productivity Center
Head, Industrial Engineering Department
Oregon State University
Corvallis, OR 97331
(503) 754-4645

PROGRAM DESCRIPTION/OBJECTIVES:
A total productivity program that involves managers and workers. It is heavily oriented to technical training and employee involvement. Features a unique productivity measurement system.

PROGRAM INITIATED:
1980

LENGTH OF STUDY FOR PARTICIPANT:
6 months – 1 year

LENGTH OF CONTRACT:
6 months – 1 year

LOCATION:
At plant site

PARTICIPANTS:
400+ employees and managers

PROGRAM COSTS PROVIDED BY:
Variable, depends on need

PRINTED MATERIALS AVAILABLE FROM:
Institution

* Representative entry—complete list available from institution.

MANUFACTURERS HANOVER TRUST COMPANY
with
HERBERT H. LEHMAN COLLEGE/CUNY

COOPERATIVE EDUCATION PROGRAM

COMPANY CONTACT:
Christine Hobrecht
Assistant Secretary
Manufacturers Hanover Trust Company
320 Park Avenue
New York, NY 10022
(212) 350-3300

INSTITUTIONAL CONTACT:
Joseph Enright
Director of Cooperative Education
Herbert H. Lehman College
Bronx, NY 10468
(212) 960-8366

PROGRAM DESCRIPTION/ OBJECTIVES:
To provide a high quality liberal arts education by creatively combining work experience with theoretical learning. To improve the career opportunities of students. To provide employers with higher quality workers and potential recruits.

PROGRAM INITIATED:
1980

LENGTH OF STUDY FOR PARTICIPANT:
1 semester or 1 semester + summer

LENGTH OF CONTRACT:
1 semester with renewal option

LOCATION:
Not reported

PARTICIPANTS:
300 sophomore, junior, and senior liberal arts majors annually

PROGRAM COSTS PROVIDED BY:
Institution: 100%

PRINTED MATERIALS AVAILABLE FROM:
Institution

NOT REPORTED*
with
MARSHALL UNIVERSITY

COOPERATIVE EDUCATION PROGRAM IN CHEMISTRY AND GEOLOGY

COMPANY CONTACT:
Specific company not identified

INSTITUTIONAL CONTACT:
E.S. Hanrahan
Dean, College of Science
Marshall University
Huntington, WV 28701
(304) 696-2372

PROGRAM DESCRIPTION/ OBJECTIVES:
To improve maturity and employability of graduates and improve relationships with industries.

PROGRAM INITIATED:
1971

LENGTH OF STUDY FOR PARTICIPANT:
Not reported

LENGTH OF CONTRACT:
Informal agreement

LOCATION:
Not reported

PARTICIPANTS:
6–10 interns

PROGRAM COSTS PROVIDED BY:
None

PRINTED MATERIALS AVAILABLE FROM:
Institution

* Representative entry—complete list available from institution.

MARRIOTT'S GREAT AMERICA
with
COLLEGE OF LAKE COUNTY

PREVENTING RETAIL THEFT

COMPANY CONTACT:
Mike Newton
Training and Development Manager
Marriott's Great America
Interstate 94 and Route 132
Gurnee, IL 60031
(312) 249-1776

INSTITUTIONAL CONTACT:
Keri Thiessen
Business/Industry Training Coordinator
Open Campus
College of Lake County
Grayslake, IL 60030
(312) 223-3616

PROGRAM DESCRIPTION/ OBJECTIVES:
Customized course providing information on shoplifter methods and operation, preventive tactics to be taken, and legal considerations of the employee and shoplifter.

PROGRAM INITIATED:
1981

LENGTH OF STUDY FOR PARTICIPANT:
1 day

LENGTH OF CONTRACT:
1 day

LOCATION:
Marriott's Great America

PARTICIPANTS:
27 managers and security personnel

PROGRAM COSTS PROVIDED BY:
Company: $95.20

PRINTED MATERIAL AVAILABLE FROM:
Institution

MARTINDALE-HUBBELL, INC.
with
KEAN COLLEGE OF NEW JERSEY*

CENTER FOR CORPORATE EDUCATION

COMPANY CONTACT:
Suzanne Durang
Vice President
Martindale-Hubbell, Inc.
630 Central Avenue
New Providence, NJ 07974
(201) 464-6800

INSTITUTIONAL CONTACT:
Ethel J. Madsen
Director
Special Programs
Kean College of New Jersey
Morris Avenue
Union, NJ 07083
(201) 527-2163

PROGRAM DESCRIPTION/ OBJECTIVES:
Advisory committee made up of representatives from various companies and from the college assist in conducting needs assessments, designing programs to meet specific needs, providing instruction for credit and non-credit courses, review evaluations, overall planning.

PROGRAM INITIATED:
1979

LENGTH OF STUDY FOR PARTICIPANT:
Varies

LENGTH OF CONTRACT:
Varies

LOCATION:
On campus and on company sites

PARTICIPANTS:
Varying number of employees

PROGRAM COSTS PROVIDED BY:
Institution: 5%
Company: 75%
Participant: 20%

PRINTED MATERIALS AVAILABLE FROM:
Institution

* Representative entry—complete list available from institution.

MARYLAND FEDERAL EMERGENCY MANAGEMENT AGENCY
with
DUNDALK COMMUNITY COLLEGE

FUNDAMENTAL COURSE FOR RADIOLOGICAL RESPONSE TEAMS

COMPANY CONTACT:
Susan Linde
Public Safety, MEMA
Sudbrook Lane and Reisterstown Road
Pikesville, MD 21208
(301) 486-4422

INSTITUTIONAL CONTACT:
Louise Kennard
Coordinator Program Development,
  Office of Continuing Education
Dundalk Community College
7200 Sollers Point Road
Dundalk, MD 21222
(301) 522-5859

PROGRAM DESCRIPTION/ OBJECTIVES:
Courses provides information learning about the latest procedures in measuring radioactive materials in disaster areas. (non-credit)

PROGRAM INITIATED:
January 1985

LENGTH OF STUDY FOR PARTICIPANT:
24 hours

LENGTH OF CONTRACT:
3 days (Friday, Saturday, Sunday)

LOCATION:
Dundalk Community College

PARTICIPANTS:
Number: 25
Type: Employed adult students

PROGRAM COSTS PROVIDED BY:
Other Source: Agency pays tuition

PRINTED MATERIALS AVAILABLE FROM:
Company

COMMONWEALTH OF MASSACHUSETTS DEPARTMENT OF SOCIAL SERVICES
with
UNIVERSITY OF MASSACHUSETTS

UNDERGRADUATE PROGRAM

COMPANY CONTACT:
Douglas Shatkin
Director of Training
Department of Social Services
150 Causeway Street
Boston, MA 02114
(617) 727-0900

INSTITUTIONAL CONTACT:
Barbara M. Buchanan
Director of Field Education
College of Public and Community
  Service
University of Massachusetts

Downtown Center
Boston, MA 02125
(617) 956-1014

PROGRAM DESCRIPTION/ OBJECTIVES:
To provide a curriculum relevant to the career needs of the Department's non-credentialed workers; to impact positively on service delivery through improved worker skills and knowledge; to provide access to the BA degree.

PROGRAM INITIATED:
1981

LENGTH OF STUDY FOR PARTICIPANT:
To completion of BA degree, if desired

LENGTH OF CONTRACT:
12 months with renewal

LOCATION:
University of Massachusetts

PARTICIPANTS:
20–30 non-credential social service staff each semester

PROGRAM COSTS PROVIDED BY:
Institution: 35%
Company: 55%
Participant: 10%

PRINTED MATERIALS AVAILABLE FROM:
Institution and company

MASSILON CITY HOSPITAL
with
KENT STATE UNIVERSITY

HEALTH ASSESSMENT SKILLS

COMPANY CONTACT:
Randy Hilscher
Massilon City Hospital
875 8th Street, NE
Massilon, OH 44646

INSTITUTIONAL CONTACT:
Karen Rylander
Director, Continuing Education

Kent State University
327 Rockwell Hall
Kent, OH 44242
(216) 672-3100

PROGRAM DESCRIPTION/ OBJECTIVES:
Parallels basic health assessment course taught by School of Nursing.

PROGRAM INITIATED:
1982

LENGTH OF STUDY FOR PARTICIPANT:
60 hours

LENGTH OF CONTRACT:
60 hours

LOCATION:
Massilon City Hospital

PARTICIPANTS:
12 registered nurses

PROGRAM COSTS PROVIDED BY:
Company: 100%

PRINTED MATERIALS AVAILABLE FROM:
Institution

MATTHEW BENDER AND COMPANY, INC.*
with
SIENA COLLEGE

INTERNATIONAL STUDIES, FOREIGN LANGUAGES AND BUSINESS PROGRAM

COMPANY CONTACT:
Paul Carter
Director
International Division
Matthew Bender and Company, Inc.
1275 Broadway
Albany, NY 12204
(518) 462-3331

INSTITUTIONAL CONTACT:
James S. Dalton
Program Director, Assistant

Dean, Arts Division
Siena College
Loudonville, NY 12211
(518) 783-2325

PROGRAM DESCRIPTION/ OBJECTIVES:
To provide understanding of and training in international studies and business through the study of language, culture and business practice.

PROGRAM INITIATED:
1980

LENGTH OF STUDY FOR PARTICIPANT:
4 years (certificate program)

LENGTH OF CONTRACT:
Internship semester (120–150 hours for 3 credits)

LOCATION:
Various

PARTICIPANTS:
20–30 students annually

PROGRAM COSTS PROVIDED BY:
Institution: 90%
Company: 10%

PRINTED MATERIALS AVAILABLE FROM:
Institution

* Representative entry—complete list available from institution.

MAYVILLE METALS PRODUCTS COMPANY
with
CENTRAL ARIZONA COLLEGE

MAYVILLE METALS I

COMPANY CONTACT:
Tom Wallangk
Administrative Manager
Mayville Metals Products Company
999 Thornton Road
P.O. Box 999
Casa Grande, AZ 85222
(602) 836-5544

INSTITUTIONAL CONTACT:
Francis E. Colgan
Occupational Dean
Technology Department
Central Arizona College
Woodruff at Overfield Road
Coolidge, AZ 85228
(602) 723-4141

PROGRAM DESCRIPTION/ OBJECTIVES:
Precision measurement tools; precision sheetmetal, frame, blueprint; quality assurance, safety practice and work ethic.

PROGRAM INITIATED:
1982

LENGTH OF STUDY FOR PARTICIPANT:
8 weeks

LENGTH OF CONTRACT:
8 weeks; renewable

LOCATION:
In-plant classroom

PARTICIPANTS:
12 per shift, 2 shifts; all production skills

PROGRAM COSTS PROVIDED BY:
Institution: 25%
Company: 50%
Other Source: 25% (state aid)

PRINTED MATERIALS AVAILABLE FROM:
Institution

MERCY CATHOLIC MEDICAL CENTER
with
GWYNEDD-MERCY COLLEGE

COMPREHENSIVE HOSPITALWIDE EDUCATION PROGRAM

COMPANY CONTACT:
Joseph Malonoski
Vice President Human Resources
Mercy Catholic Medical Center
Lansdowne Avenue and Baily Road

Darby, PA 19023
(215) 237-4000
INSTITUTIONAL CONTACT:
Patricia A. Jackson
Director, HRD
Edmonda Campus
Gwynedd-Mercy College
Lansdowne Avenue and Baily Road
Darby, PA 19023
(215) 237-0440
PROGRAM DESCRIPTION/ OBJECTIVES:
To provide staff development and continuing education to Medical Center employees and community residents.
PROGRAM INITIATED:
1979
LENGTH OF STUDY FOR PARTICIPANT:
Ongoing
LENGTH OF CONTRACT:
Ongoing
LOCATION
Gwynedd Valley, PA
PARTICIPANTS:
2,000 employees of the Medical Center and residents of the community
PROGRAM COSTS PROVIDED BY:
Company: 200,000
PRINTED MATERIALS AVAILABLE FROM:
Institution and company

METROPOLITAN LIFE INSURANCE COMPANY
with
PRINCE GEORGE'S COMMUNITY COLLEGE

PROPERTY AND CASUALTY INSURANCE TRAINING
COMPANY CONTACT:
John Dunn
General Manager
Career Success School
Metropolitan Life Insurance Company
Metropolitan Plaza
Tampa, FL 33607
(813) 871-3174
INSTITUTIONAL CONTACT:
Veronica S. Norwood
Director, Contract Services
Prince George's Community College
301 Largo Road
Largo, MD 20772
(301) 322-0726
PROGRAM DESCRIPTION/ OBJECTIVES:
To provide training which will enable the participants to successfully complete the state of Maryland Insurance Agency Brokers License Qualification Examination.
PROGRAM INITIATED:
1980
LENGTH OF STUDY FOR PARTICIPANT:
96 hours (1 8-hour class per week)
LENGTH OF CONTRACT:
12 weeks
LOCATION:
Prince George's Community College
PARTICIPANTS:
15 insurance salesmen per session
PROGRAM COSTS PROVIDED BY:
Company: 32%
Other Source: 68% (state funds)
PRINTED MATERIALS AVAILABLE FROM:
Institution

METROVISION, INC. AND STORER CABLE, INC.
with
PRINCE GEORGE'S COMMUNITY COLLEGE

CABLE COMMUNICATION WORKSHOP

COMPANY CONTACT:
Susan Wallace
Director, Community Relations
Metrovision, Inc.
211 Perimeter Center Parkway
Suite 930
Atlanta, GA 30346
(800) 241-9271

and

John Margieson
Assistant Manager
Storer Cable of Prince George's County
4314 Farragut Street
Hyattsville, MD 20781
(301) 699-8881

INSTITUTIONAL CONTACT:
Jacques Dubois
Director, Special Academic Areas
Prince George's Community College
301 Largo Road
Largo, MD 20772
(301) 322-0785

PROGRAM DESCRIPTION/OBJECTIVES:
Communicate the potential of cable television as a comprehensive communications resource for business, civic, community, and education uses.

PROGRAM INITIATED:
1982

LENGTH OF STUDY FOR PARTICIPANT:
8 hours

LENGTH OF CONTRACT:
1 day

LOCATION:
Prince George's Community College

PARTICIPANTS:
250 business, community, government, and education leaders.

PROGRAM COSTS PROVIDED BY:
Institution: Time and effort
Company: $1,000 each

PRINTED MATERIALS AVAILABLE FROM:
Institution

MICHIGAN MOLECULAR INSTITUTE
with
CENTRAL MICHIGAN UNIVERSITY

GRADUATE STUDIES IN MACRO-MOLECULAR SCIENCE

COMPANY CONTACT:
Robert Hefner
Acting Director
Michigan Molecular Institute
1910 West St. Andrews Road
Midland, MI 48640
(517) 832-5555

INSTITUTIONAL CONTACT:
Thomas J. Delia
Chairman
Department of Chemistry
Central Michigan University
Mt. Pleasant, MI 48859
(517) 774-3981

PROGRAM DESCRIPTION/OBJECTIVES:
Graduate training in macro-molecular science.

PROGRAM INITIATED:
1973

LENGTH OF STUDY FOR PARTICIPANT:
2 years

LENGTH OF CONTRACT:
12 months with renewal option

LOCATION:
Michigan Molecular Institute

PARTICIPANTS:
3 chemistry graduate students per year

PROGAM COSTS PROVIDED BY:
Company: 100%

PRINTED MATERIALS AVAILABLE FROM:
Institution and company

MICHIGAN REFORMATORY
with
CENTRAL MICHIGAN UNIVERSITY

PRISON EDUCATION PROGRAM

COMPANY CONTACT:
Joseph Wittebols
Treatment Director
Michigan Reformatory
P.O. Box 500
Ionia, MI 48846
(616) 527-2500

INSTITUTIONAL CONTACT:
Lawrence R. Murphy
Director
Institute for Personal and Career
  Development
Central Michigan University
Mt. Pleasant, MI 48859
(517) 774-3865

PROGRAM DESCRIPTION/ OBJECTIVES:
Baccalaureate Degree completion programs: BS in Management and Supervision, Community Development, and on-site counseling and instruction.

PROGRAM INITIATED:
Not reported

LENGTH OF STUDY FOR PARTICIPANT:
Approximately 3 full years

LENGTH OF CONTRACT:
Ongoing

LOCATION:
Michigan Reformatory

PARTICIPANTS:
Approximately 50 incarcerated individuals with AA or equivalent

PROGRAM COSTS PROVIDED BY:
Institution: 55%
Participant: 45%

PRINTED MATERIALS AVAILABLE FROM:
Institution

INDUSTRIAL COMPANIES IN THE STATE OF MICHIGAN
with
THE INSTITUTE OF SCIENCE AND TECHNOLOGY SPECIAL PROJECTS DIVISION THE UNIVERSITY OF MICHIGAN

ECONOMIC DEVELOPMENT ADMINISTRATION (EDA)

COMPANY CONTACT:
N/A

INSTITUTIONAL CONTACT:
Larry Crockett
Director
EDA University Center
Institute of Science and Technology
The University of Michigan
2200 Bonisteel Boulevard
Ann Arbor, MI 48109
(313) 763-9000

PROGRAM DESCRIPTION/ OBJECTIVES:
The Center's main objective is to utilize the technical and business skills available at The University of Michigan and other universities to assist in economic development with an objective of creating or saving jobs in Michigan. The principal form of business assistance is personal consulting and referral of problems to the most qualified available university specialist or other source of assistance.

PROGRAM INITIATED:
1978

LENGTH OF CONTRACT:
1 year, renewed annually

LOCATION:
The University of Michigan or company location

PARTICIPANTS:
Michigan industrial firms

PROGRAM COSTS PROVIDED BY:
The U.S. Department of Commerce
The University of Michigan Participating company

PRINTED MATERIALS AVAILABLE FROM:
Institution

MANUFACTURING FIRMS IN MICHIGAN, OHIO, AND INDIANA
with
THE INSTITUTE OF SCIENCE AND TECHNOLOGY
SPECIAL PROJECTS DIVISION
THE UNIVERSITY OF MICHIGAN

GREAT LAKES TRADE ADJUSTMENT ASSISTANCE CENTER

COMPANY CONTACT:
N/A

INSTITUTIONAL CONTACT:
Mr. Marian Krzyzowski
Director
Great Lakes TAAC
Institute of Science and Technology
The University of Michigan
2200 Bonisteel Boulevard
Ann Arbor, MI 48109
(313) 763-4085

PROGRAM DESCRIPTION/OBJECTIVES:
The program is authorized by the Trade Act of 1974, and managed by the U.S. Department of Commerce to help manufacturing firms hurt by direct import competition.

PROGRAM INITIATED:
January, 1983

LENGTH OF CONTRACT:
1 year, renewed annually

LOCATION:
The University of Michigan or company location

PARTICIPANTS:
Manufacturing firms in Michigan, Ohio, or Indiana hurt by foreign competition from directly competitive products.

PROGRAM COSTS PROVIDED BY:
The U.S. Department of Commerce Participating firms

PRINTED MATERIALS AVAILABLE FROM:
Institution

MASSACHUSETTS INFORMATION SCANNING UNIT
with
RESOURCE CENTER-SALEM STATE COLLEGE

ESSENTIAL DATA FOR GROWING ENTERPRISES

COMPANY CONTACT:
Salvatore Meringold
Head
Massachusetts Information Scanning Unit
University of Massachusetts
University Library
Amherst, MA 01003
(413) 545-4299

INSTITUTIONAL CONTACT:
Maureen Johnson
Director
Resource Center for Business
Salem State College
Alumni House
Salem, MA 01970
(617) 745-0556

PROGRAM DESCRIPTION/OBJECTIVES:
EDGE is a professional research and information service designed to meet the information and research needs of business and industry in such areas as marketing technology, domestic and international competition, etc.

LENGTH OF CONTRACT:
On-going fee based service

LOCATION:
Salem State College

PARTICIPANTS:
Number: 100+ annually (estimate)
Type: North Shore Businesses and Industrial Concerns/Management

PROGRAM COSTS PROVIDED BY:
Company and Participant: Negotiable based upon request.

PRINTED MATERIALS AVAILABLE FROM:
Institution

MIDAS INTERNATIONAL CORPORATION
with
NEW YORK CITY COLLEGE

MIDAS BRAKE SERVICE COURSE

COMPANY CONTACT:
Doug Haviland
Regional Director of Training
Training Department
Midas International Corporation
1525 Jersey Avenue
North Brunswick, NJ 08902
(201) 828-8228

INSTITUTIONAL CONTACT:
Wilford Saunders
Director of Applied Research
Continuing Education
New York City Technical College
450 West 41 Street
New York, NY 10036
(212) 239-1665

PROGRAM DESCRIPTION/OBJECTIVES:
A 42-hour course in brake service covering theory and function of drum and disc brakes; analysis of drum and disc brake design; mechanical and hydraulic systems; fault diagnosis; use of Midas Brake Catalog and Estimating Forms; removal, replacement, and rebuilding procedures; selling brake service; and customer relations.

LENGTH OF STUDY FOR PARTICIPANT:
42 hours

LENGTH OF CONTRACT:
6 weeks

LOCATION:
Voorhees Campus, Room 100

PARTICIPANTS:
Number: 7
Type: Employees of Midas International Corp., mostly mechanics

PROGRAM COSTS PROVIDED BY:
Company: 100%

PRINTED MATERIALS AVAILABLE FROM:
Institution and company

MIDLAND GLASS COMPANY
with
OKLAHOMA STATE TECH

BASIC ELECTRICITY, INTRODUCTION TO MOTORS AND CONTROLS, INTRODUCTION TO ELECTRICAL WIRING

COMPANY CONTACT:
Jim Glynn
Personnel Director
Midland Glass Company
Henryetta, OK 74437
(918) 652-9631

INSTITUTIONAL CONTACT:
Bill J. Lyons
Department Head
Electrical-Electronics Technology
Oklahoma State Tech
4th and Mission
Okmulgee, OK 74447
(918) 756-6211, X252

PROGRAM DESCRIPTION/ OBJECTIVES:
Shorter training time for entry level electricians, training in areas of expertise not available at Midland Glass Company.

PROGRAM INITIATED:
1981

LENGTH OF STUDY FOR PARTICIPANT:
Not reported

LENGTH OF CONTRACT:
Not reported

LOCATION:
Not reported

PARTICIPANTS:
30 employees annually

PROGRAM COSTS PROVIDED BY:
Company: 100%

PRINTED MATERIALS AVAILABLE FROM:
Not available

MIDSTATE TELEPHONE COMPANY
with
JAMESTOWN COMMUNITY COLLEGE

PLANNING FOR YOUR RETIREMENT

COMPANY CONTACT:
William Kelly
Director of Training
Midstate Telephone Company
525 Falconer Street
Jamestown, NY 14701
(716) 665-5220

INSTITUTIONAL CONTACT:
Rose M. Scott
Continuing Education Assistant
Jamestown Community College
525 Falconer Street
Jamestown, NY 14701
(716) 665-5220

PROGRAM DESCRIPTION/ OBJECTIVES:
This program affords company employees approximately 50 years of age and/or older, the vehicle through which they can take a serious look at retirement. Participants of the program will be made aware of a wide scope of retirement interests including such matters as the potential for future opportunities (and pitfalls), good health, where to live, legal security, optimum financial security, preparations for changing role and expansion of new interests, a possible second (or third) career, techniques of good personal management, and preparation for widowhood.

PROGRAM INITIATED:
Not reported

LENGTH OF STUDY FOR PARTICIPANT:
8 weeks

LENGTH OF CONTRACT:
12 months — renewal option

LOCATION:
Midland Telephone Company

PARTICIPANTS:
24 personnel ten years away from retirement or closer per class

PROGRAM COSTS PROVIDED BY:
Institution: 40%
Company: 20%
Other Source: 20%

PRINTED MATERIALS AVAILABLE FROM:
Not available

MID METRO ECONOMIC DEVELOPMENT GROUP
with
TRITON COLLEGE

MID METRO ECONOMIC DEVELOPMENT GROUP

COMPANY CONTACT:
Conrad Kiebles
Executive Director
Mid Metro
714 Lake Street
Oak Park, IL 60301
(312) 524-8770

INSTITUTIONAL CONTACT:
Dr. David Kozlowski
Associate Vice President
Economic Development
Triton College
2000 5th Avenue
River Grove, IL 60171
(312) 456-0300

PROGRAM DESCRIPTION/ OBJECTIVES:
This is a joint effort to promote and improve economic development in western Cook county. Offering federal procurement assistance, general business assistance, site selection and obtainment for new business.

PROGRAM INITIATED:
1983

LOCATION:
Oak Park, IL

PRINTED MATERIALS AVAILABLE FROM:
Company

CITY OF MILWAUKEE*
with
ALVERNO COLLEGE

OFF CAMPUS EXPERIENTIAL LEARNING

COMPANY CONTACT:
Barry Zalben
Research Coordinator
Legislative Reference Bureau
City of Milwaukee
Milwaukee, WI 53202
(414) 278-2295

INSTITUTIONAL CONTACT:
Marilyn Thanos
Director
Off Campus Experiential Learning Program
Alverno College
3401 S. 39 Street
Milwaukee, WI 53215
(414) 647-3792

PROGRAM DESCRIPTION/ OBJECTIVES:
Both liberal arts and professional area students work in business or service agencies. Business mentor benefits from student involvement; student learns to learn in non-academic setting.

PROGRAM INITIATED:
1971

LENGTH OF STUDY FOR PARTICIPANT:
Mentor, 3 hour orientation session; student, concurrent seminar

LENGTH OF CONTRACT:
1 semester each

LOCATION:
Alverno College and businesses

PARTICIPANTS:
100–125 students, professionals in particular fields each semester

PROGRAM COSTS PROVIDED BY:
Absorbed by institution and businesses in operating expenses.

PRINTED MATERIALS AVAILABLE FROM:
Institution

* Representative entry—complete list available from institution.

MINNESOTA MINING & MANUFACTURING
with
LAKEWOOD COMMUNITY COLLEGE

3M-LAKEWOOD COOPERATIVE PROGRAM

COMPANY CONTACT:
Ray Haas
Director
Education & Training
Minnesota Mining & Manufacturing
St. Paul, MN 55144
(612) 733-1110

INSTITUTIONAL CONTACT:
Monica Manning
Dean of Community Service
Lakewood Community College
3401 Century Avenue North
White Bear Lake, MN 55110
(612) 770-1331, X140

PROGRAM DESCRIPTION/ OBJECTIVES:
To provide college courses, academic advising and recognition by credit for on-the-job experience leading to an Associate of Arts degree and transfer to a baccalaureate institution.

PROGRAM INITIATED:
1982

LENGTH OF STUDY FOR PARTICIPANT:
6 months–3 years

LENGTH OF CONTRACT:
12 months

LOCATION:
3M Center

PARTICIPANTS:
Employees of information systems and data processing

PROGRAM COSTS PROVIDED BY:
Institution: $4,000
Company: $10,000 + tuition

PRINTED MATERIALS AVAILABLE FROM:
Institution

MISSISSIPPI POWER COMPANY*
with
MISSISSIPPI STATE UNIVERSITY

COOPERATIVE EDUCATION PROGRAM

COMPANY CONTACT:
Gene Lowery
Personnel Representative
Human Resources
Mississippi Power Company
Box 4079
Gulfport, MS 39501
(601) 865-5511

INSTITUTIONAL CONTACT:
Luther Epting
Director of Cooperative Education
Mississippi State University
P.O. Box M
Mississippi State, MS 39762
(601) 325-3823

PROGRAM DESCRIPTION/ OBJECTIVES:
To provide students an opportunity to receive relevant work experience directly related to the major field of study; to provide employing organizations a quality source of motivated mature employees that may be retained at graduation.

PROGRAM INITIATED:
1955

LENGTH OF STUDY FOR PARTICIPANT:
5 years inclusive of minimum of 1 year of practical experience obtained by alternating semesters of school and work.

LENGTH OF CONTRACT:
No formal contract required

LOCATION:
Throughout the United States

PARTICIPANTS:
502 students of various majors except architecture annually**

PROGRAM COSTS PROVIDED BY:
Institution: $200.00 per student
Company: Pays students a salary plus fringe benefits
Participants: $35.00 per each work semester

PRINTED MATERIALS AVAILABLE FROM:
Institution

* Representative entry—complete list available from institution.
** Figures given reflect the entire program.

MOBIL OIL CORPORATION
with
PRINCETON UNIVERSITY

TEN DAYS AT PRINCETON

COMPANY CONTACT:
Jack Ballard
Foreign Executive Development Program
Fund for Multinational Management Education
684 Park Avenue
New York, NY 10021
(212) 535-9386

INSTITUTIONAL CONTACT:
William H. O'Brien, Jr.
Director, Center for Visitor and Conference Services
Prospect House
Princeton, NJ 08544
(609) 452-3371

PROGRAM DESCRIPTION/OBJECTIVES:
To provide an intensive study of American society in a scholarly atmosphere which presents a picture of American society to assist foreign national executives obtain a better perspective on U.S. management styles.

PROGRAM INITIATED:
1979

LENGTH OF STUDY FOR PARTICIPANT:
10 days

LENGTH OF CONTRACT:
Not reported

LOCATION:
Princeton University

PARTICIPANTS:
40 foreign executives annually

PROGRAM COSTS PROVIDED BY:
Institution: $2,500
Participant: $2,100
Other Source: Mobil Corporation

PRINTED MATERIALS AVAILABLE FROM:
Company

MONTANA DAKOTA UTILITIES
with
UNIVERSITY OF NORTH DAKOTA

RENEWABLE ENERGY INSTITUTE

COMPANY CONTACT:
Warren Saterlee
Montana Dakota Utilities
Bismarck, ND 58501
(701) 258-0005

INSTITUTIONAL CONTACT:
Don V. Mathsen
Acting Director

Engineering Experiment Station
University of North Dakota
Box 8103, University Station
Grand Forks, ND 58202
(701) 777-3120

PROGRAM DESCRIPTION/ OBJECTIVES:
To research and develop concepts on renewable energy from the view point of the electric utility and the consumer.

PROGRAM INITIATED:
1981

LENGTH OF STUDY FOR PARTICIPANT:
Dependent on participant and project

LENGTH OF CONTRACT:
Renewed annually

LOCATION:
University of North Dakota

PARTICIPANTS:
About 15 students and faculty in mechanical engineering

PROGRAM COSTS PROVIDED BY:
Institution: 30%
Company: 70%

PRINTED MATERIALS AVAILABLE FROM:
Institution

MONSANTO COMPANY
with
WASHINGTON UNIVERSITY

PRODUCTIVITY IMPROVEMENT/ PROCESS OPTIMIZATION

COMPANY CONTACT:
G.T. Kennedy
Director of Training
Corporate Training Department
Monsanto Company
800 North Lingbergh Blvd.
St. Louis, MO 63166
(314) 694-1000

INSTITUTIONAL CONTACT:
M.P. Dudukovic
Program Director
Chemical Engineering Department
Washington University
Campus Box 1198
St. Louis, MO 63130
(314) 869-6082

PROGRAM DESCRIPTION/ OBJECTIVES:
This program is designed to broaden the background of those with previous engineering degrees, particularly chemical, electrical, and mechanical engineering and for those with career experience in or with the desire to enter a full-time career in the area of process control. Course materials are uniquely tailored to match the skills and knowledge required for the chemical engineer participant, primarily emphasizing process control, computer control, industrial electronics, and analytical instrumentation. Emphasis for the electrical and mechanical engineer will, in addition, include courses to provide the understanding of chemical process control systems.

PROGRAM INITIATED:
1977

LENGTH OF STUDY FOR PARTICIPANT:
1 year (93 trimesters and a 2-week pre-course review)

LENGTH OF CONTRACT:
1 year renewable

LOCATION:
Washington University

PARTICIPANTS:
10 senior chemical, electrical, and mechanical Monsanto engineers annually (Program also open to employees of other companies.)

PROGRAM COSTS PROVIDED BY:
Institution: Course design
Company: 100%

PRINTED MATERIALS AVAILABLE FROM:
Institution

PRINTED MATERIALS AVAILABLE FROM:
Institution

MONTANA POWER COMPANY
with
MILES COMMUNITY COLLEGE

POWER PLANT TECHNOLOGY

COMPANY CONTACT:
Blair Ricks
Director of Employee Development
Montana Power Company
40 East Broadway
Butte, MT 59701
(406) 723-5421, X2830

INSTITUTIONAL CONTACT:
Dr. John Koch
Dean of College Services
Miles Community College
2715 Dickinson
Miles City, MT 59301
(406) 232-3031, X16

PROGRAM DESCRIPTION/ OBJECTIVES:
To train entry level personnel for coal fired electrical generation facilities (mechanic, operator, business administration).

PROGRAM INITIATED:
1978

LENGTH OF STUDY FOR PARTICIPANT:
3 years

LENGTH OF CONTRACT:
Open-ended

LOCATION:
Colstrip

PARTICIPANTS:
40 employees

PROGRAM COSTS PROVIDED BY:
Institution: $25,000
Company: $100,000
Other Source: $20,000

MT. SINAI HOSPITAL
with
UNIVERSITY OF HARTFORD

MANAGEMENT TRAINING FOR HOSPITAL NURSES

COMPANY CONTACT:
Ronald Waack
Director of Nursing
Mt. Sinai Hospital
Blue Hills Avenue
Hartford, CT 06112
(203) 242-4431

INSTITUTIONAL CONTACT:
M. Brady/B. Koerner
Director, Continuing Education
Division of Adult Educational Services
University of Hartford
200 Bloomfield Avenue
West Hartford, CT 06117
(203) 243-4387

PROGRAM DESCRIPTION/ OBJECTIVES:
Introduction to management principles and practices for first line supervisors and middle managers in acute hospital nursing.

PROGRAM INITIATED:
1982

LENGTH OF STUDY FOR PARTICIPANT:
8 weeks with follow-up (30 hours)

LENGTH OF CONTRACT:
1 time (pilot) with possible renewal

LOCATION:
Mt. Sinai Hospital

PARTICIPANTS:
25 professional nurses

PROGRAM COSTS PROVIDED BY:
Company: 100%

DIRECTORY OF CAMPUS-BUSINESS LINKAGES   193

PRINTED MATERIALS AVAILABLE FROM:
Institution

NASA, GODDARD SPACE FLIGHT CENTER
with
PRINCE GEORGE'S COMMUNITY COLLEGE

BEGINNING AND INTERMEDIATE FRENCH FOR TECHNICAL PERSONNEL

COMPANY CONTACT:
Carolyn Casey
Employee Development Specialist
NASA Goddard Space Flight Center
Greenbelt, MD 20771
(301) 344-5086

INSTITUTIONAL CONTACT:
Veronica S. Norwood
Director, Contract Services
Prince George's Community College
301 Largo Road
Largo, MD 20772
(301) 322-0726

PROGRAM DESCRIPTION/OBJECTIVES:
To provide beginning and intermediate French language and culture instruction for personnel subject to foreign assignment, to enable them to communicate with citizens of French-speaking countries.

PROGRAM INITIATED:
1978

LENGTH OF STUDY FOR PARTICIPANT:
Beginning: 80 hours (2 1-hour classes per week); Intermediate: 40 hours (1 1-hour class per week)

LENGTH OF CONTRACT:
40 weeks

LOCATION:
Goddard Space Flight Center

PARTICIPANTS:
10 technical personnel per class

PROGRAM COSTS PROVIDED BY:
Company: 64%
Other Source: 36% (state fund)

PRINTED MATERIALS AVAILABLE FROM:
Institution

NASA
with
UNIVERSITY CITY SCIENCE CENTER (U.C.S.C.)

BIOPROCESSING AND PHARMACEUTICAL RESEARCH CENTER

COMPANY CONTACT:
Dr. Richard E. Halpern
Director, Microgravity Science & Applications Division
National Aeronautics & Space Administration (NASA)
Code EN, NASA Headquarters
Washington, DC 20546

INSTITUTIONAL CONTACT:
Dr. Paul Todd
Director
Bioprocessing and Pharmaceutical Research Center
3401 Market Street
Philadelphia, PA 19104
(215) 386-9600

PROGRAM DESCRIPTION:
The NASA-related Bioprocessing and Pharmaceutical Center is a Center of Excellance with a focus on the communication of research expertise and knowledge to industrial and academic researchers.

LENGTH OF STUDY:
3 years

LOCATION:
UCSC

PARTICIPANTS:
Number: 50 annually
Type: Senior corporate and university biomedical, microbiological, medical, immunological, electrical, mechanical researchers.

PROGRAM COSTS PROVIDED BY:
Institution: $100,000
Company: $1,350,000
Participant: $250,000
Other Sources: $500,000

PRINTED MATERIALS AVAILABLE FROM:
Institution

NATIONAL ASSOCIATION OF BANK WOMEN
with
MUNDELEIN COLLEGE

NABW/MUNDELEIN COLLEGE MANAGEMENT PROGRAM

COMPANY CONTACT:
Anne L. Bryant
Educational Director
National Association of Bank Women
500 North Michigan Avenue
Suite 1400
Chicago, IL 60611
(312) 661-1700

INSTITUTIONAL CONTACT:
Vivian Wilson, BVM
Assistant Director, Admissions
Mundelein College
6363 North Sheridan Road
Chicago, IL 60660
(312) 262-8100, X473

PROGRAM DESCRIPTION/ OBJECTIVES:
To provide management major in a quick format for people in banking and other financial institutions.

PROGRAM INITIATED:
1977

LENGTH OF STUDY FOR PARTICIPANT:
12 weeks spread over 3 years at 2-week sessions twice each year

LENGTH OF CONTRACT:
Ongoing

LOCATION:
Mundelein College

PARTICIPANTS:
Between 20 and 40 promotable banking employees per 2-week session

PROGRAM COSTS PROVIDED BY:
$1,575 per 2-week session provided by either company or participant

PRINTED MATERIALS AVAILABLE FROM:
Institution

NATIONAL ASSOCIATION OF BANK WOMEN
with
SIMMONS COLLEGE

NATIONAL ASSOCIATION OF BANK WOMEN/SIMMONS COLLEGE BACHELOR'S DEGREE PROGRAM

COMPANY CONTACT:
Anne Bryant
Educational Director
National Association of Bank Women
500 North Michigan Avenue
Suite 1400
Chicago, IL 60611
(312) 661-1700

INSTITUTIONAL CONTACT:
Louise Comeau
Program Director
Continuing Education
Simmons College
300 The Fenway
Boston, MA 02115
(617) 738-2141

DIRECTORY OF CAMPUS-BUSINESS LINKAGES

PROGRAM DESCRIPTION/ OBJECTIVES:
To provide a high quality curriculum in management which leads to a Bachelor's degree for women who are employed full-time. Students learn on a part-time basis by attending 6 2-week institutes.

PROGRAM INITIATED:
1976

LENGTH OF STUDY FOR PARTICIPANT:
3–5 years

LENGTH OF CONTRACT:
3–5 years

LOCATION:
Simmons College

PARTICIPANTS:
4 middle management women

PROGRAM COSTS PROVIDED BY:
Company: Approximately $3,200 to $4,800
Participant: Partial payment by some participants

PRINTED MATERIALS AVAILABLE FROM:
Institution

NATIONAL ASSOCIATION OF CREDIT MANAGEMENT
with
UNIVERSITY OF HARTFORD

BUSINESS CREDIT MANAGEMENT PROGRAM

COMPANY CONTACT:
Maurice Margotta
Director of Education
Nat. Assoc. of Credit Management
475 Park Avenue South
New York, NY
(212) 578-4433

INSTITUTIONAL CONTACT:
A.L. Zander
Director
Office of University College/Continuing
  Prof. Development
University of Hartford
200 Bloomfield Avenue
West Hartford, CT 06117
(203) 243-4371

PROGRAM DESCRIPTION/ OBJECTIVES:
The University offers 4 different professional level certificate programs for adults who work in and aspire to careers in commercial/industrial credit and finance.

PROGRAM INITIATED:
1984

LENGTH OF CONTRACT:
An annual offering

LOCATION:
University of Hartford

PARTICIPANTS:
Entry level and credit persons with some job experience in the field and a degree in marketing, economics, accounting management, finance, general business administration or liberal arts.

PROGRAM COSTS PROVIDED BY:
Company and Participant

PRINTED MATERIALS AVAILABLE FROM:
Institution

NATIONAL CREDIT UNION INSTITUTE
with
UNIVERSITY OF WISCONSIN EXTENSION

CREDIT UNION ACCOUNTING (A58)

COMPANY CONTACT:
Glenn C. Hoyle
Director
National Credit Union Institute
Credit Union National Association, Inc.
P.O. Box 431

Madison, WI 53701
(608) 231-4051

INSTITUTIONAL CONTACT:
Phil Rowin
Program Assistant
Business and Management/Economics
University of Wisconsin-Extension
One South Park Street, Room 759
Madison, WI 53706
(608) 262-4876

PROGRAM DESCRIPTION/ OBJECTIVES:
To provide participants with knowledge necessary to function at a higher level of understanding and problem-solving within their credit union in the area of accounting.

PROGRAM INITIATED:
1979

LENGTH OF STUDY FOR PARTICIPANT:
1 year

LENGTH OF CONTRACT:
6 months with renewal option

LOCATION:
University of Wisconsin—Extension

PARTICIPANTS:
300 credit union employees in each course

PROGRAM COSTS PROVIDED BY:
Institution: 50%
Company: 50%

PRINTED MATERIALS AVAILABLE FROM:
Institution and company

NATIONAL CREDIT UNION INSTITUTE
with
UNIVERSITY OF WISCONSIN— EXTENSION

CREDIT UNION MANAGEMENT (M55)

COMPANY CONTACT:
Glenn C. Hoyle
Director
National Credit Union Institute
Credit Union National Association, Inc.
P.O. Box 431
Madison, WI 53701
(608) 231-4051

INSTITUTIONAL CONTACT:
Phil Rowin
Program Assistant
Business and Management/Economics
University of Wisconsin-Extension
One South Park Street, Room 759
Madison, WI 53706
(608) 262-4876

PROGRAM DESCRIPTION/ OBJECTIVES:
To provide participants with knowledge necessary to function at a higher level of understanding and problem-solving within their credit union in the area of management.

PROGRAM INITIATED:
1971

LENGTH OF STUDY FOR PARTICIPANT:
1 year

LENGTH OF CONTRACT:
6 months with renewal option

LOCATION:
University of Wisconsin-Extension

PARTICIPANTS:
300 credit union employees in each course

PROGRAM COSTS PROVIDED BY:
Institution: 50%
Company: 50%

PRINTED MATERIALS AVAILABLE FROM:
Institution and company

NATIONAL LIFE OF VERMONT AT JOHNSON STATE COLLEGE

A.B. DEGREE AT NATIONAL LIFE OF VERMONT

COMPANY CONTACT:
Elmer Kelley
Personnel Management, Development and Training
National Life of Vermont
National Life Drive
Montpelier, VT 05656
(802) 229-3333

INSTITUTIONAL CONTACT:
William A. Cook
Academic Dean
Academic Affairs
Johnson State College
Johnson, VT 05656
(802) 635-2356, ext. 220

PROGRAM DESCRIPTION/OBJECTIVES:
Associate of Science degree program in general business offered on location for employees at National Life of Vermont. Objectives: provide convenient and complete degree program related to employee needs and business needs.

PROGRAM INITIATED:
1983

LENGTH OF STUDY FOR PARTICIPANT:
5 years

LENGTH OF CONTRACT:
Not limited

LOCATION:
Montpelier, VT

PARTICIPANTS:
Number: 70+ National Life employees per semester.
Type: 30 degree, 40 non-degree

PROGRAM COSTS PROVIDED BY:
Company: 67%
Participant: 33%

PRINTED MATERIALS AVAILABLE FROM:
Institution

NATIONAL MINE SAFETY AND HEALTH ACADEMY with MARSHALL UNIVERSITY

MASTER'S DEGREE PROGRAM IN MINE SAFETY EDUCATION

COMPANY CONTACT:
Not reported

INSTITUTIONAL CONTACT:
James Stone
Associate Professor
Marshall University
Harris Hall
Huntington, WV 25701
(304) 696-2380

PROGRAM DESCRIPTION/OBJECTIVES:
To improve the safety record in mines (coal, etc.).

PROGRAM INITIATED:
1979

LENGTH OF STUDY FOR PARTICIPANT:
Not reported

LENGTH OF CONTRACT:
Not reported

LOCATION:
Not reported

PARTICIPANTS:
80 full-time

PROGRAM COSTS PROVIDED BY:
Institution: $40,000

PRINTED MATERIALS
AVAILABLE FROM:
Not reported

NATIONAL TOOLING AND MACHINING ASSOCIATION, RHODE ISLAND/ SOUTHEASTERN MASSACHUSETTS CHAPTER
with
COMMUNITY COLLEGE OF RHODE ISLAND

MACHINE PROCESSES, PROGRAMS FOR APPRENTICES AND JOURNEYMEN

COMPANY CONTACT:
Mrs. Whitney Frost
Executive Secretary
Rhode Island/Southeastern
  Massachusetts Chapter
National Tooling and Machining
  Association
RFD Bayview Road
Bradford, RI 02808
(401) 322-7669

INSTITUTIONAL CONTACT:
Richard P. Anderson
Coordinator
Business and Industry
Community College of Rhode Island
Flanagan Campus
Louis Quisset Pike
Lincoln, RI 02865
(401) 333-7128

PROGRAM DESCRIPTION/
OBJECTIVES:
The program satisfies the 144 hour/year of related instruction required by the Bureau of Apprenticeship and Training. Apprentices receive college credit for the classroom theory portion of the apprenticeship program and on-the-job training of individuals completing the program requirements.

LENGTH OF STUDY FOR
PARTICIPANTS:
3 years, part time, evenings

LENGTH OF CONTRACT:
Continuing

LOCATION:
Community College of Rhode Island, Knight Campus, Warwick, RI 02886

PARTICIPANTS:
Number: 125
Type: Apprentices and journeymen machinists and toolmakers

PROGRAM COSTS PROVIDED BY:
Participants: $32 per credit hour

PRINTED MATERIALS
AVAILABLE FROM:
Institution

NAVAL UNDERWATER SYSTEMS CENTER, NEWPORT, RI
with
COMMUNITY COLLEGE OF RHODE ISLAND

INTRODUCTION TO SIGN LANGUAGE I AND II

COMPANY CONTACT:
Mr. Walter Mey
Employee Development Officer
Code 085
Naval Underwater Systems Center
Building 109
Newport, RI
(401) 841-4602

INSTITUTIONAL CONTACT:
Richard P. Anderson
Coordinator
Business and Industry
Community College of Rhode Island
Flanagan Campus
Louis Quisset Pike
Lincoln, RI 02865
(401) 333-7128

PROGRAM DESCRIPTION/ OBJECTIVES:
To provide supervisors and staff on N.V.S.C. with skills which enable them to communicate in sign English, both expressively and receptively. Participants are expected to attain competency with 500 signs and a working knowledge of American Sign Language.

PROGRAM INITIATED:
October 1984

LENGTH OF CONTRACT:
2 12-week sessions

LOCATION:
Naval Underwater Systems Center, Newport, RI

PARTICIPANTS:
Number: 15
Type: Supervisors and staff

PROGRAM COSTS PROVIDED BY:
Company

PRINTED MATERIALS AVAILABLE FROM:
Institution

NCR CORPORATION
with
CORNELL UNIVERSITY

TRAINING AND DEVELOPMENT PROGRAM: AN OVERVIEW

COMPANY CONTACT:
Theodore J. Settle
Program Development and Evaluation Director
NCR Management College and Career Development Center
NCR Corporation
101 West Schantz
Dayton, OH 45479
(513) 445-2346

INSTITUTIONAL CONTACT:
Dr. Donald Kane
Program Director
School of Industrial and Labor Relations
Cornell University
P.O. Box 1000
Ithaca, NY 14853
(607) 256-4462

PROGRAM DESCRIPTION/ OBJECTIVES:
Provide an overview and experience with the critical elements of the course development process.

PROGRAM INITIATED:
1981

LENGTH OF STUDY FOR PARTICIPANT:
4 consecutive days

LENGTH OF CONTRACT:
1 program

LOCATION:
NCR Corporate Education Center, Dayton, OH

PARTICIPANTS:
20 NCR educators

PROGRAM COSTS PROVIDED BY:
Company: 100%

PRINTED MATERIALS AVAILABLE FROM:
Institution

NCR CORPORATION
with
OHIO STATE UNIVERSITY

FIELD ENGINEER EDUCATION

COMPANY CONTACT:
Theodore J. Settle
Program Development and Evaluation Director
NCR Management College and Career Development Center
NCR Corporation
101 West Schantz
Dayton, OH 45479
(513) 445-2346

INSTITUTIONAL CONTACT:
James Buffer
Director, Office of Research and
  Development Service
College of Education
Ohio State University
1945 North High Street
Columbus, OH 43210
(614) 422-7231

PROGRAM DESCRIPTION/ OBJECTIVES:
Improving systems to develop instructional program which prepare field engineers to become acquainted with new products.

PROGRAM INITIATED:
1981

LENGTH OF STUDY FOR PARTICIPANT:
Not available

LENGTH OF CONTRACT:
1 year

LOCATION:
Dayton, OH

PARTICIPANTS:
Not available

PROGRAM COSTS PROVIDED BY:
Company: 100%

PRINTED MATERIALS AVAILABLE FROM:
Institution

NCR CORPORATION
with
OHIO UNIVERSITY/
EDUCATIONAL TESTING
SERVICE

COMPUTERIZED CAREER GUIDANCE SYSTEM FOR ADULTS

COMPANY CONTACT:
Anne Ayres-Gerhart
Corporate Career Planning and
  Development
NCR Corporation
101 West Schantz
Dayton, OH 45479
(513) 445-2376

INSTITUTIONAL CONTACT:
Betty Menson
Director, Adult Learning Services
Ohio University
Tupper Hall 309
Athens, OH 45701
(614) 594-6569

PROGRAM DESCRIPTION/ OBJECTIVES:
To develop a computerized career guidance system for adults which is patterned after SIGI, a current system which is oriented toward high school and early college-age students.

PROGRAM INITIATED:
1982

LENGTH OF STUDY FOR PARTICIPANT:
Not available

LENGTH OF CONTRACT:
Not available

LOCATION:
Princeton, NJ

PARTICIPANTS:
Not available

PROGRAM COSTS PROVIDED BY:
Other Source: 100% (ETS/Kellogg)

PRINTED MATERIALS AVAILABLE FROM:
Institution: (ETS)

NCR CORPORATION*
with
TRI-COUNTY TECHNICAL
COLLEGE

ELECTRONICS TECHNICIAN (FAST TRACK)

COMPANY CONTACT:
Fred Parks
Manufacturing Engineer

NCR Corporation
1150 Anderson Drive
Liberty, SC 29657
(803) 843-2711

INSTITUTIONAL CONTACT:
Ronald N. Talley
Director, Comprehensive Manpower Training
Tri-County Technical College
P.O. Box 587
Pendleton, SC 29670
(803) 646-8361

PROGRAM DESCRIPTION/ OBJECTIVES:
To provide accelerated training for electronics technicians. Eligible applicants are selected from among persons who are currently unemployed.

PROGRAM INITIATED:
1981

LENGTH OF STUDY FOR PARTICIPANT:
12 months

LENGTH OF CONTRACT:
12 months

LOCATION:
Tri-County Technical College

PARTICIPANTS:
18 electronic technicians annually

PROGRAM COSTS PROVIDED BY:
Institution: Indirect
Company: Indirect
Other Source: $65,131 (federal funds)

PRINTED MATERIALS AVAILABLE FROM:
Institution

* Representative entry—complete list available from institution.

NCR CORPORATION
with
UNIVERSITY OF DAYTON

EXECUTIVE DEVELOPMENT PROGRAM

COMPANY CONTACT:
Theodore J. Settle
Program Development and Evaluation Director
NCR Management College and Career Development Center
NCR Corporation
101 West Schantz
Dayton, OH 45479
(513) 445-2346

INSTITUTIONAL CONTACT:
William Hoben
Dean, School of Business Administration
University of Dayton
Dayton, OH 45469
(513) 229-3731

PROGRAM DESCRIPTION/ OBJECTIVES:
To increase managers' awareness of the legal, political, technological, social, and cultural environments and their impact on a multinational company.

PROGRAM INITIATED:
1980

LENGTH OF STUDY FOR PARTICIPANT:
8 weeks, 3 hours per week

LENGTH OF CONTRACT:
1 program

LOCATION:
University of Dayton

PARTICIPANTS:
50 high level executives per program

PROGRAM COSTS PROVIDED BY:
Company: 100%

PRINTED MATERIALS AVAILABLE FROM:
Company

NCR CORPORATION
with
UNIVERSITY OF MICHIGAN

CAREER MOVEMENT OF NCR EMPLOYEES

COMPANY CONTACT:
Theodore J. Settle
Program Development and Evaluation Director
NCR Management College and Career Development Center
NCR Corporation
101 West Schantz
Dayton, OH 45479
(513) 445-2346

INSTITUTIONAL CONTACT:
Andrea Foote
Institute of Labor and Industrial Relations
University of Michigan and Wayne State University
401 Fourth Street
Ann Arbor, MI 48103
(313) 763-1187

PROGRAM DESCRIPTION/OBJECTIVES:
A comprehensive research study of career movement of NCR employees to identify career paths.

PROGRAM INITIATED:
1981

LENGTH OF STUDY FOR PARTICIPANT:
Not available

LENGTH OF CONTRACT:
12 months

LOCATION:
University of Michigan

PARTICIPANTS:
Not available

PROGRAM COSTS PROVIDED BY:
Company: 100%

PRINTED MATERIALS AVAILABLE FROM:
Institution and company

NEW YORK TELEPHONE COMPANY
with
NEW YORK CITY TECHNICAL COLLEGE

N.Y. TELEPHONE DEVELOPMENTAL STUDIES

COMPANY CONTACT:
Julie Dimler
Staff Manager
Education Career Development
New York Telephone Company
11 West 42nd Street Room 1309
New York, NY 10036
(212) 398-7383

INSTITUTIONAL CONTACT:
Barbara Ritchin
Director of Contract Programs
Continuing Education
New York City Technical College
450 West 41st Street Room 501
New York, NY 10036
(212) 239-1664

PROGRAM DESCRIPTION/OBJECTIVES:
The New York Telephone Developmental Studies Program is composed of three types of skills development: basic skills, professional career skills, and technical skills. Within these three areas, the following courses are offered: math, writing, language skills, public speaking, problem solving and decision making, professional report writing; interpersonal skills, basic and advanced typing, basic electricity, basic electronics, word processing, computer literacy, office procedures, and grammar and usage. While most courses are non-credit, one has been granted college credit. In addition, 2 certificate training programs will be offered: technical training and clerical training.

LENGTH OF STUDY FOR PARTICIPANT:
Each course has individual requirements with hours ranging from 28 to 120 total

meeting hours. Students take a variety of courses each semester.

LENGTH OF CONTRACT:
Contract lasts for 1 year, renewable each year. Contract has been in existence between the 2 organizations since 1981.

LOCATION:
Classes meet at N.Y.C.T.C.'s 2 campuses, Manhattan and Brooklyn.

PARTICIPANTS:
Number: Approximately 700–800 each year
Type: Program open to all employees at New York Telephone—clerical, craft, supervisory, etc.

PROGRAM COSTS PROVIDED BY:
Company: 75%
Participant: 25%

PRINTED MATERIALS AVAILABLE FROM:
Institution

THE NORTH AMERICAN COAL CORPORATION*
with
MARY COLLEGE

ENERGY MANAGEMENT/AREA OF EMPHASIS

COMPANY CONTACT:
Richard Espeland
Director of Personnel
The North American Coal Corporation
Kirkwood Office Tower
Bismarck, ND 58501
(701) 258-2200

INSTITUTIONAL CONTACT:
Fran Gronberg
Coordinator, Areas of Emphasis
Mary College
Apple Creek Road
Bismarck, ND 58501
(701) 255-4681, X328

PROGRAM DESCRIPTION/OBJECTIVES:
Designed to qualify persons in supervisory and management roles in the energy industry. May term courses give general background in the energy field, with the internships providing guaranteed summer employment and on-location learning experiences with a major energy company or agency.

PROGRAM INITIATED:
1979

LENGTH OF STUDY FOR PARTICIPANT:
3 May terms and 3 3-month internships

LENGTH OF CONTRACT:
12 month renewable

LOCATION:
May term at Mary College; internships at business location

PARTICIPANTS:
12 business administration/accounting undergraduate majors annually

PROGRAM COSTS PROVIDED BY:
Institution: 50%
Company: 50%

PRINTED MATERIALS AVAILABLE FROM:
Institution

* Representative entry—complete list available from institution.

NORTHEAST UTILITIES
with
UNIVERSITY OF HARTFORD

ON-SITE MBA COURSES

COMPANY CONTACT:
William Naughton
Northeast Utilities
P.O. Box 270
Hartford, CT 06101
(203) 249-5711

INSTITUTIONAL CONTACT:
William T. George
Program Development Consultant
Division of Adult Educational Services
University of Hartford
200 Bloomfield Avenue
West Hartford, CT 06117
(203) 243-4507/4381

PROGRAM DESCRIPTION/ OBJECTIVES:
8 to 10 courses from the CORE MBA sequence.

PROGRAM INITIATED:
1981

LENGTH OF STUDY FOR PARTICIPANT:
Self-paced

LENGTH OF CONTRACT:
2 years

LOCATION:
Berlin, CT

PARTICIPANTS:
Approximately 80 employees

PROGRAM COSTS PROVIDED BY:
Company: 75%
Participant: 25%

PRINTED MATERIAL AVAILABLE FROM:
Institution

NORTHERN KENTUCKY UNIVERSITY
with
COLLEGE OF BUSINESS

SMALL BUSINESS DEVELOPMENT CENTER

INSTITUTIONAL CONTACT:
Roger C. Marshall
Director
Management & Marketing
Northern Kentucky University
Highland Heights, KY 41076
(606) 572-6558

PROGRAM DESCRIPTION/ OBJECTIVES:
To provide individualized counseling and training to small business people in the eight county Area Development District of Northern Kentucky.

LENGTH OF STUDY FOR PARTICIPANT:
Average of 20 hours individual counseling first 90 days

LENGTH OF CONTRACT:
Continuing

LOCATION:
BEP 461

PARTICIPANTS:
Number: 120 current (over 400 Past)
Type: Small businesses of all varieties

PROGRAM COSTS PROVIDED BY:
Institution: $15,000
Other Sources: $36,000

PRINTED MATERIALS AVAILABLE FROM:
Institution

NORTHERN KENTUCKY UNIVERSITY
with
ECONOMICS AND FINANCE DEPARTMENT

REAL ESTATE PROGRAM

COMPANY CONTACT:
Dr. Tom Cate
Chairperson
Economics & Finance
Northern Kentucky University
Nunn Drive
Highland Heights, KY 41076
(606) 572-5153

INSTITUTIONAL CONTACT:
Dr. Roger C. Meade
Director
Economics & Finance
Northern Kentucky University
Nunn Drive

Highland Heights, KY 41076
(606) 572-5370

PROGRAM DESCRIPTION/ OBJECTIVES:
To provide an associate degree in real estate

LENGTH OF STUDY FOR PARTICIPANT:
2 years

LOCATION:
Northern Kentucky University

PARTICIPANTS:
Number: 35 per class

PROGRAM COSTS PROVIDED BY:
Institution: $34,571 and/or 54%
Other Sources: $29,700 and/or 46%

PRINTED MATERIALS AVAILABLE FROM:
Institution

NORTHERN STATES POWER
with
UNIVERSITY OF
NORTH DAKOTA

RENEWABLE ENERGY INSTITUTE

COMPANY CONTACT:
Conrad Aas
Northern State Power
Minneapolis, MN 55440
(612) 330-5500

INSTITUTIONAL CONTACT:
Don V. Mathsen
Acting Director
Engineering Experiment Station
University of North Dakota
Box 8103, University Station
Grand Forks, ND 58202
(701) 777-3120

PROGRAM DESCRIPTION/ OBJECTIVES:
To research and develop concepts on renewable energy from the viewpoint of the electric utility and the consumer.

PROGRAM INITIATED:
1981

LENGTH OF STUDY FOR PARTICIPANT:
Dependent on participant and project

LENGTH OF CONTRACT:
Renewed annually

LOCATION:
University of North Dakota

PARTICIPANTS:
About 15 students and faculty in mechanical, electrical, and chemical engineering

PROGRAM COSTS PROVIDED BY:
Institution: 30%
Company: 70%

PRINTED MATERIALS AVAILABLE FROM:
Institution

NORTHWEST FOOD PROCESSORS ASSOCIATION*
with
OREGON STATE UNIVERSITY

PRODUCTIVITY BY OBJECTIVES

COMPANY CONTACT:
Dave Click
Executive Director
Northwest Food Processors Association
2828 SW Corbett
Portland, OR 97201
(503) 226-2848

INSTITUTIONAL CONTACT:
Jim Riggs
Director, Oregon Productivity Center
Head, Industrial Engineering
  Department
Oregon State University
Corvallis, OR 97331
(503) 754-4645

PROGRAM DESCRIPTION/ OBJECTIVES:
Provides company with opportunity for productivity interfirm comparisons.

PROGRAM INITIATED:
1980

LENGTH OF STUDY FOR PARTICIPANT:
6 months to 1 year

LENGTH OF CONTRACT:
6 months to 1 year

LOCATION:
At plant site

PARTICIPANTS:
400+ employees and managers

PROGRAM COSTS PROVIDED BY:
Variable, depends on need

PRINTED MATERIALS AVAILABLE FROM:
Institution

* Representative entry—complete list available from institution.

NORSK HYDRO ALUMINUM COMPANY*
with
BREVARD COMMUNITY COLLEGE

TRAINING OF ON-LINE EMPLOYEES FOR ALUMINUM EXTRUSION COMPANY

COMPANY CONTACT:
Charles Hayes
Plant Manager
Norsk Hydro Aluminum Company
Rockledge, FL 32955
(305) 636-8147

INSTITUTIONAL CONTACT:
Maurice F. Buckner
Dean, Continuing Education
Brevard Community College
1519 Clearlake Road
Cocoa, FL 32922
(305) 632-1111, X263

PROGRAM DESCRIPTION/ OBJECTIVES:
To provide specialized skills in operation of extrusion processes.

PROGRAM INITIATED:
1979

LENGTH OF STUDY FOR PARTICIPANT:
5 weeks

LENGTH OF CONTRACT:
12 months, non-renewable

LOCATION:
Brevard Community College

PARTICIPANTS:
92 laborers to skilled machinists

PROGRAM COSTS PROVIDED BY:
Institution: $3,000
Company: $3,000
Other Source: $12,850 (Industrial Services grant from Florida Department of Education)

PRINTED MATERIALS AVAILABLE FROM:
Institution

* Representative entry—complete list available from institution.

NORTON COMPANY
with
WORCESTER STATE COLLEGE

COLLABORATIVE MANAGEMENT DEVELOPMENT PROGRAM

COMPANY CONTACT:
John Conn
Manager, Organizational and Employee Development
Norton Company
One New Bond Street
Worcester, MA 01606
(617) 853-1000

INSTITUTIONAL CONTACT:
Dr. David H. Quist
Dean, Division of Graduate and Continuing Education
Worcester State College
486 Chandler Street

Worcester, MA 01602
(617) 793-8100

PROGRAM DESCRIPTION/OBJECTIVES:
To develop a new continuing education pool while meeting the needs of local companies; to provide practical training for entry-level managers; careerpath development, college credit, skill development.

PROGRAM INITIATED:
1981

LENGTH OF STUDY FOR PARTICIPANT:
21 credits; 2 years average

LENGTH OF CONTRACT:
Agreement has no termination date

LOCATION:
Norton Company plant and WSC campus

PARTICIPANTS:
50–60 entry-level and middle managers

PROGRAM COSTS PROVIDED BY:
Institution: $845 per participant
Company: $845 per participant
Participant: $100

PRINTED MATERIALS AVAILABLE FROM:
Institution

NUTRI-SYSTEMS
with
COLLEGE OF LAKE COUNTY

THE ART OF DRAWING BLOOD
COMPANY CONTACT:
Robert Sheridan
Manager
Nutri-Systems
2424 Washington
Waukegan, IL 60085
(312) 662-0615

INSTITUTIONAL CONTACT:
Keri Thiessen
Business/Industry Training Coordinator

Open Campus
College of Lake County
Grayslake, IL 60030
(312) 223-3616

PROGRAM DESCRIPTION/OBJECTIVES:
To provide nurses with phlebotomy techniques to be utilized on weight reducing clientele.

PROGRAM INITIATED:
1982

LENGTH OF STUDY FOR PARTICIPANT:
1 day

LENGTH OF CONTRACT:
1 day

LOCATION:
Nutri-Systems

PARTICIPANTS:
6 nurses

PROGRAM COSTS PROVIDED BY:
Company: $31.00

PRINTED MATERIALS AVAILABLE FROM:
Institution

OAKLAND POLICE DEPARTMENT
with
MERRITT COLLEGE

JOINT POLICE ACADEMY
COMPANY CONTACT:
R. Crawford
Sergeant, Training
Oakland Police Department
455 Washington Street
Oakland, CA 94607
(415) 273-3552

INSTITUTIONAL CONTACT:
Kenneth Giles
Assistant Dean
Technical Division
Merritt College
12500 Campus Drive

Oakland, CA 94619
(415) 436-2427
**PROGRAM DESCRIPTION/
OBJECTIVES:**
Training of police officers with pre-police students. Allows for students to receive training prior to becoming a police officer.
PROGRAM INITIATED:
1981
LENGTH OF STUDY FOR PARTICIPANT:
1 year
LENGTH OF CONTRACT:
1 year
LOCATION:
Oakland Police Department
PARTICIPANTS:
7 Administration of Justice students
PROGRAM COSTS PROVIDED BY:
Institution: $12,000
Company: $12,000
PRINTED MATERIALS AVAILABLE FROM:
Institution

OAKLAND YOUTH WORKS
with
MERRITT COLLEGE

OAKLAND YOUTH WORKS
COMPANY CONTACT:
Joan Dark
Director
Oakland Youth Works
1515 Webster Street
Oakland, CA 94612
(415) 763-9890
INSTITUTIONAL CONTACT:
Wesley Ingram
Counselor
Career Center
Merritt College
12500 Campus Drive

Oakland, CA 94619
(415) 436-2447
**PROGRAM DESCRIPTION/
OBJECTIVES:**
Place students ages 17–21 in part-time jobs related to their studies. Provide screening preemployment and supportive services in order to give employer a better performing employee.
PROGRAM INITIATED:
1980
LENGTH OF STUDY FOR PARTICIPANT:
At least 1 semester
LENGTH OF CONTRACT:
At least 1 semester
LOCATION:
Merritt College
PARTICIPANTS:
6 business, primarily data processing and electronics students per semester
PROGRAM COSTS PROVIDED BY:
Institution: Staff salary
Company: Youth Works support staff
Other Source: Placement companies provide student salaries
PRINTED MATERIALS AVAILABLE FROM:
Institution and company

OCCIDENTAL EXPLORATION &
PRODUCTION COMPANY
with
CALIFORNIA STATE COLLEGE,
BAKERSFIELD

MANAGEMENT INTERNSHIP
PROGRAM
COMPANY CONTACT:
Julie Pinsent
Recruiting Representative
Employee Relations
Occidental Exploration & Production
 Company
5000 Stockdale Highway

Bakersfield, CA 93309
(805) 395-8586

INSTITUTIONAL CONTACT:
Thomas J. Orr, II
Coordinator
Management Internship Program
California State College, Bakersfield
9001 Stockdale Highway
Bakersfield, CA 93311-1099
(805) 833-2151

PROGRAM DESCRIPTION/ OBJECTIVES:
Provide opportunity for students to gain relevant, career-related experience. Interns gain experience in the working world and have an exceptional opportunity to personally participate in career and management-related positions.

PROGRAM INITIATED:
1979

LENGTH OF STUDY FOR PARTICIPANT:
3 quarters

LENGTH OF CONTRACT:
12 months with grant renewal option

LOCATION:
California State College, Bakersfield

PARTICIPANTS:
Number: 20
Type: Juniors, seniors, and graduates

PROGRAM COSTS PROVIDED BY:
Other Source: Federal grant monies

PRINTED MATERIALS AVAILABLE FROM:
Institution

OHIO EDISON*
with
THE UNIVERSITY OF AKRON

COOPERATIVE EDUCATION

COMPANY CONTACT:
Herb Lowelien
Director of Personnel
Ohio Edison
76 South Main Street
Akron, OH 44308
(216) 382-2607

INSTITUTIONAL CONTACT:
Ralph B. McNerney
Director, Cooperative Education
The University of Akron
212 Gardner Student Center
Akron, OH 44235
(216) 375-6723

PROGRAM DESCRIPTION/ OBJECTIVES:
Alternating and parallel system co-op programs available. Students seek co-op employment in career related, paid work experiences. The university seeks to place 4,000 students between 1981 and 1986.

PROGRAM INITIATED:
1913

LENGTH OF STUDY FOR PARTICIPANT:
¾ semester

LENGTH OF CONTRACT:
1 semester with renewal option

LOCATION:
Nationwide

PARTICIPANTS:
575 students currently available from 4 colleges, in 28 major fields annually

PROGRAM COSTS PROVIDED BY:
Institution: $67,000
Other Source: $94,000 (federal grant)

PRINTED MATERIALS AVAILABLE FROM:
Institution

* Representative entry—complete list available from institution

OKC REFINING COMPANY
with
OKLAHOMA STATE TECH

INTRODUCTION TO MOTORS AND CONTROLS, INTERMEDIATE MOTORS AND CONTROLS

COMPANY CONTACT:
Not available

INSTITUTIONAL CONTACT:
Bill J. Lyons
Department Head
Electrical-Electronics Technology
Oklahoma State Tech
4th and Mission
Okmulgee, OK 74447
(918) 756-6211, X252

PROGRAM DESCRIPTION/OBJECTIVES:
To enhance the employee's competence in the regular routine maintenance of the facilities.

PROGRAM INITIATED:
1980

LENGTH OF STUDY FOR PARTICIPANT:
Not reported

LENGTH OF CONTRACT:
Not reported

LOCATION:
Not reported

PARTICIPANTS:
24 employees annually

PROGRAM COSTS PROVIDED BY:
Company: 100%

PRINTED MATERIALS AVAILABLE FROM:
Not available

OKLAHOMA ASSOCIATION OF DRYCLEANERS
with
OKLAHOMA STATE TECH

OKLAHOMA ASSOCIATION OF DRYCLEANERS ANNUAL SEMINAR/WORKSHOP

COMPANY CONTACT:
Dorothy Bennett
Executive Secretary
State Drycleaners Board
4001 North Lincoln
Oklahoma City, OK 73105
(405) 521-2395

INSTITUTIONAL CONTACT:
Lloyd Bennett
Supervisor, Drycleaning Program
Small Business Trades Department
Oklahoma State Tech
4th and Mission
Okmulgee, OK 74447
(918) 756-6211, X207

PROGRAM DESCRIPTION/OBJECTIVES:
To promote greater appreciation of drycleaning procedures; provide students opportunities to gain better understanding of industry procedures; enhance job placement prospects for students and provide institutional advertisement.

PROGRAM INITIATED:
1981

LENGTH OF STUDY FOR PARTICIPANT:
Not reported

LENGTH OF CONTRACT:
Not reported

LOCATION:
Not reported

PARTICIPANTS:
115 annually

PROGRAM COSTS PROVIDED BY:
Institution: 20%
Company: 80%

PRINTED MATERIALS AVAILABLE FROM:
Institution

OLD BEN COAL COMPANY
with
REND LAKE COLLEGE

UNDERGROUND REPAIRMAN TRAINING PROGRAM

COMPANY CONTACT:
Jim Spiller
Director of Training
Old Ben Coal Company
Main Office
Benton, IL 62812
(618) 435-8176

INSTITUTIONAL CONTACT:
Carroll Turner
Dean, Vocational Technical Education
Rend Lake College
RR 1
Ina, IL 62846
(618) 437-5321

PROGRAM DESCRIPTION/OBJECTIVES:
To provide skill training for underground miners going from laborer classification to repairman.

PROGRAM INITIATED:
1975

LENGTH OF STUDY FOR PARTICIPANT:
29 weeks

LENGTH OF CONTRACT:
Ongoing with termination notice

LOCATION:
Rend Lake College

PARTICIPANTS:
466 underground repairmen over the past 6 years

PROGRAM COSTS PROVIDED BY:
Company: 25% (facilities and equipment)
Other Source: 75% (state and local funds)

PRINTED MATERIALS AVAILABLE FROM:
Not available

ORE-IDA FOODS, INC.
with
THE UNIVERSITY OF AKRON

TAKING OFF

COMPANY CONTACT:
Nancy Brannon
Safety and Personnel Director
Ore-Ida Foods, Inc.
P.O. Box 567
Massillon, OH 44646
(216) 833-4151

INSTITUTIONAL CONTACT:
Pauline Russell
Program Associate
Adult Resource Center
The University of Akron
Akron, OH 44235
(216) 275-7448

PROGRAM DESCRIPTION/OBJECTIVES:
To help participants develop knowledge about themselves, adult development, and opportunities for growth. To develop skills in communication, time management, decision making, and goal setting.

PROGRAM INITIATED:
1981

LENGTH OF STUDY FOR PARTICIPANT:
10 hours

LENGTH OF CONTRACT:
1 workshop

LOCATION:
Ore-Ida Foods

PARTICIPANTS:
12 staff of all levels

PROGRAM COSTS PROVIDED BY:
Company: 100%

PRINTED MATERIALS AVAILABLE FROM:
Not available

OUR WAY, INC.
with
GEORGIA INSTITUTE OF TECHNOLOGY

INSTRUCTING TECHNIQUES

COMPANY CONTACT:
Don Hood
Employee Relations Mgr.
Personnel
Our Way, Inc.
P.O. Box 267
Tucker, GA 30085
(404) 491-1577

INSTITUTIONAL CONTACT:
Dr. Roberson
Director
Industrial Education
Ga. Institute of Technology
225 North Avenue
Atlanta, GA 30332
(404) 894-3950

PROGRAM DESCRIPTION/ OBJECTIVES:
To develop supervisory training skills. Includes emphasis on safety, proper physical placement during training, positive reinforcement.

LENGTH OF STUDY FOR PARTICIPANT:
16 hours

LENGTH OF CONTRACT:
16 hours

LOCATION:
Our Way, Inc.

PARTICIPANTS:
Number: 7
Type: Supervisory

PROGRAM COSTS PROVIDED BY:
Institution: $690
Company: $1,150

PRINTED MATERIALS AVAILABLE FROM:
Institution

PENNSYLVANIA ELECTRIC COMPANY
with
INDIANA UNIVERSITY OF PENNSYLVANIA

PENELEC/IUP PERSONNEL DEVELOPMENT TRAINING PROGRAM

COMPANY CONTACT:
Denny Strawmire
Coordinator of Training
Pennsylvania Electric Company
1001 Broad Street
CEED Building
Johnstown, PA 15907
(814) 533-8425

INSTITUTIONAL CONTACT:
Director, Business, Industry and Labor
School of Continuing Education
Indiana University of Pennsylvania
Stright Hall
Indiana, PA 15705
(412) 357-2227

PROGRAM DESCRIPTION/ OBJECTIVES:
CPM courses (3 courses in purchasing and materials management); contract law course; grievance resolution; water treatment for boilers and cooling towers; and other training areas.

PROGRAM INITIATED:
1976

LENGTH OF STUDY FOR PARTICIPANT:
8 weeks—1 semester

LENGTH OF CONTRACT:
Semester and annual with renewal option

LOCATION:
Various industrial sites and IUP campus

PARTICIPANTS:
100+ office personnel, generation personnel, supervisors, and middle management annually

PROGRAM COSTS PROVIDED BY:
Institution: $3,150
Company: $10,500 (course-by-course basis determines fee structure)

PRINTED MATERIALS AVAILABLE FROM:
Institution

PENNSYLVANIA POWER & LIGHT CO.
with
LUZERNE COUNTY COMMUNITY COLLEGE

COMPANY CONTACT:
James White
Supervisor, Training Support
Nuclear Department
Pennsylvania Power and Light Co.
P.O. Box 467
Berwick, PA 18603
(717) 542-3512

INSTITUTIONAL CONTACT:
Nancy Kosteleba
Luzerne County Community College
(717) 829-7353

PROGRAM DESCRIPTION/OBJECTIVES:
Provide courses in the basic sciences, arts/humanities to support associate degree in nuclear power plant operations. Courses will be available on micro computer system.

LENGTH OF STUDY FOR PARTICIPANTS:
Courses average 3 credit hours each.

LENGTH OF CONTRACT:
3 years

LOCATION:
Nanticoke, PA

PARTICIPANTS:
Number: 12
Type: Plant operators, I & C technicians, H/P Technicians

PRINTED MATERIALS AVAILABLE FROM:
Institution

PENNSYLVANIA POWER AND LIGHT
with
WILKES COLLEGE AND PENNSYLVANIA STATE UNIVERSITY—HAZLETON

ON-SITE COLLEGE CREDIT COURSES

COMPANY CONTACT:
James White
Supervisor
Training Support Services
Nuclear Department
Pennsylvania Power and Light
P.O. Box 467
Berwick, PA 18603
(717) 542-2149

INSTITUTIONAL CONTACT:
Larry Gingrich
Assistant Director
Continuing Education
Pennsylvania State University—Hazleton
Highacres
Hazleton, PA 18201
(717) 454-8731

PROGRAM DESCRIPTION/OBJECTIVES:
Provide college credit courses at a convenient location and time.

PROGRAM INITIATED:
1981

LENGTH OF CONTRACT:
Informal agreement

LOCATION:
Susquehanna Training Center

PARTICIPANTS:
Approximately 70 employees

PROGRAM COSTS PROVIDED BY:
Company: $180 per person
Participant: Books

PRINTED MATERIALS AVAILABLE FROM:
Not available

PETROSERVE
with
MARYMOUNT COLLEGE OF VIRGINIA

INTENSIVE ENGLISH INSTRUCTION

COMPANY CONTACT:
Mr. Abdulaziz Gabel
Training Supervisor
PETROSERVE
Computer Sciences Corporation
Herndon, VA 22072

INSTITUTIONAL CONTACT:
Mrs. Nyla Carney
Coordinator, Intensive English Program
Marymount College of Virginia
Arlington, VA 22207

LENGTH OF STUDY FOR PARTICIPANT:
1 year

LENGTH OF CONTRACT:
2 years

PROGRAM COSTS PROVIDED BY:
Institution: $36,000
Company: $48,000

PFIZER, INC.
with
MARYMOUNT MANHATTAN COLLEGE

PFIZER/MARYMOUNT MANHATTAN COLLEGE PROGRAM

COMPANY CONTACT:
Steve Shapiro
Training Department
Pfizer, Inc.
235 East 42nd Street
New York, NY 10021
(212) 573-7268

INSTITUTIONAL CONTACT:
Joyce Kaffel
Director, Corporate Education Programs
Marymount Manhattan College
New York, NY 10021
(212) 472-3800

PROGRAM DESCRIPTION/OBJECTIVES:
To provide Pfizer employees with an opportunity to take courses leading to a baccalaureate degree, a certificate in business management, or specific courses deemed valuable for career development. Courses are offered at the company training center at convenient hours.

PROGRAM INITIATED:
1977

LENGTH OF STUDY FOR PARTICIPANT:
Academic year

LENGTH OF CONTRACT:
Ongoing

LOCATION:
Pfizer, Inc.

PARTICIPANTS:
As of 1982, 80 participants of various educational levels and backgrounds.

PROGRAM COSTS PROVIDED BY:
Company: 100% of current tuition.

PHILIP MORRIS, U.S.A.
with
JOHN TYLER COMMUNITY COLLEGE

PHILIP MORRIS CERTIFICATE IN MANAGEMENT STUDIES

COMPANY CONTACT:
Carson Tucker
Manager, Management Development
Philip Morris, U.S.A.
P.O. Box 26603
Richmond, VA 23261
(804) 274-3404

INSTITUTIONAL CONTACT:
Samuel L. Hancock
Director, Continuing Education
Division of Continuing Education
John Tyler Community College
13101 Jefferson Davis Highway
Chester, VA 23831
(804) 796-4111

PROGRAM DESCRIPTION/ OBJECTIVES:
To provide a core management training program for employees who currently are in, or who may wish in the future to fill, key leadership and management positions at Philip Morris.

PROGRAM INITIATED:
1980

LENGTH OF STUDY FOR PARTICIPANT:
10 quarters, 1 course each quarter

LENGTH OF CONTRACT:
Ongoing

LOCATION:
Richmond, VA

PARTICIPANTS:
25 company employees

PROGRAM COSTS PROVIDED BY:
Institution: Instructors' salaries
Company: Tuition, books, and facilities

PRINTED MATERIALS AVAILABLE FROM:
Institution

PHILLIPS PETROLEUM COMPANY
with
OKLAHOMA STATE TECH

BASIC INSTRUMENTATION

COMPANY CONTACT:
Rex Miller
Gas Measurement and Instrument Superintendent
Phillips Petroleum Company
Okmulgee, OK 74447
(918) 756-4151

INSTITUTIONAL CONTACT:
Bill J. Lyons
Department Head
Electrical-Electronics Technology
Oklahoma State Tech
4th and Mission
Okmulgee, OK 74447
(918) 756-6211, X252

PROGRAM DESCRIPTION/ OBJECTIVES:
Petroleum and natural gas pump station operators in the process and control of facilities similar to those to which they are presently assigned.

PROGRAM INITIATED:
1982

LENGTH OF STUDY FOR PARTICIPANT:
Not reported

LENGTH OF CONTRACT:
Not reported

LOCATION:
Not reported

PARTICIPANTS:
48 employees annually

PRINTED MATERIALS AVAILABLE FROM:
Institution

PROGRAM COSTS PROVIDED BY:
Company: 100%

PRINTED MATERIALS PROVIDED BY:
Not available

PICKENS FOOTWARE COMPANY
with
GEORGIA INSTITUTE OF TECHNOLOGY

COMMUNICATIONS FOR MANAGEMENT

COMPANY CONTACT:
Milton Isenberg
Vice-President of Manufacturing
Pickens Footware Company
800 Hood Road
Jasper, GA 30143
(404) 692-2401

INSTITUTIONAL CONTACT:
Dr. Roberson
Director
Industrial Education Department
Ga. Institute of Technology
225 North Avenue
Atlanta, GA 30332
(404) 894-3950

PROGRAM DESCRIPTION/OBJECTIVES:
Theory and case studies in communication.

LENGTH OF STUDY FOR PARTICIPANT:
4 hours total length

LOCATION:
Jasper, Georgia

PARTICIPANTS:
Number: 30
Type: All management levels

PROGRAM COSTS PROVIDED BY:
Company: $464.00

PRINTED MATERIALS AVAILABLE FROM:
Institution

PIONEER HI-BRED INTERNATIONAL
with
IOWA STATE UNIVERSITY

THE MUTATOR SYSTEM AND TRANSPOSABLE ELEMENTS IN MUTATOR-PIONEER LINE OF MAIZE

COMPANY CONTACT:
Mr. Jack Cavanah
Pioneer Hi-Bred International, Inc.
P.O. Box 38
Johnston, IA 50131

INSTITUTIONAL CONTACT:
David W. Morris and Donald S. Robertson
Department of Genetics
Iowa State University
8 Curtiss Hall
Ames, IA 50011

PROGRAM DESCRIPTION/OBJECTIVES:
An investigation into the origin of Mutator systems and transposable Mul elements in maize. Mutator is characterized by its ability to induce mutations at a large number of loci at rates 30 to 50 times higher than other maize lines. A thorough understanding of what Mutators are, where they come from, and how prevelant they are in commercial and other lines of maize.

PROGRAM INITIATED:
1983

LENGTH OF STUDY FOR PARTICIPANT:
2 years

LENGTH OF CONTRACT:
1 year, renewable

LOCATION:
Iowa State University, Genetics Lab

PARTICIPANTS:
Number: 4
Type: 2 professors; 1 technician, research; 1 graduate student

PROGRAM COSTS PROVIDED BY:
Institution: 40%
Company: 60%

PRINTED MATERIALS AVAILABLE FROM:
Institution

PORTAGE COUNTY CETA
with
KENT STATE UNIVERSITY

STAFF DEVELOPMENT

COMPANY CONTACT:
Maureen Frederick
Portage County CETA
449 Meridian
Ravenna, OH 44266
(216) 297-5741

INSTITUTIONAL CONTACT:
Karen Rylander
Director, Continuing Education
Kent State University
327 Rockwell Hall
Kent, OH 44242
(216) 672-3100

PROGRAM DESCRIPTION/OBJECTIVES:
Includes overviews of communication skills, motivation, problem-solving, time management, and team building.

PROGRAM INITIATED:
1981

LENGTH OF STUDY FOR PARTICIPANT:
8 hours

LENGTH OF CONTRACT:
8 hours

LOCATION:
Portage County CETA

PARTICIPANTS:
25 staff members

PROGRAM COSTS PROVIDED BY:
Company: 100%

PRINTED MATERIALS AVAILABLE FROM:
Institution

PRATT & WHITNEY AIRCRAFT
with
MANCHESTER COMMUNITY COLLEGE

MANCHESTER COMMUNITY COLLEGE/PRATT & WHITNEY AIRCRAFT COOPERATIVE PROGRAM

COMPANY CONTACT:
Robert C. Barnes
Manager, Educational Programs
Pratt & Whitney Aircraft
400 Main Street
East Hartford, CT 06108
(203) 565-7008

INSTITUTIONAL CONTACT:
R. Dianne K. McHutchinson
Director, Contract and Grants
Community Services Division
Manchester Community College
MS #5, P.O. Box 1046
Manchester, CT 06040
(203) 646-5838

PROGRAM DESCRIPTION/OBJECTIVES:
Cooperative on-site instructional program providing credit and non-credit courses to employees of Pratt & Whitney Aircraft.

PROGRAM INITIATED:
1976

LENGTH OF STUDY FOR PARTICIPANT:
Varies; need to complete 30 credits

LENGTH OF CONTRACT:
5 years

LOCATION:
On-site at Pratt & Witney Aircraft

PARTICIPANTS:
350–400 graduate apprentices, salaried employees, and non-apprentice hourly workers per semester

PROGRAM COSTS PROVIDED BY:
Not reported

PRINTED MATERIALS AVAILABLE FROM:
Institution and company

PRATT & WHITNEY AIRCRAFT
with
SOUTH CENTRAL COMMUNITY COLLEGE

OFF CAMPUS CREDIT EXTENSION PROGRAM

COMPANY CONTACT:
Barbara Oliva
Educational Assistance Coordinator
Pratt & Whitney Aircraft
400 Main Street
East Hartford, CT 06108
(203) 565-7789

INSTITUTIONAL CONTACT:
Louis S. D'Antonio
Director of Community Services
South Central Community College
60 Sargent Drive
New Haven, CT 06511
(203) 789-7069

PROGRAM DESCRIPTION/ OBJECTIVES:
To provide credit courses that can be applied toward an associate's degree in business administration

PROGRAM INITIATED:
1980

LENGTH OF STUDY FOR PARTICIPANT:
1 semester

LENGTH OF CONTRACT:
12 months with renewal

LOCATION:
Pratt & Whitney Aircraft

PARTICIPANTS:
150 hourly and salaried employees

PROGRAM COSTS PROVIDED BY:
Company: 75%
Participant: 25%

PRINTED MATERIALS AVAILABLE FROM:
Institution

PRINCE GEORGE'S COUNTY GOVERNMENT
with
PRINCE GEORGE'S COMMUNITY COLLEGE

STAFF DEVELOPMENT TRAINING

COMPANY CONTACT:
Betty Austin
Training and Development Specialist
Prince George's County Government
County Administration Building
Upper Marlboro, MD 20772
(301) 952-3750

INSTITUTIONAL CONTACT:
Veronica S. Norwood
Director, Contract Services
Prince George's Community College
301 Largo Road
Largo, MD 20772
(301) 322-0726

PROGRAM DESCRIPTION/ OBJECTIVES:
To provide staff development training in communications, supervisory and management techniques, time management, delegation skills, business writing, oral presentation skills, problem solving/decision making and performance appraisal.

PROGRAM INITIATED:
1975

LENGTH OF STUDY FOR PARTICIPANT:
12–24 hours

LENGTH OF CONTRACT:
12 months with renewal option

LOCATION:
County Administration Building

PARTICIPANTS:
25 supervisors, managers, and administrative support personnel per session

PROGRAM COSTS PROVIDED BY:
Company: 53%
Other Source: 47% (state funds)

PRINTED MATERIALS AVAILABLE FROM:
Institution

PRIVATE INDUSTRY COUNCIL
with
CENTRE COLLEGE OF KENTUCKY

MANAGEMENT TRAINING PROGRAM

COMPANY CONTACT:
Joseph Paterno
Executive Director
Private Industry Council
71 Wilkinson Blvd.
Frankfort, KY 40601
(502) 227-9002

INSTITUTIONAL CONTACT:
W.E. Jackson III
Lorraine Downs
Program Director
Economics Department
Centre College of Kentucky
Danville, KY 40422
(606) 236-5211, X254

PROGRAM DESCRIPTION/ OBJECTIVES:
To assist in developing a pool of well-trained personnel in the local business community by teaching them interpersonal and supervisory skills.

PROGRAM INITIATED:
1982

LENGTH OF STUDY FOR PARTICIPANT:
1 quarter

LENGTH OF CONTRACT:
4 months with renewal pending

LOCATION:
Centre College

PARTICIPANTS:
15 pre-supervisory personnel per quarter

PROGRAM COSTS PROVIDED BY:
Institutional: Not available
Company: $33,000 or est. 80% (contributions from 3 firms who are PIC)

PRINTED MATERIALS AVAILABLE FROM:
Not yet available

PROVIDENT NATIONAL BANK
with
PEIRCE JUNIOR COLLEGE

PROVIDENT/PIC/PEIRCE CLERICAL TRAINING PROGRAM

COMPANY CONTACT:
Robert L. Schoonmaker
Vice President and Director
Training, Development and Employee Relations
Provident National Bank
100 South Broad Street
Philadelphia, PA 19101
(215) 585-6620

INSTITUTIONAL CONTACT:
Carolyn Francesconi
Director, Peirce Center for Training and Development
Peirce Junior College
1420 Pine Street
Philadelphia, PA 19102
(215) 545-6400

PROGRAM DESCRIPTION/ OBJECTIVES:
To provide pre-employment clerical training in basic skills (English, math, typing, etc.) for adult trainees from disadvantaged backgrounds.

PROGRAM INITIATED:
1981

LENGTH OF STUDY FOR PARTICIPANT:
12 weeks

LENGTH OF CONTRACT:
12 weeks with renewal option

LOCATION:
Peirce Junior College

PARTICIPANTS:
12 unemployed adults each session

PROGRAM COSTS PROVIDED BY:
Other Source: Private Industry Council, Philadelphia, PA

PRINTED MATERIALS AVAILABLE FROM:
Institution and Private Industry Council, 101 South Broad Street, Philadelphia, PA 19101

PUBLIC UTILITY COMPANY
with
GEORGIA INSTITUTE OF TECHNOLOGY

EVERY SUPERVISOR A TRAINER

COMPANY CONTACT:
H. Ben Roberson
Director, Industrial Education Department
Georgia Institute of Technology
Atlanta, GA 30332
(404) 894-3950

INSTITUTIONAL CONTACT:
H. Ben Roberson
Director, Industrial Education
  Department
Georgia Institute of Technology
Atlanta, GA 30332
(404) 894-3950

PROGRAM DESCRIPTION/ OBJECTIVES:
The program is a train-the-trainer program dealing with objectives, lesson plans, teaching techniques. The objective is for the participants to plan and deliver a 10-minute lesson using skills and knowledge gained in the course.

PROGRAM INITIATED:
Not reported

LENGTH OF STUDY FOR PARTICIPANT:
24 hours

LENGTH OF CONTRACT:
4 weeks

LOCATION:
In-plant

PARTICIPANTS:
12 foremen

PROGRAM COSTS PROVIDED BY:
Institution: 25%
Company: 75%

PRINTED MATERIALS AVAILABLE FROM:
Institution

PULP AND PAPER FOUNDATION
(156 paper and supplier companies)
with
UNIVERSITY OF MAINE AT ORONO

PULP AND PAPER FOUNDATION

COMPANY CONTACT:
Stanley N. Marshall, Jr.
Executive Director
University of Maine Pulp and Paper Foundation
217 Jenness Hall
Orono, ME 04469
(207) 581-7559

INSTITUTIONAL CONTACT:
Stanley N. Marshall, Jr.
Executive Director
University of Main Pulp and Paper Foundation
217 Jenness Hall
Orono, ME 04469
(207) 581-7559

PROGRAM DESCRIPTION/ OBJECTIVES:
Attract students to paper-related technical careers; provide a capable well-motivated faculty; promote an interest in production-management; provide financial assistance to students and to the university.

PROGRAM INITIATED:
1952

LENGTH OF STUDY FOR PARTICIPANT:
4 years

LENGTH OF CONTRACT:
Renewable annually (35-year-old foundation)

LOCATION:
Orono, ME

PARTICIPANTS:
125 students and 156 companies

PROGRAM COSTS PROVIDED BY:
Institution: $4,500
Company: $300,000
Other Source: $200,000 (investment funds)

PRINTED MATERIALS AVAILABLE FROM:
Institution

PURITAN LIFE INSURANCE COMPANY
with
COMMUNITY COLLEGE OF RHODE ISLAND

BUSINESS WRITING

COMPANY CONTACT:
Diana VandenDorpel
Training Director
Personnel Department
Puritan Life Insurance Company
Allendale Park
Johnston, RI 02916
(401) 456-6979

INSTITUTIONAL CONTACT:
Robert Danilowicz
Coordinator
Missing Link Project
Off Campus Credit Programs
Community College of Rhode Island
Flanagan Campus
Louisquisset Pike
Lincoln, RI 02865
(401) 333-7127

PROGRAM DESCRIPTION/ OBJECTIVES:
Course includes correspondence, general policies of all business correspondence, abstract and precise writing, and some report writing. Objective to improve skills of company personnel.

PROGRAM INITIATED:
1981

LENGTH OF STUDY FOR PARTICIPANT:
1 semester

LENGTH OF CONTRACT:
1 semester

LOCATION:
Puritan Life Insurance Company

PARTICIPANTS:
20 mid-management

PROGRAM COSTS PROVIDED BY:
Company: $1,525

PRINTED MATERIALS AVAILABLE FROM:
Institution and company

RAYTHEON, INC.
with
UNIVERSITY OF MASSACHUSETTS-AMHERST

VIDEOTAPE INSTRUCTION PROGRAM FOR ENGINEERS

COMPANY CONTACT:
Raytheon, Inc.
through

John Gillespie, Jr.
Bay State Skills Corporation
McCormack Office Building
One Ashburton Place
Room 2110
Boston, MA 02108
(617) 727-5431

INSTITUTIONAL CONTACT:
Harvey Stone
Director, Office of Extended
Engineering Education
113 Engineering Building East
University of Massachusetts
Amherst, MA 01003
(413) 545-0063

PROGRAM DESCRIPTION/ OBJECTIVES:
A videotape instructional program in engineering areas and computer technology providing graduate level training in CAD/CAM, management, microwave, computer systems, and computer communications.

PROGRAM INITIATED:
1982

LENGTH OF STUDY FOR PARTICIPANT:
Self-paced

LENGTH OF CONTRACT:
6 months

LOCATION:
Raytheon, Inc.

PARTICIPANTS:
200 engineers

PROGRAM COSTS PROVIDED BY:
Company: $100,000
Other Source: $97,969 (Bay State Skills Corporation)

PRINTED MATERIALS AVAILABLE FROM:
Company

RHODE ISLAND HOSPITAL
with
UNIVERSITY OF RHODE ISLAND

EMPLOYEE EDUCATIONAL OPPORTUNITIES

COMPANY CONTACT:
Barbara Parker
Manager, Employee Education
Rhode Island Hospital
Eddy Street
Providence, RI 02908
(401) 277-8353

INSTITUTIONAL CONTACT:
Hollis B. Farnum
Coordinator of Academic Programs
College of Continuing Education
University of Rhode Island
Promenade Street
Providence, RI 02908
(401) 277-3810

PROGRAM DESCRIPTION/ OBJECTIVES:
To make university credit courses available to hospital staff on the hospital grounds.

PROGRAM INITIATED:
1982

LENGTH OF STUDY FOR PARTICIPANT:
1 semester per course

LENGTH OF CONTRACT:
Academic year; renegotiable each academic year

LOCATION:
Rhode Island Hospital

PARTICIPANTS:
12 hospital staff members

PROGRAM COSTS PROVIDED BY:
Participant: 100%

PRINTED MATERIALS AVAILABLE FROM:
Company

CITY OF RICHMOND, VIRGINIA
with
VIRGINIA COMMONWEALTH UNIVERSITY

RICHMOND REVITALIZATION PROGRAM

COMPANY CONTACT:
Charles Peters
Director, Planning and Community Development
City Hall
900 East Broad Street
Richmond, VA 23219
(804) 780-4346

INSTITUTIONAL CONTACT:
Morton B. Gulak
Director, Urban Studies and Planning
Virginia Commonwealth University
812 West Franklin Street
Richmond, VA 23284
(804) 257-1134

PROGRAM DESCRIPTION/OBJECTIVES:
To stimulate revitalization in the city through assessment of selected areas in the city and the involvement of the private sector and the involvement of students at the university.

PROGRAM INITIATED:
1980

LENGTH OF STUDY FOR PARTICIPANT:
1 year

LENGTH OF CONTRACT:
3 years, ongoing through other sources

LOCATION:
Virginia Commonwealth University

PARTICIPANTS:
70 graduate urban planning, communication arts, interior design, business, architecture students annually

PROGRAM COSTS PROVIDED BY:
Institution: 10%
Company: 45%
Participant: 45%

PRINTED MATERIALS AVAILABLE FROM:
Institution

RICHMOND PRIVATE INDUSTRY COUNCIL AND RICHMOND PUBLIC SCHOOLS
with
VIRGINIA COMMONWEALTH UNIVERSITY

NEW HORIZONS

COMPANY CONTACT:
Jona McKee
New Horizons Coordinator
Richmond Private Industry Council
Franklin Street
Richmond, VA 23220
(804) 643-0864

INSTITUTIONAL CONTACT:
Thomas A. Hephner
Associate Professor
Educational Studies
Virginia Commonwealth University
1015 West Main Street
Richmond, VA 23284
(804) 257-1332

PROGRAM DESCRIPTION/OBJECTIVES:
A cooperative program among the Richmond Private Industry Council, Richmond Public Schools, and Virginia Commonwealth University to train disadvantaged youth for entry level jobs.

PROGRAM INITIATED:
1980

LENGTH OF STUDY FOR PARTICIPANT:
Up to 2 years

LENGTH OF CONTRACT:
Year-to-year grant

LOCATION:
Richmond, VA

PARTICIPANTS:
100 high school students

PROGRAM COSTS PROVIDED BY:
Company: 100%

PRINTED MATERIALS AVAILABLE FROM:
Institution and company

RISDON CORPORATION
with
UNIVERSITY OF HARTFORD

EFFECTIVE WRITING SKILLS FOR FINANCIAL MANAGERS
(3 Programs)

COMPANY CONTACT:
Kenneth Baldyga
Manager, Corporate Personnel
Risdon Corporation
1 Risdon Street
Naugatuck, CT 06770
(203) 729-8231

INSTITUTIONAL CONTACT:
Gilbert J. Maffeo
Program Development Consultant
Division of Adult Educational Services
University of Hartford
200 Bloomfield Avenue
West Hartford, CT 06117
(203) 243-4350

PROGRAM DESCRIPTION/ OBJECTIVES:
To upgrade current skills of financial managers in the areas of acquisition, monthly reports, yearly reports, and planning documents.

PROGRAM INITIATED:
1981

LENGTH OF STUDY FOR PARTICIPANT:
2-3 days

LENGTH OF CONTRACT:
Ongoing

LOCATION:
On-site or at a neutral site

PARTICIPANTS:
10-20 line management to vice presidents

PROGRAM COSTS PROVIDED BY:
Company: 100%

PRINTED MATERIALS AVAILABLE FROM:
Institution and company

A.H. ROBINS COMPANY
with
VIRGINIA COMMONWEALTH UNIVERSITY

EMPLOYEE IMPROVEMENT AND EDUCATION AT A.H. ROBINS COMPANY

COMPANY CONTACT:
Bette H. Kellehay
Manager, Personnel Training and Library Service
A.H. Robins Company
1407 Cummings Drive
Richmond, VA 23220
(804) 257-2858

INSTITUTIONAL CONTACT:
John B. Callander
Coordinator for Off-Campus Credit
Continuing Education and Public Service
Virginia Commonwealth University
901 West Franklin Street
Richmond, VA 23284
(804) 257-6032

PROGRAM DESCRIPTION/ OBJECTIVES:
To provide training for professional research personnel in pharmacology, computer science, and general research.

PROGRAM INITIATED:
1978

LENGTH OF STUDY FOR PARTICIPANT:
1 semester continuing

LENGTH OF CONTRACT:
Semester with renewal

LOCATION:
A.H. Robins Company

PARTICIPANTS:
Approximately 50 chemical research personnel annually

PROGRAM COSTS PROVIDED BY:
Institution: 10%
Company: 90%

PRINTED MATERIALS AVAILABLE FROM:
Not available

LENGTH OF CONTRACT:
Ongoing

LOCATION:
Rockwell Factory

PARTICIPANTS:
30 per semester

PROGRAM COSTS PROVIDED BY:
Institution and company

PRINTED MATERIALS AVAILABLE FROM:
Institution

ROCKWELL INTERNATIONAL
with
NORTHERN KENTUCKY UNIVERSITY

ROCKWELL CERTIFICATE PROGRAM

COMPANY CONTACT:
Barbara Cline
Personnel
Rockwell International
Florence Industrial Park
Dixie Highway
Florence, KY 40142
(606) 525-3557

INSTITUTIONAL CONTACT:
Susan Kemper
Director
Credit Continuing Education
Northern Kentucky University
1401 Dixie Highway
Covington, Kentucky 41011
(606) 572-5601

PROGRAM DESCRIPTION/OBJECTIVES:
Provides credit courses which can be applied toward certificate.

LENGTH OF STUDY FOR PARTICIPANT:
Individual

ROYSTON CORPORATION, INC.
with
GEORGIA INSTITUTE OF TECHNOLOGY, INDUSTRIAL EDUCATION DEPT.

WORKING EFFICIENTLY AND EFFECTIVELY

COMPANY CONTACT:
Paul Crawford
Personnel Director
Personnel
Royston Corp.
P.O. Box 7
Royston, GA 30662
(404) 245-6116

INSTITUTIONAL CONTACT:
Dr. Ben Roberson
Director
Industrial Education Dept.
Georgia Institute of Technology
225 North Avenue
Atlanta, GA 30332
(404) 894-3950

PROGRAM DESCRIPTION/OBJECTIVES:
To stimulate the interest of employees in job improvement and working smarter. Content includes: the questioning attitude and approach, design of work stations, methods improvement, task analysis, motion economy, work values.

PROGRAM INITIATED:
September, 1985

LENGTH OF STUDY FOR PARTICIPANT:
12 hours

LENGTH OF CONTRACT:
12 hours

LOCATION:
Royston Corporation, Royston, GA

PARTICIPANTS:
Number: 40
Type: Production employees and first line managers.

PROGRAM COSTS PROVIDED BY:
Institution: 40%
Company: 60%

PRINTED MATERIALS AVAILABLE FROM:
Institution

CITY OF SAN DIEGO
with
MIRAMAR COLLEGE

REGIONAL BASIC FIRE ACADEMY

COMPANY CONTACT:
Donald W. Farney
Director, Personnel and Training
San Diego Fire Department
1222 First Avenue
San Diego, CA 92101
(714) 236-6475

INSTITUTIONAL CONTACT:
Thoyd Latham
Dean of Instruction
Fire Science
Miramar College
10440 Black Mountain Road
San Diego, CA 92126
(714) 230-6512

PROGRAM DESCRIPTION/OBJECTIVES:
To provide required basic fire fighting training to persons seeking employment with the San Diego Fire Department prior to being hired.

PROGRAM INITIATED:
1981

LENGTH OF STUDY FOR PARTICIPANT:
10 weeks

LENGTH OF CONTRACT:
12 months with renewal option

LOCATION:
Miramar College

PARTICIPANTS:
144 entry level firefighters annually

PROGRAM COSTS PROVIDED BY:
Institution: $80,000 or 66%
Company: $40,000 or 33%

PRINTED MATERIALS AVAILABLE FROM:
Institution

ST. JOSEPH HOSPITAL
with
NATIONAL COLLEGE OF EDUCATION

BACHELOR OF ARTS DEGREE PROGRAM IN APPLIED BEHAVIORAL SCIENCES

COMPANY CONTACT:
Tom Hounihan
Director
Training and Development
St. Joseph Hospital
2900 North Lakeshore Drive
Chicago, IL 60657
(312) 985-3190

INSTITUTIONAL CONTACT:
Edward Storke
Assistant Dean
Field Experience Program
National College of Education
2 S 361 Glen Park Road
Lombard, IL 60148
(312) 629-5320

PROGRAM DESCRIPTION/ OBJECTIVES:
This program is a series of courses and work-realted projects leading to the completion of a baccalaureate degree or a masters degree. The emphasis is on interpersonal and supervisory skills related to job performance.

PROGRAM INITIATED:
1981

LENGTH OF STUDY FOR PARTICIPANT:
1 year

LENGTH OF CONTRACT:
1 year (oral agreement)

LOCATION:
St. Joseph Hospital

PARTICIPANTS:
26 supervisors and head nurses

PROGRAM COSTS PROVIDED BY:
Institution: 15%
Company: 75%
Participant: 10% (Shared by company and participant based on the length of employment at company. Some students also receive government assistance.)

PRINTED MATERIALS AVAILABLE FROM:
Institution

ST. LAWRENCE COUNTY ECONOMIC DEVELOPMENT OFFICE
with
SUNY AGRICULTURAL AND TECHNICAL COLLEGE AT CANTON

MACHINE TRADES PROGRAM

COMPANY CONTACT:
David Williams
Director of Training
St. Lawrence County Economic Development Office
Courthouse Building
Canton, NY 13617
(315) 379-2291

INSTITUTIONAL CONTACT:
Robert Mattice
Project Director
Office of Sponsored Research
SUNY Agricultural and Technical College at Canton
Canton, NY 13617
(315) 386-7210

PROGRAM DESCRIPTION/ OBJECTIVES:
To prepare individuals for careers as machine operators in local and regional industry.

PROGRAM INITIATED:
1978

LENGTH OF STUDY FOR PARTICIPANT:
450 hours

LENGTH OF CONTRACT:
6 months with renewal option

LOCATION:
SUNY Agricultural and Technical College at Canton

PARTICIPANTS:
Approximately 15–18 operators annually

PROGRAM COSTS PROVIDED BY:
Company: Approximately $50,000

PRINTED MATERIALS AVAILABLE FROM:
Institution

ST. MICHAEL'S MEDICAL CENTER
with
RUTGERS, THE STATE UNIVERSITY OF NEW JERSEY

PRIMARY AFFILIATION

COMPANY CONTACT:
Norah McCarthy
Vice President
Nursing Services

St. Michael's Medical Center
306 High Street
Newark, NJ 07102
(201) 877-5359

INSTITUTIONAL CONTACT:
Lucille Joel
Associate Dean for Clinical Affairs
College of Nursing
Rutgers, The State University of New Jersey
University Avenue
Newark, NJ 07102
(201) 648-5298

PROGRAM DESCRIPTION/ OBJECTIVES:
Manpower sharing; student placement.

PROGRAM INITIATED:
1982

LENGTH OF STUDY FOR PARTICIPANT:
Academic year

LENGTH OF CONTRACT:
10 months

LOCATION:
St. Michael's Medical Center and Rutgers

PARTICIPANTS:
2

PROGRAM COSTS PROVIDED BY:
Shared equally by exchange of time between company and institution

PRINTED MATERIALS AVAILABLE FROM:
Institution

SCHENECTADY EMPLOYMENT AND TRAINING ADMINISTRATION
with
SCHENECTADY COUNTY COMMUNITY COLLEGE

CAREER DEVELOPMENT NETWORK

COMPANY CONTACT:
Anthony Insogna
Assistant to County Manager for SETA
Schenectady Employment and Training Administration
240 Broadway
Schenectady, NY 12306
(518) 382-3567

INSTITUTIONAL CONTACT:
Sanford E. Lake
Director, Career Life Skills Center
Schenectady County Community College
78 Washington Avenue
Schenectady, NY 12305
(518) 346-6211, X205

PROGRAM DESCRIPTION/ OBJECTIVES:
To measurably improve "employability" of participants through counseling and training in self-assessment skills, interviewing techniques, resume writing, and general socio-behavioral skills areas, as well as in occupational-specific areas of instruction.

PROGRAM INITIATED:
1980

LENGTH OF STUDY FOR PARTICIPANT:
Varies (6–26 weeks)

LENGTH OF CONTRACT:
Varies

LOCATION:
Schenectady County Community College

PARTICIPANTS:
Maximum 15 unskilled generalists, clerical, retailing, nurses' aides, culinary arts individuals per program group

PROGRAM COSTS PROVIDED BY:
Company: CETA 70%; Schenectady ETA 20%
Other Source: Pell Grants 5%, Schenectady 5%

PRINTED MATERIALS AVAILABLE FROM:
Not reported

LENGTH OF CONTRACT:
10 + 1 hour individual follow-up

LOCATION:
Schneller and Associates

PARTICIPANTS:
12 sales representatives

PROGRAM COSTS PROVIDED BY:
Company: 100%

PRINTED MATERIALS AVAILABLE FROM:
Institution

SCHNELLER AND ASSOCIATES
with
KENT STATE UNIVERSITY

EFFECTIVE BUSINESS WRITING

COMPANY CONTACT:
Donald Strange
Schneller and Associates
P.O. Box 670
Kent, OH 44240
(216) 673-1400

INSTITUTIONAL CONTACT:
Karen Rylander
Director, Continuing Education
Kent State University
327 Rockwell Hall
Kent, OH 44242
(216) 672-3100

PROGRAM DESCRIPTION/OBJECTIVES:
Provides a practical review of the fundamentals of written communication for professionals in business and industry. It emphasizes the application of successful strategies for writing persuasive and efficient prose in the various business forms.

PROGRAM INITIATED:
1981

LENGTH OF STUDY FOR PARTICIPANT:
10 hours + 1 hour individual follow-up

SEATT CORP
with
COLLEGE OF DUPAGE

SEATT TRAINING

COMPANY CONTACT:
James Reilly
Vice President of Manufacturing
Seatt Corporation
Downers Grove, IL 60515
(312) 963-1550

INSTITUTIONAL CONTACT:
Joan Bevelacqua
Director
Business and Professional Institute
Open College
College of DuPage
Glen Ellyn, IL 60137
(312) 858-6870

PROGRAM DESCRIPTION/OBJECTIVES:
To provide training for 61 new employees. (Jobs created by an expansion.) The training is on the job and classroom. It is designed to prepare the employee to be productive on the job.

PROGRAM INITIATED:
1979

LENGTH OF STUDY FOR PARTICIPANT:
2–3 months

LENGTH OF CONTRACT:
1 year

LOCATION:
In plant

PARTICIPANTS:
61 entry level electronic manufacturing personnel, office staff, and data processing staff

PROGRAM COSTS PROVIDED BY:
Other Source: $150,000 (Illinois Board of Higher Education High Impact Training Grant)

PRINTED MATERIALS AVAILABLE FROM:
Institution

BRONX COMMUNITY COLLEGE
with
SEE CLEAR MAINTENANCE CORP.

MANAGEMENT UPGRADING

COMPANY CONTACT:
Charles Smith, Jr.
President
See Clear Maintenance Corp.
4417 Third Avenue
Bronx, NY 10417
(212) 364-2410

INSTITUTIONAL CONTACT:
Rafael Infante
Director, Contracts & Training
Continuing Education
Bronx Community College
University Avenue and 181 Street
Bronx, NY 10453
(212) 220-6424

PROGRAM DESCRIPTION/ OBJECTIVES:
To provide modern management procedures & state-of-the-art office machinery to build maintanance companies

LENGTH OF STUDY FOR PARTICIPANT:
18 weeks

LENGTH OF CONTRACT:
18 weeks

LOCATION:
See Clear Corporate offices

PARTICIPANTS:
Number: 13
Type: management

PROGRAM COSTS PROVIDED BY:
Company: $15,480
Other Sources: $15,060

PRINTED MATERIALS AVAILABLE FROM:
Institution

SMITHERS-OASIS
with
KENT STATE UNIVERSITY

BASIC SUPERVISORY TRAINING

COMPANY CONTACT:
David Otto
Smithers-Oasis
P.O. Box 118
Kent, OH 44240
(216) 673-5831

INSTITUTIONAL CONTACT:
Karen Rylander
Director, Continuing Education
Kent State University
327 Rockwell Hall
Kent, OH 44242
(216) 672-3100

PROGRAM DESCRIPTION/ OBJECTIVES:
Includes an overview of communication skills, motivation, problem-solving, time-management, and team building.

PROGRAM INITIATED:
1980

LENGTH OF STUDY FOR PARTICIPANT:
28 hours

LENGTH OF CONTRACT:
28 hours

DIRECTORY OF CAMPUS-BUSINESS LINKAGES

LOCATION:
Smithers-Oasis

PARTICIPANTS:
20 first-line supervisors

PROGRAM COSTS PROVIDED BY:
Company: 100%

PRINTED MATERIALS AVAILABLE FROM:
Institution

SOCIAL SECURITY ADMINISTRATION*
with
BOWLING GREEN STATE UNIVERSITY

COOPERATIVE EDUCATION

COMPANY CONTACT:
Lloyd Borer
Manager
Social Security Administration
Bowling Green, OH 43402
(419) 352-8481

INSTITUTIONAL CONTACT:
Bruce W. Smith
Director
Cooperative Education Program
Bowling Green State University
Bowling Green, OH 43403-0026
(419) 372-2451

PROGRAM DESCRIPTION/ OBJECTIVES:
To place college students in cooperative education assignments in the public and private sectors.

PROGRAM INITIATED:
1978

LENGTH OF STUDY FOR PARTICIPANT:
Multiple semesters

LENGTH OF CONTRACT:
Ongoing

LOCATION:
Bowling Green, OH

PARTICIPANTS:
740 college students annually

PROGRAM COSTS PROVIDED BY:
Institution: 100%
Company: Student salaries

PRINTED MATERIALS AVAILABLE FROM:
Institution

* Representative entry—complete list available from institution.

SOCIETY OF DIE CAST ENGINEERS
with
TRITON COLLEGE

TRITON COLLEGE/SOCIETY OF DIE CAST ENGINEERS PARTNERSHIP

COMPANY CONTACT:
James Cannon
Executive Director
Society of Die Cast Engineers
2000 Fifth Avenue
River Grove, IL 60171
(312) 452-0700

INSTITUTIONAL CONTACT:
David Kozlowski
Associate Vice President
Triton College
2000 Fifth Avenue
River Grove, IL 60171
(312) 456-0300, X538

PROGRAM DESCRIPTION/ OBJECTIVES:
Triton built and leased back to the SDCE a facility to their specifications. Triton uses facility to conduct die casting classes and seminars at no cost. SDCE uses college staff and support services.

PROGRAM INITIATED:
1982

LENGTH OF STUDY FOR PARTICIPANT:
2 years, seminars are 1 to 5 days

LENGTH OF CONTRACT:
10 years with reopener for second 10 years

LOCATION:
Triton College

PARTICIPANTS:
Not available

PROGRAM COSTS PROVIDED BY:
Institution: Building loan
Company: $43,200 per year lease

PRINTED MATERIALS AVAILABLE FROM:
Institution

LENGTH OF STUDY FOR PARTICIPANT:
Varies

LENGTH OF CONTRACT:
12 months

LOCATION:
Chula Vista Chamber of Commerce

PARTICIPANTS:
Varies

PROGRAM COSTS PROVIDED BY:
Other Source: JTPA

PRINTED MATERIALS AVAILABLE FROM:
Institution

SOUTH BAY CHAMBER OF COMMERCE
with
SOUTHWESTERN COLLEGE

BUSINESS EXPANSION TRAINING (BET)

COMPANY CONTACT:
Neil Slijk
Executive Director
Chula Vista Chamber of Commerce
233 4th Ave.
Chula Vista, CA 92010
(714) 420-6602

INSTITUTIONAL CONTACT:
Mary Wylie
Assistant Dean
Vocational & Community Education
Southwestern College
900 Otay Lakes Road
Chula Vista, CA 92016
(714) 421-6700 X259

PROGRAM DESCRIPTION/ OBJECTIVES:
Assist small businesses to expand through training, job referrals, and referral to other resources for capital funding, government regulations, etc.

PROGRAM INITIATED:
1984

STANDARD OIL COMPANY*
with
INTERNATIONAL FOUNDATION OF EMPLOYEE BENEFIT PLANS

I.F. INTERNS

COMPANY CONTACT:
C.E. Webb
Manager, Benefits Administration and Payroll Accounting
Standard Oil Company
200 East Randolph Street
P.O. Box 5738
Chicago, IL 60680
(312) 856-6355

INSTITUTIONAL CONTACT:
Robert D. Cooper
Director, Research International Foundation of Employee Benefit Plans
18700 West Bluemound Road
Brookfield, WI 53005
(414) 786-6700

PROGRAM DESCRIPTION/ OBJECTIVES:
Pilot project in Chicago with expansion to Milwaukee, 1983 and New York City, 1984. Professional development program that recruits high quality students from several universities and prepares them for careers in benefits administration and

counseling through education and on-the-job training.

PROGRAM INITIATED:
1981

LENGTH OF STUDY FOR PARTICIPANT:
2 years (part-time) including 2 full-time summer experiences

LENGTH OF CONTRACT:
Not available

LOCATION:
Principally Chicago

PARTICIPANTS:
30+ college juniors and seniors

PROGRAM COSTS PROVIDED BY:
Institution: $75,000
Company: $4,500 per year, per student

PRINTED MATERIALS AVAILABLE FROM:
Institution

* Representative entry—complete list available from institution.

THE STANLEY WORKS
with
UNIVERSITY OF HARTFORD

ASSOCIATE DEGREE IN ARTS AND SCIENCES ON-SITE

COMPANY CONTACT:
Thomas Jones
The Stanley Works
480 Myrtle Street
New Britain, CT 06050
(203) 223-9968

INSTITUTIONAL CONTACT:
William T. George
Program Development Consultant
Division of Adult Educational Services
University of Hartford
200 Bloomfield Avenue
West Hartford, CT 06117
(203) 243-4507/4381

PROGRAM DESCRIPTION/OBJECTIVES:
Associate Degree in Arts and Sciences on-site.

PROGRAM INITIATED:
1979

LENGTH OF STUDY FOR PARTICIPANT:
60 semester hours

LENGTH OF CONTRACT:
Ongoing

LOCATION:
On-site

PARTICIPANTS:
100 qualified employees

PROGRAM COSTS PROVIDED BY:
Company: 75%
Participant: 25%

PRINTED MATERIALS AVAILABLE FROM:
Institution

STEEL SPECIALTY COMPANY
with
GEORGIA INSTITUTE OF TECHNOLOGY

MANAGEMENT COMMUNICATION PROCESS TRAINING

COMPANY CONTACT:
H. Ben Roberson
Director, Industrial Education Department
Georgia Institute of Technology
Atlanta, GA 30332
(404) 894-3950

INSTITUTIONAL CONTACT:
H. Ben Roberson
Director, Industrial Education Department
Georgia Institute of Technology
Atlanta, GA 30332
(404) 894-3950

PROGRAM DESCRIPTION/OBJECTIVES:
To train managers in the steps of communication process and in the use of the process.

PROGRAM INITIATED:
Not reported

LENGTH OF STUDY FOR PARTICIPANT:
8 hours

LENGTH OF CONTRACT:
4 weeks

LOCATION:
In-plant

PARTICIPANTS:
65 foremen, area managers, managers, and plant managers

PROGRAM COSTS PROVIDED BY:
Institution: 50%
Company: 50%

PRINTED MATERIALS AVAILABLE FROM:
Institution

STOCKHAM VALVES AND FITTING*
with
BIRMINGHAM-SOUTHERN COLLEGE

CONTRACT LEARNING CENTER

COMPANY CONTACT:
Pat Swofford
Personnel Department
Stockham Valves and Fitting
P.O. Box 10325
Birmingham, AL 35202
(205) 592-6361

INSTITUTIONAL CONTACT:
Nancy Poynor
Coordinator Experiential Learning
Office of the President
Birmingham Southern College
Birmingham, AL 35254
(205) 328-5250, X394

PROGRAM DESCRIPTION/OBJECTIVES:
Designed to administer internships for Birmingham-Southern College students in local business and industry.

PROGRAM INITIATED:
1979

LENGTH OF STUDY FOR PARTICIPANT:
May be taken on a semester-by-semester basis or these may be taken in conjunction with fulfilling a contract during interim, a 4-week term between semesters.

LENGTH OF CONTRACT:
Ongoing

LOCATION:
Business site

PARTIPANTS:
192 for Spring 1982

PROGRAM COSTS PROVIDED BY:
Participant: Included in admissions fee

PRINTED MATERIALS AVAILABLE FROM:
Institution

* Representative entry—complete list available from institution.

STONE CONTAINER CORPORATION
with
JOHN TYLER COMMUNITY COLLEGE

GENERAL MECHANIC APPRENTICE

COMPANY CONTACT:
Mr. George E. Spatig
Superintendent of Maintenance
Maintenance
Stone Container Corporation
P.O. Box 210
Hopewell, VA 23860
(804) 541-9714

INSTITUTIONAL CONTACT:
Dr. Samuel Lee Hancock
Director
Division of Continuing Education
John Tyler Community College
13101 Jefferson Davis Highway
Chester, VA 23831
(804) 796-4111

PROGRAM DESCRIPTION/ OBJECTIVES:
Program designed to provide multi-craft training of a general mechanic nature with specializations in mechanical, electrical, and instrumentation.

PROGRAM INITIATED:
Fall, 1985

LENGTH OF STUDY FOR PARTICIPANT:
4 years

LENGTH OF CONTRACT:
30 to 60 instructional hours per quarter per participant

LOCATION:
Both on-site at Stone Container and on-campus

PARTICIPANTS:
Number: 8
Type: Maintenance personnel

PROGRAM COSTS PROVIDED BY:
Institution: Administrative leadership, instructional materials
Company: Equipment and materials
Participant: Time
Other Source: Virginia Training Program: instructors' salary

PRINTED MATERIALS AVAILABLE FROM:
Institution

STOUFFER FOODS
with
KENT STATE UNIVERSITY

PROFIT MANAGEMENT

COMPANY CONTACT:
John Shoupe
Stouffer Foods
29800 Bainbridge Road
Solon, OH 44139
(216) 248-3600

INSTITUTIONAL CONTACT:
Karen Rylander
Director, Continuing Education
Kent State University
327 Rockwell Hall
Kent, OH 44242
(216) 672-3100

PROGRAM DESCRIPTION/ OBJECTIVES:
Designed to introduce first and second level supervisors to concepts of performance objectives, profit planning and control, and the employees' role in achieving profit objectives. Program to be implemented by Stouffer trainers.

PROGRAM INITIATED:
1982

LENGTH OF STUDY FOR PARTICIPANT:
Program content and material development

LENGTH OF CONTRACT:
Not reported

LOCATION:
Stouffer Foods

PARTICIPANTS:
Unknown number of supervisors

PROGRAM COSTS PROVIDED BY:
Company: 100%

PRINTED MATERIALS AVAILABLE FROM:
Institution

SUMTER POLICE DEPARTMENT AND NCR CORPORATION
with
SUMTER AREA TECHNICAL COLLEGE

COMPUTERIZING CRIME INFORMATION: IS THERE AN ANALYST IN THE HOUSE?

COMPANY CONTACT:
L.W. Griffin
Chief of Police
Sumter Police Department
107 East Hampton
Sumter, SC 29150
(803) 773-1561

INSTITUTIONAL CONTACT:
Gus Becker
Dean, Continuing Education
Sumter Area Technical College
506 North Guignard Drive
Sumter, SC 29150
(803) 773-9371

PROGRAM DESCRIPTION/OBJECTIVES:
To develop a seminar for law enforcement administrators to achieve hands-on familiarity with a cost-effective computerized crime reporting/information system. Provides NCR sales representatives with real-life product evaluation.

PROGRAM INITIATED:
1981

LENGTH OF STUDY FOR PARTICIPANT:
1-day seminar

LENGTH OF CONTRACT:
Informal agreement

LOCATION:
Sumter Area Community College

PARTICIPANTS:
35 financial managers, law enforcement and NCR personnel

PROGRAM COSTS PROVIDED BY:
Institution: 20%
Company: 20%
Participant: 60%

PRINTED MATERIALS AVAILABLE FROM:
Institution

SUNBURST SYSTEMS, INC.*
with
SOUTHEASTERN MASSACHUSETTS UNIVERSITY

ENERGY MARKETING AND SALES

COMPANY CONTACT:
Rico Correia
President
Sunburst Systems, Inc.
751 Kempton Street
New Bedford, MA 02740

INSTITUTIONAL CONTACT:
Southeastern Massachusetts University (North Dartmouth)
through
John Gillespie, Jr.
Bay State Skills Corporation
McCormick Office Building
One Ashburton Place
Room 2110
Boston, MA 02108
(617) 727-5431

PROGRAM DESCRIPTION/OBJECTIVES:
To train individuals in energy sales and marketing and to provide an opportunity to observe energy retrofitting and installations.

PROGRAM INITIATED:
1982

LENGTH OF STUDY FOR PARTICIPANT:
25 weeks (35 hours per week)

LENGTH OF CONTRACT:
6 months

LOCATION:
Southeastern Massachusetts University and on-the-job training

PARTICIPANTS:
30 unemployed individuals

DIRECTORY OF CAMPUS-BUSINESS LINKAGES

PROGRAM COSTS PROVIDED BY:
Institution: $15,100
Company: $51,148
Other Source: $42,739 (Bay State Skills Corporation grant)

PRINTED MATERIALS AVAILABLE FROM:
Institution

* Representative entry—complete list available from institution.

SUPER RADIATOR COILS
with
JOHN TYLER COMMUNITY COLLEGE

MANUFACTURING APPRENTICE TRAINING PROGRAM

COMPANY CONTACT:
Mr. Ray Birk
Plant Manager
Super Radiator Coils
451 Southlake Blvd.
Richmond, VA 23236
(804) 794-2887

INSTITUTIONAL CONTACT:
Dr. Samuel Lee Hancock
Director
Division of Continuing Education
John Tyler Community College
13101 Jefferson Davis Highway
Chester, VA 23831
(804) 796-4111

PROGRAM DESCRIPTION/ OBJECTIVES:
Program is to provide theoretical and hands-on experiences for workers in a heavy manufacturing environment in the areas of blueprint reading, mathematics, electricity, and electronics.

PROGRAM INITIATED:
Fall, 1983

LENGTH OF STUDY FOR PARTICIPANT:
As needed and on-going

LENGTH OF CONTRACT:
10 instructional hours per 1 college credit

LOCATION:
On-site at Super Radiator Coils, Chesterfield County, VA.

PARTICIPANTS:
Number: 16
Type: Machine Operators

PROGRAM COSTS PROVIDED BY:
Institution: Administrative leadership
Company: Tuition, textbooks
Participant: Time
Other Source: Virginia Apprentice Training Program, instructor's salary

PRINTED MATERIALS AVAILABLE FROM:
Institution

THE TAUBMAN COMPANY*
with
HENRY FORD COMMUNITY COLLEGE

SUNRISE SEMINARS

COMPANY CONTACT:
Lin Berry
Director of Special Promotions
The Taubman Company
3270 West Big Beaver Road
Suite 300
P.O. Box 3270
Troy, MI 48099
(313) 649-5000

INSTITUTIONAL CONTACT:
Robert J. Kopecky
Director, Center for New Directions
Henry Ford Community College
Dearborn, MI 48128
(313) 271-2750, X330

PROGRAM DESCRIPTION/ OBJECTIVES:
On-site continuing education for retailers in shopping malls to develop positive attitudes, insightful solutions of business problems, effective tenant management relationships, and long range commit-

ments toward increasing shopping center profits and reducing costs.

PROGRAM INITIATED:
1980

LENGTH OF STUDY FOR PARTICIPANT:
4 weeks

LENGTH OF CONTRACT:
4 weeks

LOCATION:
Shopping center restaurant

PARTICIPANTS:
30 managers and assistant managers in mall stores per seminar

PROGRAM COSTS PROVIDED BY:
Company: $1,200 per series

PRINTED MATERIALS AVAILABLE FROM:
Institution

* Representative entry—complete list available from institution.

TEACHERS' INSURANCE & ANNUITY ASSOCIATION
with
NEW YORK CITY TECHNICAL COLLEGE

T.I.A.A. BUSINESS WRITING

COMPANY CONTACT:
Teachers' Insurance and Annuity Association
Training and Development Specialist
Personnel, Training and Development
Teachers' Insurance and Annuity Association
730 Third Avenue, 19th Floor
New York, New York 10017
(212) 916-4582

INSTITUTIONAL CONTACT:
Barbara Ritchin
Director of Contract Programs
Continuing Education
New York City Technical College
450 West 41st Street Room 501
New York, New York 10036
(212) 239-1664

PROGRAM DESCRIPTION/ OBJECTIVES:
Business writing class offered to first and second level supervisory personnel. Course objective is to assist students to write effective office memos employing correct capitalization, punctuation, grammar, sentence structure, and paragraph organization skills.

LENGTH OF STUDY FOR PARTICIPANT:
18 hours

LENGTH OF CONTRACT:
New contract for each cycle

LOCATION:
On site at T.I.A.A.

PARTICIPANTS:
Number: 10 each cycle
Type: First and second level supervisory

PROGRAM COSTS PROVIDED BY:
Company: 100%

PRINTED MATERIALS AVAILABLE FROM:
Institution and company

TERRE HAUTE AREA CHAMBER OF COMMERCE
with
INDIANA STATE UNIVERSITY

COMMUNITY-WIDE WORKFORCE DEVELOPMENT PROJECT

COMPANY CONTACT:
Ross Hedges
President
Terre Haute Area Chamber of Commerce
P.O. Box 689
Terre Haute, IN 47808
(812) 232-2391

INSTITUTIONAL CONTACT:
E.R. Pettebone
Director, Cooperative
Professional Practice
Indiana State University
Terre Haute, IN 47809
(812) 232-6311, X2582

PROGRAM DESCRIPTION/ OBJECTIVES:
Project involves creation of a mechanism capable of meeting the long term quantitative and qualitative workforce needs of the employing community through mutual cooperative effort.

PROGRAM INITIATED:
Project in formative stage

LENGTH OF STUDY FOR PARTICIPANT:
Variable

LENGTH OF CONTRACT:
Not available

LOCATION:
Vigo County, IN

PARTICIPANTS:
Not available

PROGRAM COSTS PROVIDED BY:
Not yet determined

PRINTED MATERIALS AVAILABLE FROM:
Not yet available

TEXAS GULF SULPHUR
with
WHARTON COUNTY JUNIOR COLLEGE

INDUSTRIAL TRAINING FIELD DEPARTMENT TEXAS GULF SULPHUR

COMPANY CONTACT:
Mr. Edgar Roades
Training Supervisor
Texas Gulf Sulphur
New Gulf, TX 77462
(713) 657-4481, X240

INSTITUTIONAL CONTACT:
Dr. John E. Brooks
Dean, Continuing Education
Wharton County Junior College
911 Boling Highway
Wharton, TX 77488
(713) 532-4560, X237

PROGRAM DESCRIPTION/ OBJECTIVES:
To develop a training module for personnel to be employed in the pipeline department. The module uses visual, oral, and written techniques of instruction. It is individualized and programmed for individual or group presentation. It allows for open-entry and exit.

PROGRAM INITIATED:
1981

LENGTH OF STUDY FOR PARTICIPANT:
Not available

LENGTH OF CONTRACT:
Open-ended

LOCATION:
New Gulf, TX

PARTICIPANTS:
70–100 field maintenance and pipelining of sulphur personnel

PROGRAM COSTS PROVIDED BY:
Institution: Undetermined at this time
Company: Open

PRINTED MATERIALS AVAILABLE FROM:
Institution

TEXAS INSTRUMENTS, INC.
with
NORTH LAKE COLLEGE OF THE DALLAS COUNTY COMMUNITY COLLEGE DISTRICT

PRECISION OPTICS TECHNOLOGY

COMPANY CONTACT:
John H. Pulliam
Manager
Optics Manufacturing and Materials
Texas Instruments, Inc.
P.O. Box 226015
Dallas, TX 75266
(214) 995-2011

INSTITUTIONAL CONTACT:
Clif Weaver
Associate Dean
Technology/Occupation Programs
North Lake College
5001 MacArthur Boulevard
Irving, TX 75062
(214) 659-5233

PROGRAM DESCRIPTION/OBJECTIVES:
Graduates of this program will be able to perform the basic, entry-level skills of precision optics technicians including the manufacturing of precision optics lenses and assisting in engineering tasks related to lens manufacture.

PROGRAM INITIATED:
1981

LENGTH OF STUDY FOR PARTICIPANT:
4 semesters

LENGTH OF CONTRACT:
12 months with renewal option

LOCATION:
North Lake College

PARTICIPANTS:
20 to 25 entry-level employees annually

PROGRAM COSTS PROVIDED BY:
Institution: 40%
Company: 60%

PRINTED MATERIALS AVAILABLE FROM:
Institution

THE TIMKEN COMPANY
with
KENT STATE UNIVERSITY

EFFECTIVE BUSINESS WRITING

COMPANY CONTACT:
Gerry Woltman
The Timken Company
1835 Duebar Avenue, SW
Canton, OH 44706
(216) 438-3487

INSTITUTIONAL CONTACT:
Karen Rylander
Director, Continuing Education
Kent State University
327 Rockwell Hall
Kent, OH 44242
(216) 672-3100

PROGRAM DESCRIPTION/OBJECTIVES:
The Effective Business Writing Seminar provides a practical review of the fundamentals of written communication for professionals in business and industry. It emphasizes the application of successful strategies for writing persuasive and efficient prose in the various business forms.

PROGRAM INITIATED:
1980

LENGTH OF STUDY FOR PARTICIPANT:
10 hours + 1 hour individual follow-up

LENGTH OF CONTRACT:
10 hours + 1 hour individual follow-up

LOCATION:
The Timken Company

PARTICIPANTS:
81 management employees

PROGRAM COSTS PROVIDED BY:
Company: 100%

**PRINTED MATERIALS
AVAILABLE FROM:**
Institution

**PRINTED MATERIALS
AVAILABLE FROM:**
Institution

TIMKEN MERCY
with
THE UNIVERSITY OF AKRON

MATCHING INDIVIDUAL AND ORGANIZATIONAL NEEDS

COMPANY CONTACT:
Shirley Hayes, R.N.
Faculty Development Training
Timken Mercy
1320 Timken Mercy Drive, NW
Canton, OH 44708
(216) 489-1142 or 489-1140

INSTITUTIONAL CONTACT:
Kathryn Vegso
Associate Dean
Continuing Education and Public Services
Adult Resource Center
The University of Akron
Akron, OH 44325
(216) 375-7448

**PROGRAM DESCRIPTION/
OBJECTIVES:**
To provide career/life planning to training personnel.

PROGRAM INITIATED:
1982

LENGTH OF STUDY FOR PARTICIPANT:
½ day sessions

LENGTH OF CONTRACT:
3 sessions with 3 different staffs

LOCATION:
Business site

PARTICIPANTS:
150 training personnel and support staff

PROGRAM COSTS PROVIDED BY:
Company: 100%

TOOL & DIE INSTITUTE
with
TRITON COLLEGE

ACCELERATED PRECISION METALWORKING APPRENTICESHIP PROGRAM (APMAP)

COMPANY CONTACT:
W. Jerome Baginski
Manager
Training & Education
Tool & Die Institute
777 Busse Highway
Park Ridge, IL 60068
(312) 825-1120

INSTITUTIONAL CONTACT:
Dr. David Kozlowski
Associate Vice President
Economic Development
Triton College
2000 5th Avenue
River Grove, IL 60171
(312) 456-0300

**PROGRAM DESCRIPTION/
OBJECTIVES:**
APMAP is a 32-week program designed to move individuals with a high aptitude for the precision metalworking trades to a high ability level in a relatively short time.

PROGRAM INITIATED:
1985

LENGTH OF STUDY FOR PARTICIPANT:
32 weeks

LENGTH OF CONTRACT:
NA

LOCATION:
Triton College

PARTICIPANTS:
N/A

PROGRAM COSTS PROVIDED BY:
Participant: $1,560

PRINTED MATERIALS AVAILABLE FROM:
Institution and company

TOSCO CORPORATION*
with
CALIFORNIA STATE COLLEGE-BAKERSFIELD

MANAGEMENT INTERNSHIP PROGRAM

COMPANY CONTACT:
Jan Leavitt
Personnel Administrator
Tosco Corporation
5121 Stockdale Highway
Bakersfield, CA 93309
(805) 397-2220

INSTITUTIONAL CONTACT:
Marcia Homme
Coordinator, Center for Business and Economic Research
California State College-Bakersfield
9001 Stockdale Highway
Bakersfield, CA 93309
(805) 833-2151

PROGRAM DESCRIPTION/OBJECTIVES:
Provide opportunity for students to gain relevant, career related experience. Interns gain experience in the working world and have an exceptional opportunity to personally participate in career and management related positions.

PROGRAM INITIATED:
1979

LENGTH OF STUDY FOR PARTICIPANT:
3 quarters

LENGTH OF CONTRACT:
12 months with grant renewal option

LOCATION:
California State College-Bakersfield

PARTICIPANTS:
20 juniors, seniors and graduates

PROGRAM COSTS PROVIDED BY:
Other Source: Federal grant monies

PRINTED MATERIALS AVAILABLE FROM:
Institution

* Representative entry—complete list available from institution.

TRADEWELL*
with
GREEN RIVER COMMUNITY COLLEGE

DYNAMIC SUPERVISION MANAGEMENT

COMPANY CONTACT:
Dan McIalwain
Training Director
Tradewell
7890 South 188th
Kent, WA 98031
(206) 251-8300

INSTITUTIONAL CONTACT:
Margaret Kaus
Associate Dean
Continuing Education
Green River Community College
12401 SE 320th Street
Auburn, WA 98002
(206) 833-9111, X231

PROGRAM DESCRIPTION/OBJECTIVES:
Present custom tailored supervisory communications education for employees. Addresses specific needs of personnel in food processing/grocery industry.

PROGRAM INITIATED:
1979

LENGTH OF STUDY FOR PARTICIPANT:
10 weeks

LENGTH OF CONTRACT:
10 weeks

LOCATION:
Tradewell Training Center

PARTICIPANTS:
24 office personnel

PROGRAM COSTS PROVIDED BY:
Company: $1,376 (including texts)

**PRINTED MATERIALS
AVAILABLE FROM:**
Institution book store

* Representative entry—complete list available from institution.

THE TREATY COMPANY
with
EDISON STATE COMMUNITY COLLEGE

SUPERVISION: THE ART OF MANAGEMENT

COMPANY CONTACT:
Jack Oliver
Vice President
Personnel Department
The Treaty Company
Gray Avenue
Greenville, OH 45331
(513) 548-2181

INSTITUTIONAL CONTACT:
Gary W. Wilson
Assistant Dean for Continuing Education
Edison State Community College
1973 Edison Drive
Piqua, OH 45356
(513) 778-8600

**PROGRAM DESCRIPTION/
OBJECTIVES:**
Comprehensive training experience for supervisory staff which will serve as a means of improving the varied levels of supervisory experience.

PROGRAM INITIATED:
1981

LENGTH OF STUDY FOR PARTICIPANT:
40 hours

LENGTH OF CONTRACT:
5 weeks

LOCATION:
Edison State Community College

PARTICIPANTS:
20 first-line supervisors

PROGRAM COSTS PROVIDED BY:
Institution: $2,453.64
Company: $3,036.50
Other Source: $210.00

**PRINTED MATERIALS
AVAILABLE FROM:**
Institution

TRINITY PAPER & PLASTICS CORPORATION
with
KEAN COLLEGE OF NEW JERSEY*

TRAINING COURSE FOR DEVELOPING SUPERVISORY & MANAGEMENT PERSONNEL

COMPANY CONTACT:
Robert V. Anaya
Personnel Manager
Personnel
Trinity Paper & Plastics Corporation
750 Dowd Avenue
Elizabeth, NJ 07201
(201) 351-2400

INSTITUTIONAL CONTACT:
Ethel J. Madsen
Director
Special Programs
Kean College of NJ
Morris Avenue
Union, NJ 07083
(201) 527-2163

PROGRAM DESCRIPTION/ OBJECTIVES:
To provide training for the development of supervisory and management personnel.

PROGRAM INITIATED:
1985

LENGTH OF STUDY FOR PARTICIPANT:
20 hours

LENGTH OF CONTRACT:
8 weeks

LOCATION:
In-house

* Representative entry—complete list available from institution.

PARTICIPANTS:
Number: 11
Type: Supervisors

PROGRAM COSTS PROVIDED BY:
Company

PRINTED MATERIALS AVAILABLE FROM:
Institution

TRI MARK INDUSTRIES
with
NORTHEAST IOWA TECHNICAL INSTITUTE

SPC (STATISTICAL PROCESS CONTROL) TRAINING

COMPANY CONTACT:
Duane Nelson
Plant Manager
Tri Mark Industries
New Hampton, IA 50659
(515) 394-3188

INSTITUTIONAL CONTACT:
Ken Vande Berg
Coordinator, Business and Industry Partnerships
Community Education
Northeast Iowa Technical Institute
Box 400
Calmar, IA 52132
(319) 562-3263

PROGRAM DESCRIPTION/ OBJECTIVES:
SPC is a management tool for solving production problems and profit problems. The focus is to improve quality and productivity by utilizing statistical quality testing as an ongoing process. SPC enhances creativity, fosters pride in workmanship, and begins the process of continuous improvement.

PROGRAM INITIATED:
1985

LENGTH OF STUDY FOR PARTICIPANTS:
56 hours

LENGTH OF CONTRACT:
4 months

LOCATION:
In plant, New Hampton

PARTICIPANTS:
Number: 29
Type: Management and supervisors

PROGRAM COSTS PROVIDED BY:
Company: 100%

PRINTED MATERIALS AVAILABLE FROM:
Not available

TRUSTHOUSE FORTE AIRPORT SERVICES, INC.
with
NEW YORK CITY TECHNICAL COLLEGE

CULINARY ARTS & GARDEN MANAGER

COMPANY CONTACT:
Anthony B. DaMaino
Executive Chef

Trusthouse Forte Airport Services, Inc.
147-17 Guy Brewer Boulevard
Jamaica, NY 11434
(718) 917-7782

INSTITUTIONAL CONTACT:
Beverly La Puma
Coordinator, Continuing Education and Extension Services
Continuing Education
New York City Technical College
300 Jay Street
Brooklyn, NY 11201
(718) 643-5570

PROGRAM DESCRIPTION/ OBJECTIVES:
A 30-hour course which covers basic preparation to finished product of chaudfroids, canapes, pates, timbales, galantines, and salads. Student will be shown the correct use of the knife, decorating tools, and the pastry bag. Students will receive instruction in the decoration of plates, meats and fish, vegetable sculpture, and other intricate displays.

LENGTH OF STUDY FOR PARTICIPANT:
30 hours

LENGTH OF CONTRACT:
2 weeks

LOCATION:
Namm Hall, 201

PARTICIPANTS:
Number: 6
Type: chefs

PROGRAM COSTS PROVIDED BY:
Company: 100%

PRINTED MATERIALS AVAILABLE FROM:
Institution and company

TULSA PORT OF CATOOSA
with
CLAREMORE COLLEGE

CLAREMORE COLLEGE TRAINING CENTER AT THE TULSA PORT OF CATOOSA

COMPANY CONTACT:
Bill Thomas
Director of Administration
Port Authority
Tulsa Port of Catoosa
5350 Cimarron Road
Catoosa, OK 74015
(918) 266-2291

INSTITUTIONAL CONTACT:
Kathy Callaham
Director of Community Services
Claremore College
College Hill
Claremore, OK 74017
(918) 341-7510

PROGRAM DESCRIPTION/ OBJECTIVES:
To provide college courses, credit and non-credit, at a convenient location and time for port personnel.

PROGRAM INITIATED:
1982

LENGTH OF STUDY FOR PARTICIPANT:
Not available

LENGTH OF CONTRACT:
Ongoing

LOCATION:
Tulsa Port of Catoosa

PARTICIPANTS:
Not reported

PROGRAM COSTS PROVIDED BY:
Company: 100%

PRINTED MATERIALS AVAILABLE FROM:
Institution

SEVERAL COMPANIES*
with
TURABO UNIVERSITY

GRADUATE PROGRAM IN BUSINESS ADMINISTRATION

COMPANY CONTACT:
Specific company not identified

INSTITUTIONAL CONTACT:
Josue Guzman
Program Director
Graduate Program in Business Administration
Turabo University
P.O. Box 1091
Caguas, Puerto Rico 00625
(809) 744-8792

PROGRAM DESCRIPTION/ OBJECTIVES:
Graduate program in business administration to offer high level education of quality in Puerto Rico.

PROGRAM INITIATED:
1981

LENGTH OF STUDY FOR PARTICIPANT:
3 years (part-time)

LENGTH OF CONTRACT:
3 years

LOCATION:
Turabo University

PARTICIPANTS:
75 junior executives, technicians, engineers, etc.

PROGRAM COSTS PROVIDED BY:
Company: 60%
Participant: 40%

PRINTED MATERIALS AVAILABLE FROM:
Institution

* Representative entry—complete list available from institution.

UC INDUSTRIES
with
KENT STATE UNIVERSITY

FIRST LINE SUPERVISION

COMPANY CONTACT:
Michael Weisenberg
UC Industries
P.O. Box 37
Tallmadge, OH 44278
(216) 633-5848

INSTITUTIONAL CONTACT:
Karen Rylander
Director, Continuing Education
Kent State University
327 Rockwell Hall
Kent, OH 44242
(216) 672-3100

PROGRAM DESCRIPTION/ OBJECTIVES:
This "how to" approach to supervisory training covers motivations, communication, decision making, problem solving, time management, delegation, and people skills.

PROGRAM INITIATED:
1981

LENGTH OF STUDY FOR PARTICIPANT:
14 hours

LENGTH OF CONTRACT:
14 hours

LOCATION:
UC Industries

PARTICIPANTS:
10 first-line supervisors

PROGRAM COSTS PROVIDED BY:
Company: 100%

PRINTED MATERIALS AVAILABLE FROM:
Institution

UNITED AIR LINES
with
COLLEGE OF SAN MATEO

MANAGEMENT CERTIFICATE PROGRAM

COMPANY CONTACT:
Karen Kobrosky
Training Officer
United Air Lines
San Francisco International Airport
San Francisco, CA 94101
(415) 876-5517

INSTITUTIONAL CONTACT:
Michael Kimball
Director of Instructional Services
College of San Mateo
1700 West Hillsdale Blvd.
San Mateo, CA 94402
(415) 574-6544

PROGRAM DESCRIPTION/ OBJECTIVES:
12-course program leading to a certificate in the area of management training.

PROGRAM INITIATED:
1981

LENGTH OF STUDY FOR PARTICIPANT:
1–6 semesters

LENGTH OF CONTRACT:
Informal, ongoing agreement

LOCATION:
United Air Lines

PARTICIPANTS:
Approximately 80 primarily United Airlines employees

PROGRAM COSTS PROVIDED BY:
Institution: 50%
Company: 50%

PRINTED MATERIALS AVAILABLE FROM:
Company

UNITED AUTO WORKERS
with
CENTRAL MICHIGAN UNIVERSITY

UAW STAFF COUNCIL PROGRAM

COMPANY CONTACT:
Bruce Kingery
United Auto Workers
International Headquarters
8000 East Jefferson Avenue
Detroit, MI 48214
(313) 886-7437

INSTITUTIONAL CONTACT:
Lawrence R. Murphy
Director
Institute for Personal and Career Development
Central Michigan University
Mt. Pleasant, MI 48859
(517) 774-3865

PROGRAM DESCRIPTION/ OBJECTIVES:
Provide undergraduate training in labor studies leading to a BS degree for labor organization leaders.

PROGRAM INITIATED:
Not reported

LENGTH OF STUDY FOR PARTICIPANT:
1–3 years

LENGTH OF CONTRACT:
Ongoing

LOCATION:
Dave Miller Retirement Center

PARTICIPANTS:
20–50 Staff Council members and union leaders

PROGRAM COSTS PROVIDED BY:
Company: 85%
Participant: 15%

PRINTED MATERIALS AVAILABLE FROM:
Institution

UNITED HOSPITALS MEDICAL CENTER
with
RUTGERS, THE STATE UNIVERSITY OF NEW JERSEY

PRIMARY AFFILIATION

COMPANY CONTACT:
Delores Henderson
Administrator
Nursing Services
United Hospitals Medical Center
15 South Ninth Street
Newark, NJ 07107
(201) 268-8767

INSTITUTIONAL CONTACT:
Lucille Joel
Associate Dean for Clinical Affairs
College of Nursing
Rutgers, The State University of New Jersey
University Avenue
Newark, NJ 07102
(201) 648-5298

PROGRAM DESCRIPTION/OBJECTIVES:
Manpower sharing; student placement.

PROGRAM INITIATED:
1981

LENGTH OF STUDY FOR PARTICIPANT:
Academic year

LENGTH OF CONTRACT:
10 months

LOCATION:
United Hospitals Medical Center and Rutgers

PARTICIPANTS:
2

PROGRAM COSTS PROVIDED BY:
Shared equally by exchange of time between company and institution.

PRINTED MATERIALS AVAILABLE FROM:
Institution

UNITED NUCLEAR CORPORATION
with
QUINEBAUG VALLEY COMMUNITY COLLEGE

ON-SITE EDUCATION

COMPANY CONTACT:
Stanley N. Cume
Director of Corporate Training
United Nuclear
67 Sandy Desert Road
Uncasville, CT 06382
(203) 848-1511

INSTITUTIONAL CONTACT:
Richard R. Fontaine
Director of Counseling and Training
Student and Community Services
Quinebaug Valley Community College
P.O. Box 59, Maple Street
Danielson, CT 06239
(203) 774-1130

PROGRAM DESCRIPTION/OBJECTIVES:
To make college courses conveniently available to company employees interested in the college's Industrial Supervision Program.

PROGRAM INITIATED:
1979

LENGTH OF STUDY FOR PARTICIPANT:
1 semester per course

LENGTH OF CONTRACT:
Semester by semester

LOCATION:
United Nuclear

PARTICIPANTS:
Varies, approximately 36 current and aspiring supervisors per semester

PROGRAM COSTS PROVIDED BY:
Institution: Some overhead
Company: $850 per course
Participant: Unknown

PRINTED MATERIALS AVAILABLE FROM:
Not reported

UNITED PARCEL SERVICE*
with
MERRITT COLLEGE

JOB PLACEMENT

COMPANY CONTACT:
Glenn Leydecker
Personnel
United Parcel Service
579 McCormick Avenue
San Leandro, CA 94501
(415) 635-6227

INSTITUTIONAL CONTACT:
George Ito
Placement Officer
Career Center
Merritt College
12500 Campus Drive
Oakland, CA 94619
(415) 436-2449

PROGRAM DESCRIPTION/ OBJECTIVES:
Match student job applicants to job opportunities. Particular interest in matching skills gained in Merritt training with needs of employers.

PROGRAM INITIATED:
1968

LENGTH OF STUDY FOR PARTICIPANT:
At least 1 semester

LENGTH OF CONTRACT:
Ongoing

LOCATION:
Merritt College

PARTICIPANTS:
Approximately 1,000 current student and graduate student applicants per semester

PROGRAM COSTS PROVIDED BY:
Institution: $30,000
Other Source: $10,000

PRINTED MATERIALS AVAILABLE FROM:
Institution

* Representative entry—complete list available from institution.

UNITED NUCLEAR CORPORATION
with
UNIVERSITY OF HARTFORD

IMPROVING INTERPERSONAL EFFECTIVENESS FOR MANAGERS

COMPANY CONTACT:
John C. Parker
Manager, Human Resources
United Nuclear Corporation
67 Sandy Desert Road
Uncasville, CT 06382
(203) 848-1511

INSTITUTIONAL CONTACT:
M. Brady/G. Maffeo
Director, Continuing Education
Division of Adult Educational Services
University of Hartford
200 Bloomfield Avenue
West Hartford, CT 06117
(203) 243-4387

PROGRAM DESCRIPTION/ OBJECTIVES:
Intensive 1-day seminar designed to teach managers and supervisors how to interact more effectively with subordinates, peers, and superiors.

PROGRAM INITIATED:
1981

LENGTH OF STUDY FOR PARTICIPANT:
1 training day (7 contact hours)

LENGTH OF CONTRACT:
1 time-pilot with possibility of renewal

LOCATION:
Uncasville, CT

PARTICIPANTS:
25 technical personnel, engineers, etc.

PROGRAM COSTS PROVIDED BY:
Company: 100%

PRINTED MATERIALS AVAILABLE FROM:
Institution

UNITED STATES ARMY FINANCE AND ACCOUNTING CENTER
with
CENTRAL MICHIGAN UNIVERSITY

COMPANY CONTACT:
Mr. Darrell Roth
Civilian Personnel Office
United States Army Finance and Accounting Center
Fort Benjamin Harrison
Indianapolis, IN 46249
(317) 542-2383

INSTITUTIONAL CONTACT:
Dr. Richard Potter
Assistant Director
Central Michigan University
Institute for Personal and Career Development
Rowe 130
Mt. Pleasant, MI 48859
(517) 774-7133

PROGRAM DESCRIPTION/OBJECTIVES:
Graduate Management Development Program for selected managers of USAFAC. Participants may, at their option, earn a Master of Science in Administration through participation in the program.

PROGRAM INITIATED:
Fall, 1984

LENGTH OF STUDY FOR PARTICIPANT:
30 months

LENGTH OF CONTRACT:
36 months

LOCATION:
USAFAC, Ft. Benjamin Harrison, IN

PARTICIPANTS:
32 high performance managers selected by USAFAC

PROGRAM COST PROVIDED BY:
USAFAC-100%

PRINTED MATERIALS AVAILABLE FROM:
Institution

U.S. DEPARTMENT OF HEALTH AND HUMAN SERVICES
with
PRINCE GEORGE'S COMMUNITY COLLEGE

CERTIFIED PROFESSIONAL SECRETARIAL PROGRAM

COMPANY CONTACT:
Elaine Lazaroff
EEO Specialist
Health Resources Administration
U.S. Department of Health and Human Services
3700 East-West Highway
Hyattsville, MD 20782
(301) 436-7210

INSTITUTIONAL CONTACT:
Veronica S. Norwood
Director, Contract Services
Prince George's Community College
301 Largo Road
Largo, MD 20772
(301) 322-0726

PROGRAM DESCRIPTION/OBJECTIVES:
To prepare participants to successfully complete the Certified Professional Secretary Examination and to enhance present skills and abilities, leading to positions of greater responsibility.

PROGRAM INITIATED:
1979

LENGTH OF STUDY FOR PARTICIPANT:
5 1-semester credit classes and 3 18–30 hour non-credit classes offered over a 24-month period

LENGTH OF CONTRACT:
Renewable each semester

LOCATION:
Health Resources Administration

PARTICIPANTS:
16 secretaries and clerk-typists

PROGRAM COSTS PROVIDED BY:
Company: 50%
Other Source: 50% (state funds)

PRINTED MATERIALS AVAILABLE FROM:
Institution

LENGTH OF STUDY FOR PARTICIPANT:
4 days, 8 hours each day

LENGTH OF CONTRACT:
24 hours

LOCATION:
Office of Justice Assistance and Research

PARTICIPANTS:
25 employees undergoing RIF per session

PROGRAM COSTS PROVIDED BY:
Company: 50%
Other Source: 50% (state funds)

PRINTED MATERIALS AVAILABLE FROM:
Institution

U.S. DEPARTMENT OF JUSTICE
with
PRINCE GEORGE'S COMMUNITY COLLEGE

CAREER PLANNING

COMPANY CONTACT:
Allison Howell
Office of Justice Assistance and Research
U.S. Department of Justice
633 Indiana Avenue
Washington, DC 20531
(202) 724-3154

INSTITUTIONAL CONTACT:
Veronica Norwood
Director, Contract Services
Prince George's Community College
301 Largo Road
Largo, MD 20772
(301) 322-0726

PROGRAM DESCRIPTION/ OBJECTIVES:
To familiarize participants with a career-life planning and decision-making model which can be effectively utilized in a career change situation.

PROGRAM INITIATED:
1982

U.S. POSTAL SERVICE
with
UNIVERSITY OF VIRGINIA

ADVANCED MANAGEMENT PROGRAM

COMPANY CONTACT:
Norman Buehler
General Manager
Career Development Division
HQ U.S. Postal Service
475 L'Enfant Plaza
Washington, DC 20260
(202) 245-4696

INSTITUTIONAL CONTACT:
Robert Fair
Assistant Dean
Graduate Business Administration
University of Virginia
Charlottesville, VA 22904
(804) 924-7195

PROGRAM DESCRIPTION/ OBJECTIVES:
Opportunity for selected employees to pursue college coursework to improve managerial skills at an executive level.

PROGRAM INITIATED:
1978

LENGTH OF STUDY FOR PARTICIPANT:
1 semester-1 year

LOCATION:
Campus

PARTICIPANTS:
12 selected professionals, executives and candidates

PROGRAM COSTS PROVIDED BY:
Company: 100%

PRINTED MATERIALS AVAILABLE FROM:
Institution

U.S. POSTAL SERVICE
with
INSTITUTIONS THROUGHOUT THE U.S.*

TUITION ASSISTANCE

COMPANY CONTACT:
Norman Buehler
General Manager
Career Development Division
HQ U.S. Postal Service
475 L'Enfant Plaza
Washington, DC 20260
(202) 245-4696

INSTITUTIONAL CONTACT:
Not available

PROGRAM DESCRIPTION/OBJECTIVES:
To provide tuition assistance for executives and candidates; to provide educational development and skills for improved performance at executive and managerial levels.

PROGRAM INITIATED:
1978

LENGTH OF STUDY FOR PARTICIPANT:
1 semester-1 year

LENGTH OF CONTRACT:
1 semester-1 year

LOCATION:
Varied at institutions

PARTICIPANTS:
30 Postal Service employees

PROGRAM COSTS PROVIDED BY:
Company: 100%

PRINTED MATERIALS AVAILABLE FROM:
Institution and company

* Representative entry—complete list available from institution.

U.S. SMALL BUSINESS ADMINISTRATION
with
EL PASO COMMUNITY COLLEGE

BUSINESS AND INDUSTRY CENTER

COMPANY CONTACT:
Abby H. Carter
Assistant District Director for Management Assistance
Management Assistance
U.S. Small Business Administration
10737 Gateway Blvd. W.
El Paso, TX 79935
(915) 541-7560

INSTITUTIONAL CONTACT:
Roque R. Segura
Coordinator
Small Business Center
El Paso Community College
P.O. Box 20500
El Paso, TX 79998
(915) 534-4135

PROGRAM DESCRIPTION/OBJECTIVES:
To co-sponsor entrepreneurship training and provide counseling assistance services to small business persons for growth and economic development.

PROGRAM INITIATED:
On-going

LENGTH OF STUDY FOR PARTICIPANT:
On-going

LENGTH OF CONTRACT:
Yearly

LOCATION:
Chamber of Commerce and El Paso Community College

PARTICIPANTS:
Small business
Number: Varies per training program
Type: Small business owners, managers, and employees

PROGRAM COSTS PROVIDED BY:
Institution: Staff salaries
Company: Staff salaries
Other Source: (Institutional funds, federal grants)

PRINTED MATERIALS AVAILABLE FROM:
Institution and company

LENGTH OF STUDY FOR PARTICIPANT:
3 quarters

LENGTH OF CONTRACT:
Not reported

LOCATION:
U.S. and Europe

PARTICIPANTS:
25 MBA and undergraduate business students

PROGRAM COSTS PROVIDED BY:
Company: Student salary

PRINTED MATERIALS AVAILABLE FROM:
Institution

* Representative entry—complete list available from institution.

20 OR MORE COMPANIES*
with
UNIVERSITY OF ILLINOIS-CHICAGO CIRCLE

COOPERATIVE INTERN PROGRAM

COMPANY CONTACT:
Specific company not identified

INSTITUTIONAL CONTACT:
Dr. Fred McLinmore
Associate Dean for External Affairs
University of Illinois-Chicago Circle
Chicago, IL 60680
(312) 996-0529

PROGRAM DESCRIPTION/OBJECTIVES:
To provide students with a management related experience and job contact.

PROGRAM INITIATED:
1977

VIRGINIA NATIONAL BANK
with
OLD DOMINION UNIVERSITY

RESEARCH ON DATA PROCESSING PROFESSIONAL'S PRODUCTIVITY

COMPANY CONTACT:
Truman Hester
Department Chief
Data Processing
Virginia National Bank
1 Commercial Plaza
Norfolk, VA 23510
(804) 441-4000

INSTITUTIONAL CONTACT:
Mark Chadwin
Director
Bureau of Business and Economic Research
Old Dominion University
Norfolk, VA 23508
(804) 440-4598

PROGRAM DESCRIPTION/ OBJECTIVES:
Analyze determinants of programmer performance.

PROGRAM INITIATED:
Not reported

LENGTH OF STUDY FOR PARTICIPANT:
Not available

LENGTH OF CONTRACT:
2 months with renewal option

LOCATION:
Norfolk

PARTICIPANTS:
Various numbers of data processing management, staff, programmers and systems analysts

PROGRAM COSTS PROVIDED BY:
Institution: Overhead
Company: $5,000

PRINTED MATERIALS AVAILABLE FROM:
Not yet available

VIRGINIA CREDIT UNION LEAGUE
with
JOHN TYLER COMMUNITY COLLEGE

CREDIT UNION OPERATIONS MANAGEMENT

COMPANY CONTACT:
Mr. Donald Graham
Human Resource Development Specialist
Education
Virginia Credit Union League
1207 Fenwick Drive
Lynchburg, VA 24506
(804) 237-6466

INSTITUTIONAL CONTACT:
Dr. Samuel Lee Hancock
Director
Division of Continuing Education
John Tyler Community College
13101 Jefferson Davis Highway
Chester, VA 23831
(804) 796-4111

PROGRAM DESCRIPTION/ OBJECTIVES:
The courses are designed to help the employees better understand the workings and management of a credit union operation. A second objective is career advancement for those successfully completing the 3 courses.

PROGRAM INITIATED:
Winter, 1982

LENGTH OF STUDY FOR PARTICIPANT:
3 college quarters

LENGTH OF CONTRACT:
30 instructional hours per college quarter

LOCATION:
On-campus at John Tyler Community College

PARTICIPANTS:
Number: 18–20
Type: Employees of local credit unions

PROGRAM COSTS PROVIDED BY:
Institution: Administrative leadership, instructors' salaries
Company: Coordination leadership
Participant: Time
Other Source: Local credit unions: tuition, textbooks

PRINTED MATERIALS AVAILABLE FROM:
Institution

VIRGINIA POWER
with
JOHN TYLER COMMUNITY COLLEGE

NUCLEAR FOUNDATIONS TRAINING PROGRAM

COMPANY CONTACT:
Mr. Arthur H. Friedman
Director-Training (Power Operations)

Power Training Services
Virginia Power
11201 Old Stage Road
Chester, VA 23831
(804) 748-3610, Ext. 3004

INSTITUTIONAL CONTACT:
Dr. Samuel Lee Hancock
Director
Division of Continuing Education
John Tyler Community College
13101 Jefferson Davis Highway
Chester, VA 23831
(804) 796-4111

PROGRAM DESCRIPTION/ OBJECTIVES:
The program will prepare trainees for admittance into the Nuclear Control Room Operator Development or the Health Physics Technician Development Programs.

PROGRAM INITIATED:
Fall, 1985

LENGTH OF STUDY FOR PARTICIPANT:
6 months (26 weeks)

LENGTH OF CONTRACT:
1,080 instructional contact hours

LOCATION:
On-site at the Power Operations Training Center, Chester, VA

PARTICIPANTS:
Number: 16
Type: Control Room Operator or Health Physics Technician Trainees

PROGRAM COSTS PROVIDED BY:
Institution: Administrative leadership
Company: Educational materials, equipment, supplies, training site
Participant: Time
Other Source: Virginia Apprentice Training Program: instructors' salaries

PRINTED MATERIALS AVAILABLE FROM:
Company

VITRO CORPORATION
with
UNIVERSITY OF SOUTHERN CALIFORNIA

MASTER OF SCIENCE (MS) IN SYSTEMS MANAGEMENT

COMPANY CONTACT:
Mary L. Woodworth
Supervisor
Employee Orientation and Support Programs
Vitro Corporation
14000 Georgia Avenue, TGA5-501
Silver Spring, MD 20910
(301) 231-1546

INSTITUTIONAL CONTACT:
Jon W. Whitton
Field Representative
Eastern Region
University of Southern California
5510 Columbia Pike, #200
Arlington, VA 22204
(703) 521-5025

PROGRAM DESCRIPTION/ OBJECTIVES:
The MS in Systems Management is designed to meet the graduate education needs of modern managers who seek competence in the systems approach and its use in formulation of strategy and policy decisions.

PROGRAM INITIATED:
1983

LENGTH OF STUDY FOR PARTICIPANT:
2 years

LENGTH OF CONTRACT:
Open ended

LOCATION:
Silver Spring, MD

PARTICIPANTS:
Number: 25
Type: management-level personnel

PROGRAM COSTS PROVIDED BY:
Company

PRINTED MATERIALS
AVAILABLE FROM:
Institution

VULCAN MATERIALS COMPANY
with
BIRMINGHAM-SOUTHERN
COLLEGE

EXECUTIVES IN RESIDENCE
COMPANY CONTACT:
Herbert A. Sklenar
President and CEO
Vulcan Materials Company
P.O. Box 7497
Birmingham, AL 35253
(205) 877-3000

INSTITUTIONAL CONTACT:
Natalie M. Davis
Director of Graduate Studies
Birmingham-Southern College
800 8th Avenue West
Birmingham, AL 35254
(205) 328-5250, ext. 214

PROGRAM DESCRIPTION/
OBJECTIVES:
The objectives of the program are to provide an on-campus, mini-sabbatical for local executives in business, government, industry, and social service agencies. Executives are afforded an opportunity to meet together in seminar sessions, hear outstanding speakers on pertinent topics, work on office or personal projects, conduct research in areas of professional or personal interest, and work with members of the faculty and student body.

PROGRAM INITIATED:
1978

LENGTH OF STUDY FOR
PARTICIPANT:
One week

LENGTH OF CONTRACT:
Ongoing

LOCATION:
Birmingham-Southern College

PARTICIPANTS:
Number: 30–60
Type: selected executives annually

PROGRAM COSTS PROVIDED BY:
Institution: 100%

PRINTED MATERIALS
AVAILABLE FROM:
Institution

WALTER REED ARMY MEDICAL
CENTER
with
CENTRAL MICHIGAN
UNIVERSITY

WALTER REED ARMY MEDICAL CENTER PROGRAM
COMPANY CONTACT:
Michael Burnam
Education Director
Education Center
Walter Reed Army Medical Center
Washington, DC 20044
(202) 545-6700

INSTITUTIONAL CONTACT:
Dr. Lawrence R. Murphy
Director
Institute for Personal and Career Development
Central Michigan University
Mt. Pleasant, MI 48859
(517) 774-3865

PROGRAM DESCRIPTION/
OBJECTIVES:
Provide professional training in management and supervision with a health care emphasis; leads to a MA degree.

PROGRAM INITIATED:
Not reported

LENGTH OF STUDY FOR
PARTICIPANT:
1–3 years

LENGTH OF CONTRACT:
Ongoing

LOCATION:
Walter Reed Army Medical Center

PARTICIPANTS:
Military and civilian employees of local hospitals

PROGRAM COSTS PROVIDED BY:
Participant: 100%

PRINTED MATERIALS AVAILABLE FROM:
Institution

WASHINGTON SUBURBAN SANITARY COMMISSION
with
PRINCE GEORGE'S COMMUNITY COLLEGE

SANITARY WASTEWATER TECHNOLOGY

COMPANY CONTACT:
Mona Chase
Coordinator, Training
Washington Suburban Sanitary Commission
4017 Hamilton Street
Hyattsville, MD 20781
(301) 699-4518

INSTITUTIONAL CONTACT:
Margaretta Bir
Program Assistant
Community Services
Prince George's Community College
301 Largo Road
Largo, MD 20772
(301) 322-0793

PROGRAM DESCRIPTION/OBJECTIVES:
Improve performance and assist in obtaining state license required of plant superintendents

PROGRAM INITIATED:
1982

LENGTH OF STUDY FOR PARTICIPANT:
1 semester (45 hours)

LENGTH OF CONTRACT:
1 semester and renewable as required

LOCATION:
Prince George's Community College

PARTICIPANTS:
12 plant superintendents and technical personnel

PROGRAM COSTS PROVIDED BY:
Company: $90 per student
Other Source: $89 per student (state funds)

PRINTED MATERIALS AVAILABLE FROM:
Institution

WEBER KNAPP
with
JAMESTOWN COMMUNITY COLLEGE

SHOP MATH

COMPANY CONTACT:
Thomas Madison
Personnel Assistant
Personnel Department
Weber Knapp
441 Changler Street
Jamestown, NY 14701
(716) 484-9135

INSTITUTIONAL CONTACT:
Rose M. Scott
Continuing Education Assistant
Jamestown Community College
525 Falconer Street
Jamestown, NY 14701
(716) 665-5220

PROGRAM DESCRIPTION/OBJECTIVES:
To provide a basic understanding of mathematical principles for presently employed machinists in order to maintain skills needed to keep pace with changing technology.

PROGRAM INITIATED:
Not reported

LENGTH OF STUDY FOR PARTICIPANT:
8 weeks

LENGTH OF CONTRACT:
12 months with option to renew

LOCATION:
Weber Knapp

PARTICIPANTS:
35 machinists per class

PROGRAM COSTS PROVIDED BY:
Institution: 40%
Company: 20%
Other Source: 20%

PRINTED MATERIALS AVAILABLE FROM:
Not available

WELLS FARGO BANK
with
COGSWELL COLLEGE

BUILDING SAFETY/FIRE PREPLANNING

COMPANY CONTACT:
C. Paul Bernard
AVP and Manager
Safety Department
Wells Fargo Bank
343 Sansome Street
San Francisco, CA 94163
(415) 396-5923

INSTITUTIONAL CONTACT:
Philip Alan Cecchettini
Dean
Continuing Education
Cogswell College
600 Stockton Street
San Francisco, CA 94108
(415) 433-5550

PROGRAM DESCRIPTION/ OBJECTIVES:
To provide instruction in the basics of building safety and fire preplanning techniques in compliance with Titles 19 and 24 created by the State Fire Marshall of California.

PROGRAM INITIATED:
1981

LENGTH OF CONTRACT:
6 months

LOCATION:
Cogswell College and Wells Fargo

PARTICIPANTS:
100 of a variety of designated management personnel from bank buildings annually

PROGRAM COSTS PROVIDED BY:
Institution: 10%
Company: 90%

PRINTED MATERIALS AVAILABLE FROM:
Institution

WESTVACO CORP.
with
DABNEY S. LANCASTER COMMUNITY COLLEGE

CROSS-TRAINING OF JOURNEYMEN

COMPANY CONTACT:
Homer Landis
Director of Training
Training
Westvaco Corp.
Covington, VA 24426
(703) 969-5500

INSTITUTIONAL CONTACT:
Bill Greene
Director, Business/Industry Training
Vocational Training
(Bob Meyers/Everett Mays)
Dabney S. Lancaster Community
  College
Clifton Forge, VA 24422
(703) 862-4247, Ext. 228

PROGRAM DESCRIPTION/ OBJECTIVES:
To provide welding skills for journeymen pipefitters, mechanics, millwrights.

LENGTH OF STUDY FOR PARTICIPANT:
40 hours

LENGTH OF CONTRACT:
1 year

LOCATION:
In plant and on campus

PARTICIPANTS:
Number: 50
Type: Full-time employees

PROGRAM COSTS PROVIDED BY:
Company: 100%

LENGTH OF STUDY FOR PARTICIPANT:
Minimum 15 weeks

LENGTH OF CONTRACT:
Minimum 15 weeks

LOCATION:
Depends upon internship site

PARTICIPANTS:
All junior-standing students

PROGRAM COSTS PROVIDED BY:
Participant: $50 per credit

PRINTED MATERIALS AVAILABLE FROM:
Institution and company

* Representative entry—complete list available from institution.

VARIOUS INDUSTRIES AND STATE AGENCIES*
with
WESLEY COLLEGE

ENVIRONMENTAL SCIENCES INTERNSHIP

COMPANY CONTACT:
Specific list is available

INSTITUTIONAL CONTACT:
Terrance L. Higgins
Director, Environmental Sciences Program
Wesley College
Dover, DE 19901
(302) 736-2477

PROGRAM DESCRIPTION/ OBJECTIVES:
Internship in one of a variety of positions with private industry or governmental agency. Each internship position will be structured so as to provide the student with a set of realistic learning experiences in a professional environment.

PROGRAM INITIATED:
1981

VIRGINIA DEPARTMENT OF EDUCATION
with
MARYMOUNT COLLEGE OF VIRGINIA

MATHEMATICS AND COMPUTER EDUCATION FOR CERTIFIED PUBLIC SCHOOL TEACHERS

COMPANY CONTACT:
Virginia Department of Education
P.O. Box 6Q
Richmond, VA 23216

INSTITUTIONAL CONTACT:
Dr. Ellen Hocking
Coordinator, Mathematics Program
Marymount College of Virginia
Arlington, VA 22207

LENGTH OF STUDY FOR PARTICIPANT:
1 to 2 years

LENGTH OF CONTRACT:
2 years

PROGRAM COSTS PROVIDED BY:
Institution: Costs of instruction and support services not covered by tuition
Company: Cost of tuition for participants

WEST VIRGINIA STATE POLICE
with
MARSHALL UNIVERSITY

WEST VIRGINIA STATE POLICE
COMPANY CONTACT:
John Buckalew
West Virginia State Police
Department of Public Safety
Charleston, WV 25301
(304) 348-6370

INSTITUTIONAL CONTACT:
Paul D. Hines
Vice President/Dean
Community College
Marshall University
16th Street and Hal Greer Blvd.
Huntington, WV 25701
(304) 696-3646

PROGRAM DESCRIPTION/OBJECTIVES:
To improve state police training standards.

PROGRAM INITIATED:
1977

LENGTH OF STUDY FOR PARTICIPANT:
20 or 36 weeks

LENGTH OF CONTRACT:
Ongoing

LOCATION:
Marshall University

PARTICIPANTS:
400 cadets or full-time West Virginia State Police

PROGRAM COSTS PROVIDED BY:
Shared, depending on the year

PRINTED MATERIALS AVAILABLE FROM:
Institution

WESTERN ELECTRIC COMPANY
with
FRANKLIN UNIVERSITY

COMPUTER TECHNOLOGY PROGRAM

COMPANY CONTACT:
Lynn Davis
Department Chief
Training and Development
Western Electric Company
6200 East Broad
Columbus, OH 43213
(614) 860-3991

INSTITUTIONAL CONTACT:
Peg Thomas
Director of Continuing and Management Education
Franklin University
201 South Grant Avenue
Columbus, OH 43215
(614) 224-6388

PROGRAM DESCRIPTION/OBJECTIVES:
Several courses from the computer technology area were chosen by Western Electric managers to be offered on-site. The objective is to involve interested employees in the new technology and help them begin a degree.

PROGRAM INITIATED:
1978

LENGTH OF STUDY FOR PARTICIPANT:
1–3 years

LENGTH OF CONTRACT:
Ongoing

LOCATION:
Western Electric

PARTICIPANTS:
65 company employees

PROGRAM COSTS PROVIDED BY:
Company: 100% tuition, fees

PRINTED MATERIALS AVAILABLE FROM:
Not available

WESTERN PUBLISHING COMPANY
with
UNIVERSITY OF WISCONSIN-PARKSIDE

BUSINESS/INDUSTRY LIAISON PROGRAM

INSTITUTIONAL CONTACT:
Wendi Schneider
Counselor, Community Student Services
University of Wisconsin-Parkside
Box 2000
Kenosha, WI 53141
(414) 553-2496

PROGRAM DESCRIPTION/OBJECTIVES:
Increase the number of adults attending University of Wisconsin-Parkside by providing more information about available programs and simplified registration procedures to members of the local business community. 1,100 businesses are on the mailing list, receive visits with 15 on-site registrations.

PROGRAM INITIATED:
1977

LENGTH OF STUDY FOR PARTICIPANT:
Varies

LENGTH OF CONTRACT:
Not available

LOCATION:
University of Wisconsin-Parkside

PARTICIPANTS:
40% of the student body is over 23 years old

PROGRAM COSTS PROVIDED BY:
Institution: 100%

PRINTED MATERIALS AVAILABLE FROM:
Institution

WESTMINSTER BUSINESS SYSTEMS, INC.
with
COLLEGE OF LAKE COUNTY

INFORMATION PROCESSING EQUIPMENT SERVICE TECHNICIANS OJT

COMPANY CONTACT:
Karl Lichtenberger
President
Westminster Business Systems, Inc.
999 Sherwood Drive
Lake Bluff, IL 60044
(312) 234-0506

INSTITUTIONAL CONTACT:
Keri Thiessen
Business/Industry Training Coordinator
Open Campus
College of Lake County
Grayslake, IL 60030
(312) 223-3616

PROGRAM DESCRIPTION/OBJECTIVES:
High Impact Training Service (HITS) grant which provided funds for OJT of service technicians. Westminster Business Systems, Inc. employees served as instructors in the servicing of high technology information processing equipment.

PROGRAM INITIATED:
1982

LENGTH OF STUDY FOR PARTICIPANT:
6 months

LENGTH OF CONTRACT:
6 months

LOCATION:
Westminster Business Systems

PARTICIPANTS:
Service technicians

PROGRAM COSTS PROVIDED BY:
Other Source: $8,000 (state funds)

PRINTED MATERIALS
AVAILABLE FROM:
Company

WHIRLPOOL COMPANY
with
CENTRAL MICHIGAN UNIVERSITY

WHIRLPOOL/CMU PROGRAM

COMPANY CONTACT:
Louis Mineweaser
Corporate Personnel Manager
Whirlpool Company
Research and Engineering Center
Monte Road
Benton Harbor, MI 49022
(616) 926-5000

INSTITUTIONAL CONTACT:
Lawrence R. Murphy
Director
Institute for Personal and Career Development
Central Michigan University
Mt. Pleasant, MI 48859
(517) 774-3865

PROGRAM DESCRIPTION/ OBJECTIVES:
To provide an opportunity for employees of the Whirlpool Research Division with high level of technical training for complete bachelor's degrees.

PROGRAM INITIATED:
Not reported

LENGTH OF STUDY FOR PARTICIPANT:
27 months average

LENGTH OF CONTRACT:
Ongoing

LOCATION:
Whirlpool plant

PARTICIPANTS:
20 technicians

PROGRAM COSTS PROVIDED BY:
Company: 100%

PRINTED MATERIALS
AVAILABLE FROM:
Institution

ANONYMOUS INDUSTRIAL DONOR
with
WILMINGTON COLLEGE

COOPERATIVE EDUCATION

COMPANY CONTACT:
Anonymous

INSTITUTIONAL CONTACT:
Diane Alazi
Director, Career Center
Wilmington College
Pyle Center #1306
Wilmington, OH 45177
(513) 382-6661, X299

PROGRAM DESCRIPTION/ OBJECTIVES:
An alternative process for acquiring baccalaureate level competency for careers in agriculture, business and industry by students alternating periods of study with periods of work (with progressive learning).

PROGRAM INITIATED:
1981

LENGTH OF STUDY FOR PARTICIPANT:
Typical student will require 4 years

LENGTH OF CONTRACT:
3-5 years

LOCATION:
Wilmington College

PARTICIPANTS:
Average of 15 undergraduate students annually

PROGRAM COSTS PROVIDED BY:
Company: $40,000

PRINTED MATERIALS AVAILABLE FROM:
Institution

TOWN OF WINDSOR
with
UNIVERSITY OF HARTFORD

EFFECTIVE SUPERVISORY TRAINING

COMPANY CONTACT:
Albert Ilg
City Manager
Town of Windsor
Windsor, CT 06095
(203) 688-3675

INSTITUTIONAL CONTACT:
Gilbert J. Maffeo
Program Development Consultant
Division of Adult Educational Services
University of Hartford
200 Bloomfield Avenue
West Hartford, CT 06117
(203) 243-4350/4381

PROGRAM DESCRIPTION/ OBJECTIVES:
To provide effective supervisory skills training to members of administrative staff. To upgrade managerial skills of department heads and assistants.

PROGRAM INITIATED:
1981

LENGTH OF STUDY FOR PARTICIPANT:
10–15 weeks

LENGTH OF CONTRACT:
10–15 weeks/ongoing

LOCATION:
On-site at town of Windsor

PARTICIPANTS:
10–15 varying level of management, homogeneously grouped personnel

PROGRAM COSTS PROVIDED BY:
Company: 100%

PRINTED MATERIALS AVAILABLE FROM:
Institution and company

TOWN OF WINDSOR
with
UNIVERSITY OF HARTFORD

PROMOTION ASSESSMENT PROGRAM

COMPANY CONTACT:
Maxwell Patterson
Chief of Police
Town of Windsor
Windsor, CT 06095
(213) 688-5273

INSTITUTIONAL CONTACT:
Gilbert J. Maffeo
Program Development Consultant
Division of Adult Educational Services
University of Hartford
200 Bloomfield Avenue
West Hartford, CT 06117
(203) 243-4350/4381

PROGRAM DESCRIPTION/ OBJECTIVES:
To provide personnel assessment skills to the town of Windsor.

PROGRAM INITIATED:
1980

LENGTH OF STUDY FOR PARTICIPANT:
3–6 days

LENGTH OF CONTRACT:
3–6 days

LOCATION:
On campus

PARTICIPANTS:
25 town employees

PROGRAM COSTS PROVIDED BY:
Company: 100%

PRINTED MATERIALS AVAILABLE FROM:
Institution and company

WISCONSIN TELEPHONE*
with
ALVERNO COLLEGE

VOLUNTEER ASSESSOR PROGRAM

COMPANY CONTACT:
Harold Steen
Division Staff Manager
Wisconsin Telephone
324 East Wisconsin Avenue
Milwaukee, WI 53202
(414) 678-3375

INSTITUTIONAL CONTACT:
Marilyn Thanos
Director
Assessment Center
Alverno College
3401 South 39th Street
Milwaukee, WI 53215
(414) 647-3792

PROGRAM DESCRIPTION/ OBJECTIVES:
To provide assessors to evaluate students' achievement (e.g., group problem-solving skills) who are professional, non-academic personnel; to enable assessors to remain updated on assessment art and practice.

PROGRAM INITIATED:
1971

LENGTH OF STUDY FOR PARTICIPANT:
Training and retraining sessions for assessors are ½ day. Taught by faculty.

LENGTH OF CONTRACT:
1 year; renewable

LOCATION:
Alverno College

PARTICIPANTS:
Approximately 100–125 students, professionals in particular fields each semester

PROGRAM COSTS PROVIDED BY:
Institution: Operating costs of Assessment Center

Company: Assessor time volunteered by companies

PRINTED MATERIALS AVAILABLE FROM:
Institution

* Representative entry—complete list available from institution.

WPRI-TV
with
COMMUNITY COLLEGE OF RHODE ISLAND

INTRODUCTION TO MICROCOMPUTERS

COMPANY CONTACT:
Edward Passarelli
Business Manager
WPRI-TV
25 Catamore Boulevard
East Providence, RI 02914
(401) 438-7200

INSTITUTIONAL CONTACT:
Robert Danilowicz
Coordinator
Missing Link Project
Off Campus Credit Programs
Community College of Rhode Island
Flanagan Campus
Louisquisset Pike
Lincoln, RI 02865
(401) 333-7127

PROGRAM DESCRIPTION/ OBJECTIVES:
Course was designed to familiarize students with methodology and application of microcomputers system, number systems, logic functions.

PROGRAM INITIATED:
1981

LENGTH OF STUDY FOR PARTICIPANT:
8 weeks

LENGTH OF CONTRACT:
1 semester

LOCATION:
WPRI-TV

PARTICIPANTS:
20 mid-management

PROGRAM COSTS PROVIDED BY:
Company: $200
Participant: $800

PRINTED MATERIALS AVAILABLE FROM:
Institution

WYANDOTTE GENERAL HOSPITAL
with
CENTRAL MICHIGAN UNIVERSITY

WYANDOTTE GENERAL PROGRAM

COMPANY CONTACT:
Roger Griswold
Personnel Director
Wyandotte General Hospital
2333 Biddle Avenue
Wyandotte, MI 48192
(313) 284-2400

INSTITUTIONAL CONTACT:
Lawrence R. Murphy
Director
Institute for Personal and Career Development
Central Michigan University
Mt. Pleasant, MI 48859
(517) 774-3865

PROGRAM DESCRIPTION/OBJECTIVES:
To provide an opportunity for area health care professionals to obtain master's level preparation for middle management position in the health care industry.

PROGRAM INITIATED:
Not reported

LENGTH OF STUDY FOR PARTICIPANT:
22 months average

LENGTH OF CONTRACT:
Ongoing

LOCATION:
Wyandotte General Hospital

PARTICIPANTS:
Not reported

PROGRAM COSTS PROVIDED BY:
Participant: 100%

PRINTED MATERIALS AVAILABLE FROM:
Institution

WYMAN-GORDAN COMPANY
with
WORCESTER STATE COLLEGE

ENTRY-LEVEL MANAGEMENT PROGRAM

COMPANY CONTACT:
Jane Gallagher
Director, Human Resources
Wyman-Gordon Company
244 Worcester Street
North Grafton, MA 01536
(617) 839-4441

INSTITUTIONAL CONTACT:
William O'Neil
Dean, Division of Graduate and Continuing Education
Worcester State College
486 Chandler Street
Worcester, MA 01602
(617) 793-8100

PROGRAM DESCRIPTION/OBJECTIVES:
To develop a new continuing education pool while meeting the needs of local companies; to provide practical training for entry-level managers; careerpath development, college credit, skill development.

PROGRAM INITIATED:
1982

LENGTH OF STUDY FOR PARTICIPANT:
21 credits; 2 year average

LENGTH OF CONTRACT:
Agreement has no termination date

LOCATION:
Wyman-Gordon plant and WSC campus

PARTICIPANTS:
40–60 entry-level and middle managers annually

PROGRAM COSTS PROVIDED BY:
Institution: $900 per participant
Company: $900 per participant

PRINTED MATERIALS AVAILABLE FROM:
Institution

XEROX CORPORATION*
with
UNIVERSITY OF THE STATE OF NEW YORK

NEW YORK REGENTS AND XEROX CORPORATION COOPERATE TO AWARD DEGREES

COMPANY CONTACT:
Von Haney
Manager of Operational Training
Xerox Corporation
Xerox Square
Rochester, NY 14644
(716) 423-4541

INSTITUTIONAL CONTACT:
Carrie Getty
Liaison for Employers
Office of Independent Study
Regents External Degree Program of the University of the State of New York
Cultural Education Center
Albany, NY 12230
(518) 474-3703

PROGRAM DESCRIPTION/OBJECTIVES:
To make non-residential college degree opportunities available to employees nationwide who are unable to attend conventional college for reasons of work responsibilities, travel, frequent transfers, while allowing participant to upgrade level of education and credentials.

PROGRAM INITIATED:
1980

LENGTH OF STUDY FOR PARTICIPANT:
Self-paced

LENGTH OF CONTRACT:
Informal agreement

LOCATION:
Varies

PARTICIPANTS:
70 annually

PROGRAM COSTS PROVIDED BY:
Institution: 15%
Company: 25%
Participant: 60%

PRINTED MATERIALS AVAILABLE FROM:
Institution

* Representative entry—complete list available from institution.

Subject Index

Administrator, 9, 11, 18, 35, 41, 45, 48
Agencies, 55–56, 58, 61–62, 63, 64, 68–69, 72–73, 81, 88–89, 94–95, 100–102, 105, 115–116, 124–125, 129–130, 133–134, 146, 154–155, 159–160, 174–175, 179–180, 184, 188–189, 195–196, 205–206, 207–208, 210–211, 217, 218–219, 220–221, 223–224, 226–227, 228–229, 236–237, 238–239, 247, 250–252, 257, 260, 263
Administrator, 9, 11, 18, 35, 40, 41, 45, 48
ASTD (American Society for Training and Development), 11, 16, 37
Audience, 15, 16–18, 21, 29–30

Budget: sample of, 9; section of proposal, 33; structure and procedures, 13–14
Budgetary realities, 7
Business: in-house training, 12, 28; needs and demands of, 10, 19, 21–22, 27, 36, 41; officials of, 16–18, 20–21, 24, 34, 48; roles and responsibilities, 21, 22, 32; small, 3, 12, 17; targeted for CBL, 12, 16–19, 37

Career exploration, 83, 84–85, 88, 96, 100–101, 102, 104, 105–106,

Career exploration (*cont.*) 108–110, 111, 114–115, 123–124, 125, 133–134, 159, 161–162, 168–170, 171, 174, 175, 176, 177, 180, 188–191, 200, 203, 207–208, 209, 210–211, 220–221, 231–233, 234, 242, 249, 251, 259, 260, 262–263
Career transition, 57–58, 69, 70–71, 87, 88–90, 91, 100–101, 103–104, 112, 126, 142, 146, 152, 154–155, 171, 200–201, 202, 206–207, 219–220, 251
CBL (Campus–Business Linkages): concept, 28, 46, 49–50; coordinator, 7, 10, 12, 18, 20, 24, 34–35, 49; cost effectiveness, 9, 13–14; curriculum specialist, 7, 49; organizational realities, 6–7; organizational structure, 6–7, 9; rationale for, 3–6, 9, 46; three phases of, 46–48; who initiates, 4; why initiate, 5–6
CBL Office: 6–10; budget of, 7; functions, 7–8; organizational structure, 7; responsibilities, 6, 8; staff, 7–9, 48
Certification, 60, 66–67, 106–107, 117, 134–135, 142–143, 146, 149–150, 158–159, 163, 182, 202–203, 214–215, 225, 250–251, 257

Chamber of Commerce, 11, 16, 37
Chemistry, 114–115, 119–120, 128–129, 162–163, 173, 177–178, 183–184
Civic awareness, 59–60, 71–72, 79, 81, 82, 86–87, 88–89, 93, 95, 96, 105, 114–115, 135–136, 170–171, 179, 184–185
Civic organizations, 11, 16, 37
Classes: contract vs. open market, 19, 21; credit vs. noncredit, 19, 21, 27, 37–78; first day of, 38
Communications, 23, 27, 45, 48, 57–58, 62, 74–75, 77, 97–98, 113, 119, 144, 151, 158, 163, 174–175, 185–186, 198–199, 202–203, 216, 217, 218–219, 233–234
Communications technology, 67–68, 76, 164–165, 165–166, 172–173, 183, 185–186, 187, 202–203, 224–225, 236
Company (see business)
Company profiles, 7, 10, 11–12, 17, 20
Competition, 8–9, 11–13
Computer technology, 71, 89, 108, 111, 118–119, 120, 121, 140–142, 154, 170, 188, 199–200, 202–203, 253–254, 259–260, 261–262, 264–265
Construction industry, 55, 78, 86, 131–132, 147–149, 162
Construction: meeting, 20–22; agenda, 21–22
Consumer education, 109, 181–182, 183, 205, 207
Content and learning experiences, 19, 25–26, 29–30
Contract: cancellation, 34; defined as, 31; discrepancies, 39; language, 33–34, 41, 48; major changes in, 33–34; monitoring, 34, 40; negotiations, 32–33; samples of, 9; signing of, 31, 34; writing a, 31–34
Corporate learning, 130–131, 184–186
Cost profile, 23
Costs, 9–10, 13–14, 16, 20, 21, 32, 33
Credibility, 13, 45, 50–51

Criminal justice, 61–62, 104–105, 129–130, 170–171, 178, 207–208, 236, 260, 263
Curriculum developer, 25, 27–29, 40
Curriculum development: 15, 25–30, 31, 41, 46; issues of, 25–29
Customer service, 142, 170–171, 186

Data collection: formal, 42; informal, 42
Deadlines, 16, 20–21, 23
Declining enrollment, 5, 49–50
Degree program, 55, 62–63, 64, 68, 75–77, 80–81, 85–86, 90–91, 98–100, 101–102, 104–105, 106, 107, 112–113, 115–116, 117–119, 124, 135, 145–146, 150, 154–155, 176, 177, 178–180, 184, 189, 194–195, 197, 203–205, 206–207, 212–215, 217–218, 226–227, 233, 245, 246, 247, 250, 255–257, 260, 261, 262, 265–266
Delivery, as an issue, 25, 27–28
Development Phase of CBL, 15–45, 46
Die casting, 231–232

Economic development, 49, 184–185, 188, 204, 252–253
Earth sciences, 74, 107, 170, 177–178
Electrical engineering, 129, 167, 186–187, 190–191
Electronics, 55–56, 69–70, 111, 152–53, 159–160, 165–166, 175, 200–201, 202–203, 229–230, 237
Employees, 11–12, 19, 21, 33, 42–45, 48
Employer, 41
Energy, 69, 72, 73–74, 86, 93–94, 98, 106, 108, 123, 147–149, 165, 166–167, 189, 190–191, 192, 203–204, 205, 209, 210, 211, 212–213, 215–216, 232–233, 236–237, 239, 254–255, 260
Equipment, 36
Evaluation: comprehensive, 41, 44; formative, 28, 41; goals, 26, 28, 42; issue of, 25, 28; product, 41;

SUBJECT INDEX

Evaluation (cont.)
program, 22, 34, 39, 40, 46; roles of, 26, 28; sharing results, 45; standards for, 43–44; summative, 28, 41; types, 26, 28–29; validity of, 44–45
Evaluative data: 37, 39, 40, 41–44; methods of collection, 42–44
Expected outcomes, 41
External environment (see also marketplace): 37; assessment of, 10–14

Facilities, adequacy of, 33, 35–36, 38
Faculty, 5, 8–9, 11, 13, 18, 26–29, 35, 36–37, 38, 40, 41, 43, 45, 48, 50
Faculty loan, 59–60, 83–84, 95, 96, 102, 105–106, 114, 143–144, 152–153, 160–161, 227–228, 248, 249–250, 264
Financial management, 62, 63–64, 65, 67, 68, 72–73, 77–78, 91–93, 94–95, 99–100, 115–116, 117–118, 134–135, 144–145, 149–150, 172–173, 194–195, 196–197, 204–205, 219–220, 224, 253–254, 258
Fire science, 226, 258
Follow-up: evaluations, 45; initial contacts, 18; letters, phone calls, 9, 18; ongoing programs, 46–48

Goals: evaluation, 25–26, 28; of program, 15, 18, 21, 22, 32

Health sciences, 57–58, 66, 74–75, 84–86, 96, 100–101, 102, 105–106, 120–121, 124, 133–134, 150–151, 154–155, 168–169, 170–171, 173, 180, 192–193, 207, 222, 224–225, 226–228, 241, 248, 256–257
Human resource specialists, 12, 20, 24, 34, 36, 50
Human resources, 5, 11, 12, 17–18, 21, 35

Implementation: component, 15–16, 25, 31, 41; of linkage program, 31–40
Industrial safety, 78–79, 86–87, 156, 170, 179, 212
Industrial social work, 58, 125–126
Information: dissemination, 8; management, 8–9; methods of gathering, 11, 20; sources, 11
Initial contacts, 10, 17–18
Institution (Institution of higher education): mission, 4, 46; role and responsibilities, 22, 32, 41, 51; support and commitment to CBL, 3, 4, 6, 38, 46–48, 49–50
Instruction; facilities, 35–36, 38; methods, 25–26, 27, 41; on-campus, 19, 21, 27, 32; on-site, 19, 21, 27, 32, 33
Instructional materials, 13, 25–27, 33, 35–36, 38, 41
Insurance, 64–65, 124–125, 126–127, 150, 157–158, 174–175, 182, 221
Internal Advisory Committee, 7–8, 18
IMIS (Internal Management of Information System), 8–9, 10
IMIS Specialist, 7, 9, 12
Internal operations, 37
International studies, 116, 126–127, 164–165, 180, 185–186, 190, 193, 201, 253
Issues of curriculum development: 25–29; related to rationale, 3–4

Liberal arts, 108–110, 157–158, 168–169, 213, 222
Linkage Program: components, 15–16, 25, 32–33, 41; construction, 15–24, 25, 41, 42, 46; defining the, 15–16; design, 19–20; development phase, 15, 22, 41–45, 46–47; features, 19, 21; four components of, 15–16; goals, 15, 21, 28, 32; implementation, 15, 22, 31–40, 41, 46–47; indicators for success, 3–4, 10, 28–29; objective, 26, 29, 39, 41, 44–45;

Linkage Program (*cont.*)
overview, 50; planning, 49; putting into effect, 31–34; strengths and weaknesses, 44; twelve steps to success, 35–39; types of, 50

Management, 12
Management training and development, 57–58, 62–64, 66–67, 68, 75–76, 77–78, 81–82, 88–89, 91–93, 97, 99–100, 101–102, 104, 107, 111–112, 113–114, 115, 117, 119, 121, 123, 132, 140–141, 142, 144–145, 146, 147–149, 150, 151–152, 155, 161, 163, 169, 176–177, 178–179, 190, 192–193, 194, 195–196, 199–200, 201, 203–204, 206–207, 211–212, 215, 216, 217, 218–219, 220, 221–222, 230, 233–234, 235, 237–238, 240–241, 242–244, 246, 247, 249–250, 251–253, 263, 265–266
Market potential, 10–12, 47
Marketplace (*see also* external environment) assessment, 10–14, 46
Market share, 12
Mechanical design, 160, 171–172, 186
Metallurgy, 84, 99, 167–168, 181, 206, 233–234, 241–242
Mining, 189, 197–198, 203, 211

Occupational training, 56–57, 60, 68, 69–70, 78, 84, 86, 87, 98, 103, 106–108, 122, 137–140, 152–153, 164, 165–167, 173–174, 175, 186, 198, 200–201, 202–203, 206–207, 208, 211, 216–217, 219–220, 223–224, 226, 227, 228–229, 234–235, 236–237, 257–258, 261–262
Open market classes, 19

Patience, persistence, and professionalism, 24, 34
Postdevelopment phase of CBL, 46–51
Precision optics, 240

Predevelopment phase of CBL, 3–14, 46, 49
Presentation package, 50–51
Press packet, 51
Private Industry Council, 219–220, 223–224
Procedure Manual, 9–10
Productivity, 63–64, 71, 73–74, 110–111, 130–131, 153, 159–160, 171–172, 176–177, 179–180, 186–187, 191–192, 205–206, 210, 224, 225–227, 229–232, 238–239, 243, 244, 257, 260
Professional development, 155–156, 256
Professional associations, 11, 13, 16, 37
Professionalism, 24, 48, 51
Profit motive, 13–14, 20
Program administration: 48; modification, 40, 45; modifying existing, 29, 30, 49; monitoring, 34, 38, 39–40, 48; registration for, 37–38; requirements and procedures, 22, 32
Programs: developing new, 29–30; modifying existing, 29–30, 49; tailor-made, 20; training, 21, 29, 35, 51
Promoting CBL, 50–51
Proposal: acceptance, 34; cover letter, 23; making an offer, 31; negotiations, 23, 32–33; preparing the, 22–23; presenting the, 23; purpose of, 22; quality, 22; rewrite of, 34; samples of, 9; sign-offs, 23; stipulations in, 32, 38; working copy of, 23, 32–33
Public relations, materials, 37
Public relations specialist, 7, 37, 49
Pulp and paper industry, 100, 220–221, 243–244

Quality: instructional materials, 36; issue of, 25–26; proposal, 22

Rationale for CBL, 3–6, 9, 46–47
Resources, 16, 20–21 (*see also* human resources)

SUBJECT INDEX

Retail management, 174, 178, 210–211, 237–238, 242–243
Retirement, 70–71, 79–81, 121, 128–129, 187

Safety engineering, 78–79, 197–198
Secretarial training, 64–65, 77, 134, 142–143, 202–203, 250–251
Selection and involvement of people, 8, 16, 18, 21, 27–28
Self-paced program, 203–204, 239, 266
Staff, 5, 8–9, 11, 13, 18, 35–36, 45, 48
Stress management, 109–110, 150–151
Students, 40, 41 (*see also* employees)
Support and commitment for CBL: 3, 4, 6, 14, 38, 46–48, 49–50; importance of, 49; measuring extent of, 49–50

Timetable, 20, 32, 39
Trade organizations, 11, 13, 37

Training-education dichotomy, 27–28
Training directors, 20, 29, 34, 36, 50
Transportation industry, 61–62, 66–67, 97–99, 117, 132–133, 137–140, 143–144, 145, 157, 217–218, 247

Urban development, 223

Valid judgment, 44–45
Validity, 44–45 (*see also* evaluation)

Welding, 84, 258–259
Worker attitude, 92–93, 97–98, 100–101, 109–110, 113, 127, 131, 141, 144, 163, 211–212, 225–226, 230–231, 241, 246, 249–250
Work-education program, 135–136
Writing skills, 64–65, 74–75, 77, 158, 202–203, 214, 221, 224, 229, 238, 240–241

State Index

Alabama, 58, 79–84, 93, 129–130, 234, 256
Alaska, 77–78
Arizona, 86, 122, 137–138, 155, 181

California, 55, 69–71, 76–77, 89–90, 98, 105, 123–124, 137, 152–154, 160, 175, 207–209, 226, 232, 242, 247, 249, 255–256, 258
Colorado, 109, 133
Connecticut, 66, 95, 107, 145, 150–151, 157, 169, 174–175, 192–193, 195, 217–218, 224, 233, 248, 249–250, 263

Delaware, 120–121, 124, 259
District of Columbia, 134, 161–162, 193–194

Florida, 59, 85–86, 107–108, 114, 116, 165–166, 206

Georgia, 86–87, 140–141, 212, 216, 220, 225–226

Illinois, 55, 61–62, 75–76, 114–115, 130–132, 139–140, 194–195, 211, 226, 229–230, 231–232, 241–242, 253, 261–262
Indiana, 62, 111, 162–163, 238–239
Iowa, 61, 76, 92–93, 116–117, 156–157, 164–165, 173–174, 216–217, 244

Kansas, 88–89, 169–170
Kentucky, 133, 158–159, 170–171, 204–205, 219, 255

Maine, 220–221
Maryland, 64, 78–79, 119–120, 129, 134–135, 141–143, 162, 179, 182–183, 193, 218–219, 250–251, 255–256
Massachusetts, 72, 91–92, 109–110, 112–113, 121, 135–136, 150, 168–169, 179–180, 185–186, 206–207, 221–222, 236–237, 265–266
Michigan, 62–63, 71–73, 78, 90–91, 98–102, 115–116, 126, 138–139, 155–156, 183–185, 202, 237–238, 247, 250, 256–257, 262, 265
Minnesota, 189
Mississippi, 117, 189–190
Missouri, 139, 149–150, 168, 191–192
Montana, 192

New Jersey, 68–69, 105–106, 119–120, 128–129, 178–179, 190, 227–228, 243–244, 248
New York, 58–59, 64–65, 70, 77, 84–85, 97–100, 103–104, 106–109, 124–127, 142, 147–149, 158, 160–161, 166–167, 177, 180–181, 199, 202–203, 214–215, 227, 230, 238, 244–245, 257–258
North Dakota, 190–191, 203, 241

State Index

Ohio, 57–58, 74–75, 100–101, 113–114, 132–133, 144–145, 180, 199–200, 201, 209, 211–212, 217, 229, 230–231, 235, 240–241, 243, 246, 260, 262
Oklahoma, 68–69, 73–74, 87, 108–109, 140, 174, 186–187, 210–211, 215–216, 245
Oregon, 176, 205–206

Pennsylvania, 99, 104–105, 125, 131, 156, 181–182, 212–214, 219–220

Rhode Island, 135, 198–199, 221, 222, 264–265

South Carolina, 90, 104, 136, 143–144, 176, 200–201, 236

Tennessee, 59–60, 130–131, 146
Texas, 60, 123, 239, 240, 252–253

Utah, 151–152

Vermont, 118–119, 197
Virginia, 63, 65, 66–68, 96–97, 103, 112, 118, 121–122, 132, 163, 214, 215, 223–225, 234–235, 254–255, 258–260

Washington, 242–243
West Virginia, 63–64, 67, 177–178, 197–198, 260
Wisconsin, 70–71, 94–95, 171–173, 188–189, 195–197, 261, 264

Panama, 116
Puerto Rico, 246

University Index

Alabama State University, 129–130
Alpena Community College, 78
Alverno College, 188, 264
American University, 161–162
Aurora College, 75–76

Bay De Noc Community College, 126
Bethune-Cookman College, 114
Birmingham Southern College, 79–85, 93, 234, 256–257
Borough of Manhattan Community College, 64–65
Bowling-Green State University, 231
Bradley University, 52
Brevard Community College, 165–166, 206
Brigham Young University, 151–152
Bronx Community College, 58–59, 77, 85, 142, 230
Broward Community College, 85–86
Butler County Community College, 88

California Baptist College, 55, 76–77
California State College, Bakersfield, 89–90, 208–209, 242
Cape Cod Community College, 91–92
Case Western Reserve University, 125–126
Centenary College, 117–118
Central Arizona College, 181
Central Michigan University, 62–63, 90–91, 98–99, 101–102, 116–

Central Michigan University (*cont.*) 117, 155–156, 183–184, 247, 250, 256–257, 262, 265
Centre College of Kentucky, 219
City University of New York, Herbert H. Lehman College, 108–109, 177
Claremore College, 245
Cleveland State University, 104, 145–146
Cogswell College, 258
College of Alameda, 134
College of DuPage, 229
College of Lake County, 55, 114–115, 178, 207, 261–262
College of New Rochelle, 103–104
College of San Mateo, 69–70, 247
College of Staten Island, 99–100, 106
Colorado School of Mines, 109
Columbia College, 104–105
Community College of Rhode Island, 135, 198–199, 221, 264–265
Cornell University, 199

Dabney S. Lancaster Community College, 258–259
Dallas County Community College District, 240
Danville Community College, 112
Dominican College of San Rafael, 105
Drew University, 119–120, 128–129

UNIVERSITY INDEX

Dundalk Community College, 78-79, 120, 179

Eastern Michigan University, 92
Edison State Community College, 89, 110-111, 243
El Paso Community College, 98, 252-253
El Paso Community College District, 123
Evergreen Valley College, 71, 152, 160, 175

Fairfield University, 95
Florida Junior College, 59, 107-108, 159-160, 166-168
Franklin University, 261

Gardner-Webb College, 89, 90
Georgia Institute of Technology, 86-87, 140-141, 212, 216, 220, 225-26, 233-234
Glendale Community College, 115, 122, 137, 155
Golden West College, 138
Gordon College, 109-110, 168
Green River Community College, 242-243
Greenville Technical College, 176
Gwynedd Mercy College, 181-182

Hampton Institute, 160-161
Henry Ford Community College, 237-238
Herbert H. Lehman College, 108-109, 177

Indiana State University, 162-163, 238-239
Indiana University of Pennsylvania, 131, 156, 212-213
Indiana Vocational College, 62
Iowa State University, 61, 76, 92-93, 116-117, 156-157, 164-165, 173, 216-217

Jamestown Community College, 70, 166-167, 187, 257-258

John Tyler Community College, 65, 66-67, 96-97, 132, 163, 215, 234-235, 237, 254-255
Johnson State College, 118-119, 197

Kansas City Art Institute, 169-170
Kean College of New Jersey, 178-179, 243-244
Kent State University, 57-58, 74-75, 100-101, 113-114, 144-145, 180, 217, 229, 230-231, 235, 240-241, 246

Lakeshore Technical Institute, 171-172
Lakewood Community College, 189
Luzerne Community College, 213

Macombe Community College, 138-139
Manchester Community College, 217-218
Manhattan College, 124-125, 126-127
Marshall University, 67, 72, 177-178, 197-198, 260
Mary College, 203
Marymount College of Virginia, 63, 67-68, 118, 214, 259-260
Marymount Manhattan College, 214-215
Maryville College, 59-60
Medgar Evers College, 161
Meridian Junior College, 117
Merritt College, 123-124, 152-153, 207-208, 249
Michigan Technological University, 72-73, 100
Middlesex County College, 226
Miles Community College, 192
Miramar College, 226
Mississippi State University, 189
Montgomery College, 134-135
Montgomery College, Takoma Park, 64
Mt. Wachusett Community College, 73
Mundelein College, 194

National College of Education, 226–227
North Lake College, 240
Northeast Iowa Technical Institute, 173–174, 244
Northern Kentucky University, 133, 158, 170–171, 204–205
New York City Technical College, 84, 106–107, 147–149, 158, 186, 202–203, 244–245
Northland Pioneer College, 86
Northwest Community College, 77–78

Ohio State University, 199–200
Ohio University, 200
Oklahoma State Tech, 68–69, 73–74, 87, 108, 140–141, 174, 186–187, 210–211, 215–216
Old Dominion University, 253–254
Oregon State University, 176–177, 205–206

Palomar Community College, 153
Panama Canal College, 116
Patrick Henry Community College, 121–122
Peirce Junior College, 219–220
Pennsylvania State University, Hazleton, 213
Pioneer Community College, 139, 149–150
Prince George's Community College, 119, 134, 141–143, 162–163, 182–183, 193, 218–219, 250–251, 257
Princeton University, 190

Quinebaug Valley Community College, 248–249

Regis College, 154
Rend Lake College, 211
Rutgers, the State University of New Jersey, 96, 102–103, 105–106, 227–228, 248

Salem State College, 121, 135, 185–186

San Diego Community College, 154–155
Schenectady County Community College, 228–229
Seattle Community College District, 56–57
Shippensburg State College, 104–105
Siena College, 180–181
Simmons College, 150, 194–195
South Central Community College, 218
Southeastern Massachusetts University, 236–237
Southwestern College, 232
Spartanburg Technical College, 143–144
State University College, Buffalo, 97–98, 127
State University of New York Agricultural and Technical College, Canton, 227
Sumter Area Technical College, 236

Texas State Technical Institute, 60
Tri-County Technical College, 90, 200–201
Triton College, 131–132, 139–140, 188, 231–232, 241
Tufts University, 56
Turabo University, 246
Tusculum College, 146

University of Akron, 209, 211–212, 241–242
University of Cincinnati, 132–133
University City Science Center, 193–194
University of Dayton, 201
University of Ebansville, 111
University of Hartford, 66, 95, 107, 145–146, 150–151, 157, 169, 174–175, 192–193, 195, 203–204, 224, 233, 249–250, 263
University of Illinois, 10
University of Illinois, Chicago Circle, 253
University of Maine, Orono, 220–221

University Index

University of Maryland, Baltimore County, 120–121
University of Maryland, College Park, 129
University of Massachusetts, Amherst, 221–222
University of Massachusetts, Boston, 179
University of Michigan, 184–185, 202
University of North Dakota, 190, 205
University of North Florida, 159
University of Pennsylvania, 99, 157–158
University of Rhode Island, 222
University of Southern California, 255
University of the State of New York, 266
University of Virginia, 251–252
University of Wisconsin, Madison, 94–95
University of Wisconsin, Marinette County, 70–71
University of Wisconsin, Parkside, 261
University of Wisconsin Extension, 195–197

Vanderbilt University, 130–131
Villa Maria College, 125
Virginia Commonwealth University, 223–225

Washington University, 191
Webster College, 168
Wesley College, 259
Western Michigan University, 71–72, 170
Western Wisconsin Technical Institute, 172–173
Wharton County Community College, 239
Widener University, 124
Wilmington College, 262
Worcester State College, 112–113, 206–207, 265–266
Wilkes College, 213

Organization Index

Adams Russell, 56
Alabama Department of Education, 58
Arapahoe CETA, 133
Association of American Colleges, 88

Bay State Skills Corporation, 156, 121–122, 236–237
Bradley-Business Task Force, 93–94

Charleston Higher Education Consortuim, 111, 136

Educational Testing Service, 200

Hewlett Packard, 56

International Foundation of Employee Benefit Plans, 232

Microwave Associates, 56

NCR Corporation, 199–202, 236
NASA, 193–194
National Credit Union Institute, Inc., 195–197

Police Training Institute, 61–62

Richmond Public Schools, 223–224

Storer Cable, Inc., 183